AND ON AND ON THE AGES ROLL

And On and On the Ages Roll

Yesterday, Today, Tomorrow

J. H. BAVINCK

CASCADE *Books* · Eugene, Oregon

AND ON AND ON THE AGES ROLL
Yesterday, Today, Tomorrow

Copyright © 2019 Wipf and Stock Publishers. All rights reserved. Except for brief quotations in critical publications or reviews, no part of this book may be reproduced in any manner without prior written permission from the publisher. Write: Permissions, Wipf and Stock Publishers, 199 W. 8th Ave., Suite 3, Eugene, OR 97401.

Cascade Books
An Imprint of Wipf and Stock Publishers
199 W. 8th Ave., Suite 3
Eugene, OR 97401

www.wipfandstock.com

PAPERBACK ISBN: 978-1-5326-5885-3
HARDCOVER ISBN: 978-1-5326-5886-0
EBOOK ISBN: 978-1-5326-5887-7

Cataloguing-in-Publication data:

Names: Bavinck, J. H., author.

Title: And on and on the ages roll : yesterday, today, tomorrow / J. H. Bavinck.

Description: Eugene, OR: Cascade Books, 2019

Identifiers: ISBN 978-1-5326-5885-3 (paperback) | ISBN 978-1-5326-5886-0 (hardcover) | ISBN 978-1-5326-5887-7 (ebook)

Subjects: LCSH: Bible. Revelation—Commentaries. | Bible. Revelation—Devotional literature.

Classification: BS2825.53 .B40 2019 (paperback) | BS2825.53 (ebook)

Manufactured in the U.S.A.   07/30/19

Contents

CHAPTER ONE
Between Anxiety and Ecstasy (Revelation 12) | 1
　This strange world | 1
　The great "not-yet" | 7
　The two scenarios | 11
　This demonic world | 18
　Where do we stand ourselves? | 22

CHAPTER TWO
The Road More Troubled (Revelation 2 and 3) | 26
　Where we are now | 26
　Life is dangerous | 27
　Everything is different than it seems | 33
　Caesar or Christ | 37
　In the grip of money | 42
　The very ordinary life | 47
　The only mission church | 50
　The mortal self-deceit | 53
　The road more troubled | 56

CHAPTER THREE
The Ban Is Broken (Revelation 4 and 5) | 59
　Above the earth are the vaulting heavens | 59
　The grand vision | 60
　The first rustling of the coming things | 66
　The beginning of the last things | 71
　Eternity and time | 78

CHAPTER FOUR
God's Great Disruption (Revelation 6) | 80
  The thread is unwinding | 80
  The rider with a crown | 82
  The three great disasters | 88
  The hiddenness of the last seals | 93
  The emergency signal | 100

CHAPTER FIVE
The World Advances toward Chaos (Revelation 8, 9, 10, 11) | 103
  The background of the great delay | 103
  The horizon retreats | 110
  The great panorama | 114
  The two witnesses | 118

CHAPTER SIX
The Very Last Unmasking (Revelation 13–19) | 123
  Overview | 123
  The architecture of the human kingdom | 124
  The fall of Babylon | 143
  The edge of the history of the world | 151

CHAPTER SEVEN
What Is Behind the End (Revelation 20 and 21) | 153
  The question of the 1000-year kingdom | 153
  The final finish | 155

CHAPTER EIGHT
On and On the Ages Roll | 160
  Image and counterimage | 160
  Everything becomes what it is | 165
  And what about us? | 170

CHAPTER ONE

Between Anxiety and Ecstasy
(Revelation 12)

THIS STRANGE WORLD

I am sure what we see around us is far different from what it appears at first blush. Take the universe, for instance: the Revelation of John talks about this in the verses of this chapter.

You may remember from your days at school something of the immense magnitude of the universe, something hard to visualize. Suppose that on Capitol Hill in Washington we notice a simple marble, no bigger than one mere centimeter in diameter. If that little round sparkling ball were to represent the earth, then, using the same measuring, the moon is about thirty centimeters—one single foot—away from that little plaything. Probing deeper into the universe, the sun—using the same method—is a ball a bit more than a meter big, some 3.5 feet in diameter, but much, much farther away: about 115 meters, some 120 yards. And when we continue this sort of calculation then we find out that the very closest of stars we find somewhere in China, a distance of tens of thousands of miles away. And that is the nearest of these stars. The vault of heaven of which the sun is a part has many hundreds of millions stars and is enclosed by the Milky Way that surrounds them like a belt. But beyond the Milky Way there are still more celestial wonders, stars so numerous and so far away that they dazzle the sharpest minds. That gives us an inkling of our universe. And in the midst of it all these heavenly bodies moves this little marble, our globe, the place we have been allowed to inhabit.

But on closer examination that little round toy actually appears to be remarkably large. There are mighty mountain ranges, immeasurably deep oceans as well as steppes and deserts, but also fertile river valleys, forests, cities, villages, meadows. And that earth is inhabited by humans, billions of them, everyone different—different races, different colors, different languages, different religions. But do these so different people realize that they really are so minutely tiny compared to the inexpressible distances of the universe? They imagine themselves big, they each possess their own little empire, their own interests and thoughts. In the meantime they turn around in sync with the earth around her axle, while the earth makes its daily turn around the sun. And the sun? It pursues her imperturbable, imperial path through the astronomical depths of infinite space. Do these people actually realize that they daily wander on an earth-crust beneath which broils an indescribable mass of compressed terror? When within the earth even the slightest movements occur, then the terrestrial crust trembles, then cities crumble, then people are driven away in utter terror. Just imagine if something really serious would happen to this carefully calibrated universe! Just imagine that this tiny earth in her continuous revolutions would meet up with another celestial body, however small and insignificant, what would then happen to that awesome anthill we call humanity!

We and the whole wide universe. Really when we look at both us and that infinite space we cannot help but smile. Sure, because we humans can reason and think and we exceed by far a blade of grass or a moose, go even beyond the lion and the eagle; sure, we are able to draw from the world her closely guarded secrets, and even have been able to subdue nature's forces, yet, in the final analysis we are just puny and insignificant. In the fabulous totality of the universe we are a mere worm constantly subject to annihilation.

Enter John. He writes: "A great and wondrous sign appeared in heaven: a woman clothed with the sun, with the moon under her feet and a crown of twelve stars on her head." For now we won't speculate who that woman is, but right away it is clear that she is human, a person just like we are. She is "clothed with the sun," she has "the moon under her feet," and she carries a crown of stars on her head.

I want to make sure that you understand that we here deal with symbolism and talk in images that express deep ideas. Yet this does not detract from the fact that here humanity is pictured as being at the heart of the universe. Everything points to that premise: the total focus is aimed at that situation. The innumerable celestial bodies meandering in their lonely selves through the abysses of the great out-there, dispatching their luminous rays everywhere throughout the universe, they simply are a crown on the head of that woman. They are nothing but an ornament, they only count because that woman is there, they exist only because she is alive. And the sun which consumes itself in its passionate desire to provide light, through which buds swell, flowers open up, trees grow tall, clouds gather above the waters, animals breathe, humans live, that same sun is nothing else but a dress for the woman. The sun is the framework, the outer garment for humanity. The mighty sun finds its meaning, its destination in the human race: it too is there because humanity exists.

If that is true, and John writes this quite straightforwardly, then, indeed, everything is different than it seems. There are connections in the universe we fail to detect, something that our scientific minds cannot possibly fathom. All phenomena in the universe are somehow connected to each other in a way that totally supersedes/ our thinking processes. This really means that we are more than a mere planet-crawling worm, something of ridiculous insignificance. It also means that the universe is more than limitless immensity. What it really means is that between the miniscule human and the so distant celestial entities, those starry systems of immeasurable width and extent, there exists such an intimate connection that we are incapable to produce the proper picture.

Yet we must probe to detect the proper connection. It is right away clear that this can never be established by means of natural science. Purely scientifically speaking, the sun and the moon and the total heavenly vault out there, all these light-points in the infinity of space, move totally outside the human realm. If today or tomorrow our planet would prematurely end through some sort of devastating explosion and the entire human race in one moment would vanish into nothingness, then it is highly unlikely that the sun would even feel the shock and the stars so many light-years away would not notice anything at all. Yes, all of humanity could disappear without a trace. However it is very much the question whether the vision natural science has of the universe is the only valid one, whether it really makes the correct observation regarding mother earth. John does not speak here as a scientist; no, he has a totally different view because he speaks on behalf of God and sees reality his way. That's why we can only speak about this miraculous connection in terms of theology. That really entails that we must discuss this matter using a different terminology, no longer speaking in light years and star formations, but in terms of faith and childlike acceptance. Of course John sees a definite connection between what we seem to regard as separate entities because he sees how closely it all ties to God. That same God, who is "King of the Ages," who has created this unfathomable universe, who governs the ever revolving course of the stars, that same God has a very special relationship to us, and it is this intimate connection that gives us such an exceptional place in the infinite structure of God's creation.

Before we continue contemplating this any further, we have to first more closely examine what is really meant by that "woman" who occupies such a high and honorable place that sun and moon and stars are woven into her royal attire. We already have noted that the woman takes the place of all of us humans. That is, however, only correct up to a point, but this also means that we must determine what the real meaning is behind all this. It right away is evident that very little is said about this woman, and what later is described about her, is actually not very flattering. According to verse 2 she is pregnant and "cried out in pain as she was to give birth." Later she flees into the desert. All this somehow contrasts with the indescribable magnificence that had been her earlier hallmark. Even though she is "clothed with the sun" and even though her feet stand on the moon, and she is adorned with a crown of stars, she still is a beggarly figure, hunted, suffering, a fugitive, and daily exposed to numerous dangers.

The most significant statement about this woman is that she brings a child into the world, "a male creature." In other words, she is a mother and that is her most essential feature. It is not she who is important, but it is the child that counts, the one about to be born. Of course it is beyond doubt that this child is none other than Jesus Christ. Even though in this entire chapter very little is said about him, everything indicates that his personality dominates this chapter. Yes, this woman is the mother of Jesus Christ. But does that mean that this points to Mary? The Roman Catholic Bible translation, the so-called Canisius version, comes with a footnote here: "The woman is the community of God in the Old and New Testament. She is the bearer of the divine Light. From her the Messiah is born suffering from many griefs and persecutions in the past, in the presence and in the future. She is the spiritual mother of many children who with her are persecuted by Satan. (In a spiritual sense all this is perfectly applied to Mary, the mother of Jesus, the mother of all believers, but also the mother of all sorrows.)"

From this quote it is plain that also this translation does not see in this woman only Mary, but the church of all ages. At best we can say that Mary is depicted here as the symbol of that church of all ages, and that thus, in a peculiar way, in her has been fulfilled what also applies in a very spiritual sense to that church of all ages.

In this entire matter there are indeed some facets that for a moment make us think of Mary and her child. When a bit later it is mentioned that the dragon is conniving to devour the child right after his birth, then our thoughts go to Herod, who right after the birth of Christ vied to kill him.

And when then the woman seeks refuge in the desert, this reminds us of Mary and Joseph fleeing to Egypt. Thus there are some instances in this entire episode that can be applied to the happenings around Jesus' birth as described in Luke. On the other hand there are ample other happenings that go far beyond the persecution instigated by Herod and the seeking of refuge in Egypt, indicating that it is more realistic to connect all this to realities of a far more permanent character.

This woman, representing the congregation of God, is always and ever in danger, is always imperiled, and is always on the run. The book of Revelation of John will tell us about this later in greater detail.

That this woman means the community of God, and points to his people, also explains right away why she is pictured as endowed with the sun and carrying a crown of stars. That can only be said of her because she is the mother of Jesus Christ. This description only fits her because she too is his possession, because she too is saved by him and carried by him. In other words it is the Christ who is centered in the heart of the universe. On his head the stars are weaved as a crown and it is he who is adorned with the sun. When he is born a star indicated the place of his crib, and when he is suspended on the cross, the sun is blackened out, and the universe stops breathing, and when he dies the rocks split and the earth quakes. Yes, no doubt, he is the center of the world; everything is arrayed around him. That in the spring the crocuses emerge from the soil, that the snowdrops sneak up, that also then the trees sprout tiny leaves, that the sea moves in endless rhythm, that the snow-covered mountain tops gloriously silhouette against the blue sky, that the Milky Way safely contains the starry expanse, all this points back to him who securely holds everything in check. That person we so far have discussed is not just the typical human, but points to the great, the only true human, Jesus Christ, the Son of Man. The author of the book to the Hebrews has perfectly grasped this secret. He quotes somewhere in his letter the words of Psalm 8, the hymn praising humanity: "What is man that you are mindful of him, the daughter of man that you care for her? You have made both a little lower that the heavenly beings and crowned them with glory and honor. You have made them rulers over the works of your hands." And then he continues: "Yet at present we do not see everything subject to him, but we see Him, Jesus, crowned with glory and honor." (Heb 2:9) The author of this letter evidently has visualized that same picture, the image of a human being, humanity personified, standing on the moon, and having a crown of stars on his head.

All that really throws a sharp light on what has been written here about the woman. It is she who is crowned with all that glory. But, that is only the case because she is a mother, the mother of Jesus Christ. Where we are now, in this world, it is true that all things are under her control, something that is, as yet, not the case. She still lives in the period of "not yet." As the mother of the Christ, as elected in him and saved by him, she shares in his majesty that is beyond description, but as yet we do not see that all things are subjected to her. She is not yet what she really is. As yet she does not wear the garment she is entitled to wear. The real secret of the church is the great "not yet," it is that unfathomable that she cannot yet be what she has been a long time ago, through Jesus Christ. At the moment she stands there as under threat, as an outcast, as one persecuted, as a trembling character in the midst of the world history, and yet she is the woman, clothed with the sun, with the entire universe devotedly arrayed around her.

With these words we are approaching the meaning of this revelation. John does not notice anything strange in all this, detects nothing incomprehensible. He does not see something that is not there. What does happen here is that God has given him this moment of grace that allowed him to pierce through the superficial appearance of matter and enabled him to fathom the deepest reality. He observed matters here that are the truth in the utmost sense of the word. He was allowed to penetrate through the masquerade of earthly dazzle and perceive the ultimate basics. It is precisely that which he was given and what overwhelmed his senses.

At the same time it's exactly here where we find ourselves at the center of all thinking that dominates this entire book. The things in this world are really not what they are in the final analysis. Everything in our world is fake, carries a mask, is disguised; everything is different than it is. When John paints the progress of the grand happenings then he starts with this premise that at last matters will become what they are, that their masks will be torn off. Even in the last chapter of Revelation he sounds the alarm bell: "Let those who do wrong keep on doing wrong, and those who do right continue to do so, and let those who are holy continue to be holy." Out of all the chaos and collapse at long last the truth will emerge. All camouflage will vanish and everything will at last show the true character that corresponds with its ultimate essence. That is the melody that vibrates through the entire book and makes it so engaging and vibrant. All this means that, judging by what we so far saw, this woman, the mother of Jesus Christ, standing in the heart of the universe and still displaying the image of the hunted and persecuted, has to become what she is in Christ, that is the glorified and the crownbearer. She still dwells in the "not-yet," because there still are some limiting factors that prevent her from displaying her true status. But that "not-yet" has to come to an end because God will eventually make her into what she also now may be.

THE GREAT "NOT-YET"

In the meantime we must first deal with the great "not-yet." John does not hesitate to in a few words describe its terrible nature. He begins to indicate in the sober language that this woman "cried out in pain of childbirth." This simple sentence outlines the entire history of God's people in Old Testament times: the ups and downs the people of Israel experienced. Time and again they were led astray, seduced, succumbed to temptations, persecuted, carried away into exile, almost annihilated, and swallowed up. Throughout the Old Testament books there emerge shouts of pain, of anxiety, of despair. No wonder. After all, that woman carried the great child in her bosom, the very reason why she was tortured so much. This was not because of her but because of the child. When the kings of Egypt menace Israel, try to eradicate her, when the Egyptian army chases Israel in the desert, then the aim is not Israel, but it is all about the child that will come from Israel. When the Philistines oppress Israel, then it is not the future of Israel that is at risk, but it is all about the child. When later Jerusalem is destroyed and the entire population is captured and exiled to Babylon, then again it is not that the people of Israel are threatened with demise, but again it is all about the child that even before he is born is persecuted. Of course the Pharaoh or the Philistines or Nebuchadnezzar did not have the slightest notion of their place in this: they all were convinced that their aim was to destroy the nation of Israel. But matters are different than they seem; there are more profound realities behind all these historic happenings, and those who are involved in this do not have the slightest notion what is really at stake. There are powers at work and forces behind all these happenings that have their own intentions and the people who shape these events cannot possibly fathom the real meaning. Seen in that light, we certainly can label the Old Testament the book of sorrows, the book from which cries of anxiety arise. A bit later we will see that also after the child is born, the woman is still faced with grave danger. The history of the church in the new covenant too is a chronicle from which one long cry of delivery wells up to God. From where does all this originate? What is the ultimate cause of this distress? John speaks of "another sign" seen in the heaven, "an enormous red dragon with seven heads and ten horns and seven crowns on his head." That he sees this sign in heaven means that he observes the deepest background of the phenomena happening on our earth, evident in the ever more destructive historical struggles. History always witnesses different scenarios, always causes new battles to flare up, always takes on new shapes, but in all these different appearances the only constant factor is a degree of illusion, of unreality. The real essence dominating these happenings is only sporadically visible in the far distance.

Only in God's light, only silhouetted against the heaven does John see the great "signs," history's driving forces, which show the true nature of what really takes place. And in that very light, positioned over against the woman, appears the terrible figure of the red dragon.

That image places us directly in the midst of the ancient Eastern symbolism, a symbolism we, unimaginative Westerners, have trouble understanding. It is very likely that John, seeing this dragon, did not think of all sorts of monsters such as they appear in the Babylonian and Egyptian myths, but that he primarily was focused on what is described in Genesis 3. This dragon is not the primeval ocean, not some sort of mythic monster, not the personification of the chaotic powers in the cosmos, but he is the "ancient snake," the "devil and Satan'" who "has seduced the entire world"(verse 9). That he is depicted here as "the great red dragon" must indicate that he is as red as fire as if he wants to destroy the entire cosmos in his spiteful rage. Seven heads he has and on these heads are seven crowns. He also carries ten horns on these heads. The image of the aggressively punching horn is well-known in the Bible. It points to the world's empires, as they, at times, suddenly reveal themselves as mad bulls wildly attacking everything around them. The seven heads and the seven crowns must indicate that this mysterious dragon, shown here in its frightening reality, depicts the various powerful empires in the history of the world. These empires differ from each other in size, in power, in culture, in wealth, but they all are, in a sense, identical. It is not necessary to go into detail about these empires because that's not what this is all about. John has no intention of providing us with a point-for-point outline of the course of these realms, he only wants to emphasize the single critical moment that always emerges in these mighty nations. There may be seven heads and ten horns, but there is only one dragon, one frightening monster who throughout all the ages, especially today, has only one goal: death and destruction.

In the meantime we are nevertheless faced here with a remarkable event. If we must interpret those seven heads and those seven crowns as world empires—something that, given the total context, seems the most probable—then the question arises whether these realms have been or are or will be so demonic that they can only be regarded as destructive. However, looking at them individually, this does not seem plausible. This also applies to those mentioned in the Old Testament, such as Babylon, Egypt, Persia, and Greece. They all were guardians of judicial structures, protected their cultural treasures, which were a blessing and benefit for many. That is exactly the mysterious element in the history of the world, that is to say, that in the most exact sense nothing really is what it is. Babylon was not simply Babylon in its enmity against God, but it also had a high cultural state, and within its borders order and safety were paramount. The Bible fully acknowledges that, when Daniel tells Nebuchadnezzar that: "The tree you saw, which grew large and strong, with beautiful leaves and abundant fruit, you, O King are that tree!" (Dan 4:20–22). That is the same Babylon, of which one of the Psalms says that "happy are those who grab your children and crush them against the rocks." That same Babylon was then also a bulwark of safety and strength. Yet under the surface, Babylon displayed a power that was utterly devilish. That same empire possessed a pride, a tyrannical tendency, a desire to dominate, that was boundless. And Babylon was not alone in this: in some form or another all the other world powers were of the same mind. They all possess the nature that is conveyed in the head of the dragon that from time to time becomes evident in their abhorrent appearances. Yet they also carry crowns, which indicate that they display authority and majesty. Well, that is what the masquerade of world history is all about because the powers behind all these happenings are only visible through all sorts of disguises. Not a single event is completely what it is when stripped down to the bones. The church is not yet a "woman clothed with the sun," and the world powers, Babylon, Persia, and others, are not in the full sense the heads of the red dragon. What we have to do is to see through all these outer appearances, by holding them up against the light from heaven, and so detect their true nature. Because as long as we are standing within history, they all reflect, in addition to possessing the demonic features of the beast, also something of the glow that has its source in grandeur and glory. John sees them here in their uttermost essence, against the background of the coming end time. He is of the opinion that, when all things come to their destination, the false front slowly falls away, and the full horror will be revealed. Because behind all these world empires he detects the spooky, frightening figure of the dragon, "who seduces the entire world."

That dragon stood in front of the woman. That is the solution to the riddle of history. In fact there are two realities that determine all world events: the reality of the woman and the reality of the dragon. Both still dwell in the great "not yet." Both are not yet what they are in their most profound essence. But already the relationship between these two, carry all characteristics of the stupendous struggle that is determinative for the entire world history.

This sober sketch displays the real connection between these powers from ancient times until the coming of Jesus Christ. It is possible to call this scenario a prophecy as seen in the rearview mirror, a disclosure of the ultimate meaning of matters that have taken place. In a flash all those figures of ancient times pass before our eyes: Cain who murdered his brother; Lamech spouting his haughty, offensive language; those who started to build the tower of Babel and their god-defying actions; the princes of the ancient Ur of the Chaldeans from which Abram had to flee; the Egyptian king who threatened Moses and pursued him later; Philistines, Moabites, Edom, and Ammon, all who suppressed Israel, Sanherib and Nebuchadnezzar, Antioch Epiphanes and Herod. It's a long list of kings and potentates who all in their time and in their way contributed to that single grand happening. In all this is incorporated what here in a few simple words has been described: the dragon stands before the woman in order to devour the child as soon as she has given birth. This is history exposed in all its naked reality.

After this the grand event plays out, eagerly awaited by the ages. "And she gave birth to a son, a male being, who will rule the heathens with an iron scepter" (Rev 19:15). We have to force ourselves to understand that this points to the child in the manger, that supposedly powerless and helpless child. Here we see again the lack of reality, because this child also is not yet what it is in his deepest essence. He lies there defenseless, wrapped in cloths and lying in a manger, but he is destined to triumph over all evil powers. The "iron scepter" is his sign of dominion.

What follows now is exceedingly remarkable. Without a pause John adds "And her child was snatched up to God and to his throne." In just one short sentence this depicts Jesus' entire life on earth: first his youth in Egypt and Nazareth, then his public appearances, his preaching in Galilee, his miracles in various places, his suffering because of the stubborn obstinacy of the Pharisees and the scribes. It also includes his last journey to Jerusalem, his imprisonment and judgment, and finally the cross, that rough, scraggy cross on which he suffered all the unutterable agony. But also in that one sentence there is the Easter morning of the resurrection, his appearances to his disciples, in Jerusalem and in Galilee. And then, at the very end, comes the ascension. All that rich, all that unfathomably marvelous and sorrowful happening is here depicted in a few words: the child was snatched up to God and his throne. All these stages mean that the Satan, in spite of all his tireless efforts, has not been able to get a hold of the child, was not able to triumph. He tried to seduce him, but no luck. He tried to push him over the brink of hell, wanted to crush him, but in the depth of death and abandon he came out on top. That child simply could not be conquered. He always came out as a winner because not for one instant did he deviate from the road the Father had outlined for him. That's the reason why Jesus' entire life could be condensed to one simple sentence. It is a life without detours, without twists and turns. That this Jesus in that single moment of his presence here on earth has accomplished a task of eternal significance, deserves here no further elaboration, is not even considered here at this time. The focus of this prophecy is only directed to that one surprising fact that this seemingly helpless child has victoriously ascended to God's throne in spite of all powers on earth conspiring to prevent this, and that he now is endowed with all authority in heaven and earth.

At the same time this means that it has become totally beyond the satanic powers to defeat him. No longer is Jesus Christ the reason for the battle. Now no power can prevail against him. There is no possibility for his life to be endangered. He is far, infinitely far removed from all of Satan's cunning and connivance. The intent of the dragon, for many ages so eagerly cherished, has now met with failure, all chances of success have been shattered.

We would be inclined to think that now also the woman would be out of danger. What's the use to go after her now that the Son is born and has been victorious? Now history has seen a turnaround. In Jesus Christ and in his triumph the totality of all things has taken a definite turn. Spoken from the human point of view we should conclude that from now on the world's history has come to a definite finish. The verdict is in. After all, the woman is what she is only because of the child. The concern is not about her because she is what she is through the child and in the child. She herself is completely without any significance, but through the child she is clothed with the sun and has a crown of stars on her head. That's why the enmity of the dragon is not directed against her but against the child born from her. And now that this child has been saved, now that Jesus Christ has emerged as the winner, now everything is solved, the decision has been made. With the ascension world history has ceased to exist. Everything that comes after carries the character of a postlude. The matter that really was at stake, the cardinal point around which everything revolved, that has been accomplished. Whatever now comes after cannot alter one thing, can bring nothing new. In the ultimate meaning of the word nothing can happen anymore because that which had to happen has happened. At most the results of the event may become clearer because there may be some sort of after-effect. But the event itself has been totally finalized. It is accomplished.

THE TWO SCENARIOS

It is clear that, judging by the remainder of this chapter, there's a lot yet to come. John continues to tell us some amazing matters, events about which we did not have the faintest notion.

It is right away clear that what he is about to reveal to us is presented by way of two different scenarios. There is a chain of events playing itself out in heaven and there are other happenings that take place on the earth.

Two levels are suspended above each other. In the heavenly scene powerful events take place as the result of Christ's great victory. Below, on the earth, similar overwhelming matters occur also as the result of this same victory. That means that what now is occurring can no longer be reduced to the same denominator, can no longer be mentioned in the same breath. The two threads, the heavenly one and the earthly, are both unwinding and continue to plot along parallel paths.

This idea of the two scenarios is by itself not strange. The ancient East always suspected that there were two chains of events, one in heaven and one on earth. The general notion then was that what occurs in heaven can be seen by the courses of the stars, while what takes place on earth is evident in the always occurring collisions between the different nations. These ancient Eastern people were totally convinced that the goings-on in heaven determined the earthly outcomes as well. What was visible in the stars would soon be evident on earth also. At any rate the heavenly events had in all cases priority over the earthly ones. On that subtle assumption was based the passionate preference for astrology, the divine direction inherent in the stars, a condition to which the ancient world had pledged complete allegiance.

In Old Testament prophecy we too find two scenarios, or rather two chains of events occurring simultaneously. However, in the biblical prophecy the two events are completely different from the ancient Eastern astrology. In the prophecy it is not the ever-changing courses of the stars that dominate the entire process, but it is the angelic powers battling the demons that determine the earthly happenings. And these two are not identical. We cannot equate the erratic behavior of the stars with the battle formations of the angels because the one differs completely from the other. The prophecy stipulates most clearly that in the second scenario, the heavenly one, that so mysterious situation not discernible to the human eye, matters are at play that are of invaluable importance for the life of the nations. Daniel has a word about that when he describes how the royal angel, in their conversation, assured him that "the prince of the Persian kingdom resisted me twenty one days." That prince of the Persian kingdom is probably meant to be a figure in the world of ghosts, probably representing Persia there. Supposedly in the mysterious realms above the earth there was a war going on, running parallel with what was happening in the earthly sphere, all in the course of world history (Dan 10:13). The angel who spoke with Daniel—Michael, one of the chief princes—told him also that in this ferocious war Michael was at his side (see also verse 21). This indicates that up there, in the high heavenly sphere, a struggle had taken place, wherein the prince of Persia with his mighty forces were on the one side, and the royal angel who appeared to Daniel, aided by the prince of angels, Michael, on the other side. So, there also are the two scenarios, the one on top of the other. All that later will happen on earth, the war of the Persian kings with Greece, after that the conflict with Alexander the Great that too corresponds with the overwhelming happenings that took place earlier in the heavens.

All these thoughts contain something that is both frightening and fascinating. We are so used to regard our terrestrial theater, the world's history, as something that stands alone and is self-explanatory, that we simply cannot imagine that there exists a different theater, one of a higher order, where the same conflicts are played out, but of a totally different caliber. Frankly this reduces somewhat the allure and fascination with our own world history. We now see that the world history is no longer decisive, is no longer everything, but the battle is being fought on several fronts, both in heaven and on earth. Somehow or another there are parallel series of happenings, and that robs the earth of some of its originality and deprives it of some of its importance.

Earlier we have suggested that our cosmology, our knowledge concerning the constellation of the cosmos, needs a thorough revision as we came to understand that the "woman" who will give birth to the child, the church that Christ represents, is clothed with the sun and carries a crown of stars on her head. It is now clear that what we have accepted as historic truth, must be completely revised now that we begin to understand that what is playing out here upon earth in human history is not as original as it seems at first blush, but that up there parallel events take place, occurring on a totally different plane, and that these parallel happenings have an extremely important influence on history itself.

I repeat: an extremely important influence on history itself. I will show later that under no circumstances can we suggest that what happens on earth is only a copy, a reflection of what happens in heaven. If that were the case the events down here would lose their own dynamic, their own responsibility. They would be reduced to something secondhand and thus become a matter of less importance. That certainly is not the case. The earth has its own character, it moves on its own, and, yes, it is responsible for its own unraveling. But neither is it self-sufficient, which is to say that neither is it a force that finds its explanation in and by itself. The entire history of the world contains inexplicable, completely mysterious occurrences because it is intimately connected to another series of happenings that occur in a totally different sphere, and time and again it is influenced by what takes place there. When we are ever in the position to see the entire picture with all its surprising twists and turns, with all its periods of disintegration and renewal, of ruin and renewal, with her perpetual struggle for world domination, only then we will notice that this history is merely a fragment of a far more comprehensive happening. And therefore to really see history in its proper perspective, it is necessary to delve deeper into that other scene.

In any case we cannot say that what happens in the heavenly sphere will simply be copied on earth. That's what the ancient East believed, and their real motive was the silent fear of inevitable fate. The Bible gives equal weight to both scenarios. In both cases something valuable takes place. What goes on above the earth has its repercussions on the earth. But the other way around, what has taken place on earth, in particular that astounding affair concerning the woman and the child, also directly influences what goes on in the heavenly realms. At times heaven has first call, but then again what goes on on the earth has priority with heaven experiencing the after effects. In a word, everything is much more complex and intertwined than we at first are inclined to assume.

John has not in any sense obtained authority to solve the deepest secret of this interconnectedness for us. He is only allowed to just lift the tip of the veil that covers this fascinating secret. He is permitted to recount in very sober sentences that the happenings on earth are not self-explanatory and that they neither stand alone, but that they in some obscure way are connected to the events that on a much higher order have taken place. To stand in the center of world history means to stand between two coherent entities, means to see the connection related to the earthly chain of events and simultaneously see the context of the impenetrable mystery taking place in the higher realms.

When we more closely examine what John tells us about the events in the higher regions, it is striking that we at once are confronted with conflict: "And there was war in the heaven. Michael and his angels fought against the dragon and the dragon and his angels fought back." From the entire context it is clear that the start of this war was very closely connected to what had been mentioned before: the victory of the child who at once was carried up to God and his throne. Now that the dragon, the embodiment of all demonic powers, has been unable to destroy the child, now that he has failed in that one decisive factor, the only possibility left is to wage war. This war contaminates the universe in all its spheres, it infects all facets of creation, but first of all it reveals itself in the upper regions. It is there where the first, tremendous attack is launched against that powerful empire to test whether it is subject to dissolution and destruction or whether it is solidly and firmly constructed. Now that Christ has triumphed, now that he has passed through the darkness of death and hell and gloriously risen on Easter, and now that he has occupied his royal throne in the universe, now the destroyer of the world is trying to pull down every pillar of the universal palace. And that effort to pull down the pillars begins in the heavens, begins in the mysterious world behind the impenetrable curtain.

What confronts us now is in the first place the question how it is possible for the dragon, and its demonic power, to show up in the heavens. What sort of status does he enjoy there, how is it even possible for him to be there? Would it not be difficult to move around in the midst of the angels, because he simply does not fit in the realm of eternal light? That question is not easy to answer, especially because we know so very little of that world far above ours. It is safe to say that we know that the devil or Satan appears in the Bible always under two personas. He is in the first place the great seducer who tempted humanity right from its very start in paradise. In this very chapter of the Revelation of John he is still called the Satan "who seduces the entire world" (verse 9). Jesus depicts him as the ultimate deceiver, the "father of lies" (John 8:44). He twists human thought in the web of delusion, he conjures before the human eye the mirage of salvation and grandeur and drags the people, caught in the grip of falsehoods as an easy prey to their perdition. He resembles what the people in India call Maja, the overpowering pipe dream that as a deadly poison permeates our spiritual life. He is the king of conceit, the royal champion in mind bewilderment.

But in the second place the Bible depicts this same Satan as the terrible informer, who accuses the helpless, disoriented humans before God's throne. That's how he, as a prosecutor, appears in the first chapter of the book of Job in the meeting of "the children of God." Scoffing cynically, he hisses his poisonous accusation: "Does Job fear God for nothing?" He dissects the disintegrating human life, he picks it apart, he grinds it to pieces, until there's nothing left but ruin and garbage, and then he triumphantly brings all this to God's throne to show God that everything in this world has gone to pieces. "This world, God, your own world, over which you at one time have pronounced that it was 'very good,' now this world, this same world, is, in my possession, distorted into dire destruction, everything in her is in pieces, is poisoned, is on the verge of collapse." That's why the Satan is the tireless accuser of all God's servants. He is the one that carries the title of "the great accuser of all our brothers." So, in that capacity, as the accuser of the human being, he has access to the heavenly realms. That's the case because there is so much truth in his accusations, because, as a matter of fact, he has us in his grip. Satan has, to tell the bitter truth, truth on his side. The facts show that, indeed, we humans are completely corrupt. God is no position to deny him that truth; God simply cannot ignore this as pure fiction.

It is very likely that John here, in this section, has especially seen Satan in the second function. He has a place in the heavenly realms, and that place is permanent. He can insist on some rights, can maintain himself there. The war that now rages there is a conflict that centers on these privileges. Because what Jesus has done has totally changed the situation, has deprived the Satan of his status in heaven. Since the shout of triumph has sounded on Golgotha, the place of God's children has become different as well. They are justified in Jesus Christ, they have become new creatures. The woman is in the child, she participates in the child's victory, she is "made alive in Christ," and has gained a place in the heavenly realms in Christ Jesus" (Eph 2:5–6). Now that Christ has emerged as the victor, no longer can the Satan lodge any accusations against the woman and against the people of God, because every charge comes to nothing because of the great redeeming work of Jesus Christ. No longer may he appear in the meeting of the angels with his sneering face, his sarcastic mockery, his taunts aimed at the believers. For "in all this we are more than conquerors through him who has loved us." Because we know that Jesus Christ is there, who died—more than that, who was raised to life, is at the right hand of God and is also interceding for us. "Who will bring any charge against those whom God has chosen?" (Rom 8:33).

With the victory of the child a deeply penetrating change has taken place in all the world's relationships. And the consequence of these is war. "There was war in heaven." Of course it was to be expected that the dragon would not easily surrender his former rightful place. He fights for his position with all the tenacity at his disposal, but, of course, his defeat is inevitable. He was already conquered on Calvary. The only matter still to be solved is that all that is for certain, all that is really true, now must become reality, now has to be revealed in its true light.

It is remarkable that Michael and his angels are named here as their great opponents. We know of Michael already from the book of Daniel. Apparently he is one of the archangels, one of the princes among them, and that is all we know about him. However, in this setting his name is not without significance. His name is a question: mi-cha-el?, which means "who resembles God?" We would be inclined to answer this question with "Jesus Christ," "the radiance of God's glory and the exact representation of his being" (Heb 1:3). Jesus Christ, the Word of God that has appeared in the world, because whoever has seen him has seen the Father. The question contained in the name of the angel, is answered in him, in whose service he is. That this angel Michael acts here with the authority of the victorious Christ and in his power is true beyond any doubt. He has not waged a war against the deeply entrenched powers of the demonic empire upon his own initiative, but he has started this struggle because the basic situation has changed, because Jesus Christ has ascended to heaven, because all things in the universe have been placed on a new foundation through the victory gained by the child.

That's the only reason why he has dared to start this terrible struggle without for a moment having any doubt about the final outcome.

The final score was clearly outlined in a few words. "The dragon and his angels fought back. But he was not strong enough and they lost their place in heaven." Their place in this context includes both their judicial powers and their position of authority. The dragon, in spite of all his pretensions and his filthy slander, was kicked out of heaven shorn of his power and deprived of influence. No longer is he able to stand before God's throne with clenched fists and make accusations against God's elect. He simply has lost his foothold. Totally powerless, he is banned from heaven and is thrown out as quick as lightning. "He was hurled to the earth, and his angels with him."

It serves no purpose to elaborate here because when we, small, limited people try to further fathom these secrets then we right away start to make impossible guesses, then we draw fanciful images and devise fairy-tale scenes. All this makes no sense because the Bible gives us very little to go on. Everything we try to say beyond the Bible is nothing but pure fiction. That's why it is best to refrain from further comment. Let me only say that the events taken place in the celestial regions have had immense consequences. Something totally different has changed in the overall structure of the universe through Christ's victory. Let me leave it at that. What now is of importance is the question how all this affects matters below, here on earth. We live on a totally different level. We are situated in the everyday reality of earthly happenings, where we occasionally detect the faint reflections of what has taken place up there in the heavens but we are simply unable to understand its essence.

That's the reason why we have to focus again on the earth. Our habitat is the domain of the woman who had given birth to the child. Our earth is the place where Jesus Christ himself is born, where he preached, where he performed his miracles, where he suffered and died. His body was laid in the bosom of the earth when he had fought his last struggle. This earth is the region of his resurrection, and from this earth He ascended to the place from which he came. This cruel, grim earth, this rebellious earth is the sore reality we have to deal with. The matter that is now of the utmost importance is the question: what has happened to the earth since the victory has been gained in the heavenly realms?

That's what John, after all, is aiming at. He no longer continues depicting what happened in the upper heavens but right away turns his attention to this world. Here's where the church lives, to which he sent his letter to comfort them. Here's where she is attacked, persecuted, hunted, threatened, tempted. Here's where through the ages she pursues her troubled course. Here's where she eagerly longs for her ultimate complete redemption.

THIS DEMONIC WORLD

Not for a moment are we left in uncertainty. What just now happened in heaven undoubtedly has its rebound on the earth as well. That makes perfect sense, for, in fact, the two chains of events, those up there and those down here, are two sides of the same immense and decisive situation, so overwhelming because it is being fought in every sector of the universe. That's why it is inevitable that the victory of Michael and his angels over the demonic armies must somehow in a crucial way influence the happenings on earth.

The way that this unfolds is, however, highly surprising and even, to some extent, difficult to fathom. Those who had expected that Christ's great triumph here on earth would result in a process of increasing peace and prosperity, are cruelly cured of this illusion. It is soon evident that now the world starts to become demonic in the fullest sense of the word. "But woe to the earth and the sea, because the devil has gone down to you! Filled with fury, because he knows that the time is short" (verse 12). That's what the angels sing. This means that the demonic armies have thrown themselves onto the world with such unbridled ferocity and awesome fury that it can only have the most terrible results. It right away is striking that first a passive expression was used: "the dragon was thrown on the earth," now an active verb appears, when the sentence records the word "descends." Apparently the Satan has reversed the situation: he uses his defeat to start a new activity.

It's impossible to gauge the real situation, even though from afar we can guess what some of the implications are. The real significance could well be that Christ's victory, his resurrection and ascension, form a turning point in the history of the world. As of Easter morning the history of the world has taken a decisive turn. In the background massive shifts have taken place, which are the cause that even now in the everyday events occur. However, I am sorry to say, this does not mean that everything will be better, nicer, more hopeful, or sunnier, but precisely the opposite. Easter morning gives, viewed in the total context of world history, not the first glimpses of the rising sun, not the prelude of a melodious song of triumph, but introduces events that simply must be called catastrophic. What emerges is a combination of evil powers, a frightening totality of such a highly disturbing magnitude that it will seem that on that Easter morning the bells have tolled for humanity, banning all peace and quietness forever. From now on world events will be grimmer, more frightening, accelerating with breathtaking speed, continuously assuming more ghastly proportions, dragging millions along in a maddening danse macabre, undermining all old established morals, speeding relentlessly to chaos and social upheaval. This world, indeed, is to become possessed. All factors that somehow acted as brakes to stall this development are pushed aside; now that this process is in motion it speeds up disastrously, and nothing can stop it. On Easter morning history became madness. Woe to those who are sucked into this whirlpool of evil.

We wonder what this is all about. Why? What is behind this? This makes no sense at all. When finally this battle over the universe has been victorious then, one would expect, this grandiose success would penetrate through all spheres and expressions of the universe. After all, the glorious Easter morning, because of its immense significance, can have no other outcome than a cosmic revolution, as everything must become new, different, better, as everything must take on a new shine, now that new life is powerfully pulsing through the dead body. But why do we experience something totally different? Why now when we least expect it?

These relevant questions come with no answers. There are mysteries hidden here of which we have no inkling at all. One thing seems to come through loud and clear and that is that between the two functions of the satanic powers, accusing God's people and seducing the world, there is a connection impossible to detect and with an unfathomable depth. Now that the devil has lost his honorable place, now that he no longer occupies the position in heaven as accuser of God's children, his powerful place on the planet has not automatically come to an end. On the contrary, that position seems more secure, more unassailable, and also more terrifying and threatening than ever. John too realizes that something is the matter here that is beyond human grasp, because in principle, Satan's influential position should naturally come to an end as well, as, it seems, his defeat is final and can only mean total destruction. But God has a reason for this delay, has a reason why the demonic powers are allowed space to pursue their relentless opposition; there is a reason why God has allowed a certain period for this, a time frame in which life on earth goes on as if not Satan but Michael and his angels have suffered defeat. It is here that we are confronted with the history of the world. It is this extremely remarkable phenomenon that matters are not yet what they are, that everything still looks different than it is in reality. The haze of untruthfulness hovers like a curse over the world and in that haze of uncertainty history marches on.

Therefore it makes sense for us to spend a few moments to reflect on the character of world history since Easter morning. It is an undeniable fact that since that morning history's tempo has accelerated. That is especially noticeable if we pay attention to the last five centuries. There are parts of the world where in earlier times 500 years made hardly any difference at all, where the old religions were kept in honor, and the old ancestral morals remained intact. Large parts of Asia, Africa, and South America have for centuries lived without undergoing any change at all. Occasionally they waged wars, and some regime change took place, but there was no change at all in the spiritual make-up of the people as social life retained its structure. However since the 1500s the entire world has seen a very deep transformation. Europe has been at the forefront of this wild ride. The center of gravity there has switched from the Mediterranean Sea powers to the Western countries, Germany, England, and The Netherlands in particular, partly through the discoveries of new continents and the establishment of colonial empires. That period also saw deeply penetrating social changes, urbanization, and bloody revolutions. It also witnessed the birth of a global mechanical, physical science-dominated world with all its consequences. All too evident also are the erosion of old moral principles. All too well-known are the world wars, affecting and upsetting all that lives. Never before in the history of the world has so much in such a short time been demolished and radically changed, as in the last five centuries. These immense changes were not confined to Europe and the USA, but now involve all people everywhere, imperiling the existence of all these countries and regions as they increasingly cause unrest and confusion.

In this grand scheme of changes the many discoveries especially in the area of natural physics have played a significant role. I could mention the invention of the machine, steam, the motor, electricity, atomic energy, television, just to name a few. Medical science gained new insight in the nature of diseases and the methods of healing. We saw new ways in agriculture, a great increase in world population, new methods of transportation, especially aviation, and communication such as the rise of the computer and electronic information. We also witnessed the development of new weapons and greater possibilities for destruction. And the end has not yet been reached. Every day we read about new developments. As ever the probing human brain is searching for the secrets of the universe in the quest for new discoveries. All this has meant an immense increase in human power. It almost seems as if God for centuries has blindfolded humanity to prevent them from seeing all the planetary powers and possibilities and then suddenly he ripped away the blindfold in our days, so that the one perspective after the other opens up. Earlier generations may have dreamed about these developments, but in our days they have become reality. That which the ancient myths referred to in vague terms, are now so common among us that they no longer receive any comment. This wild, unrestrained progress of human thought and discovery comes with both a good dose of triumph but also with visions of frightening nightmares. Nerves are constantly on edge, the pace of life is ever more hectic, undefined feelings of anxiety dominate the millions. We are confronted with situations, internally, spiritually, and morally that make it impossible to cope, that make us feel helpless, and that give us the unnerving notion that we are racing toward indescribable confusion and degeneration.

There is no doubt that what took place in the previous five centuries has all the hallmarks of a wild and turbulent era, overwhelming all opposition, undermining all established certainties. As a furiously cascading stream it forces a destructive path to nobody knows where. Is that what is meant when it is said that ever since the Easter morning the world resembles more and more a possessed world? Is that what is meant when John laments in these harrowing words, "Woe to the earth and the sea, because the devil has gone down to you! He is filled with fury, because he knows that his time is short" (verse 12)? Have we humans, more than ever before in these last centuries, embraced these demonic powers that sweep us along in their breathtaking course? Are these the demons whose terrible presence we more and more sense in our day and age? This entire gigantic process finds its start, its point of departure, around Easter morning, when the Roman Empire stood at the pinnacle of power, but the germs of degeneration and decomposition were clearly becoming evident. Then certain forces were loosed that as a tsunami have overwhelmed the world. Here we encounter events behind events, happening on a different level than that in which we live. Around that Easter something indescribably great took place on that different level, and its consequence is now noticeable, first slowly, but gradually with increasing tempo and ferocity. We now are in the eye of a cyclone: everything around us is cracking up, crashing, on edge and at the breaking point. "For this world in its present form is passing away" (1 Cor 7:31).

And yet—it cannot be otherwise—behind all this moaning and groaning there are hardly hidden hoots of laughter. True, they also include inexpressible anxiety, a condition that at times is augmented with doubt, but even this state of fear cannot eliminate the fact that the rage and the confusion that we as powerless people now are exposed to ultimately are the result of an overwhelming victory, God's very triumph. Above this disjointed and utterly terrified world we see the sparkling sign of the Easter morning. All our dismay and bewilderment cannot erase the overriding fact that the demonic forces in reality have suffered defeat and that's why their fury is merely a symptom of their defeat. They are fully aware that they have "little time": they have already been banned from heaven and their influence on earth is approaching its inevitable finish. That "woe on earth and sea" may be accompanied with feelings of untold anguish, yet they fully rest on the unbelievable sounds of jubilation coming from on high: "Now have come the salvation and the power and the kingdom of our God and the authority of his Christ." "He has come!" Above the screaming hurricanes emerges the overriding call to joy beyond measure. It resounds like a loud trumpet blast penetrating to the utmost parts of the universe. It also echoes in our hearts, filled with anxiety and fear.

WHERE DO WE STAND OURSELVES?

It is time to have a look at ourselves in an effort to find the meaning of all this for our personal lives. What is it actually that John wants to show us in this grand vision? What does he mean with his anxiety-provoking description of what he has observed?

It is right away clear that he has situated us between two opposing conditions: deep anxiety and profound, inexpressible joy. That's where he wants us, that's where we belong.

At first blush we are inclined to maintain that anxiety should prevail. "Woe to the earth and sea, because the devil has descended there." There's where we belong, with the earth and the sea. There's where we spend our life, there's where we were born, there's where we are engaged in our daily struggle, there's where we stand, dead tired, and anxious and also amazed. All that is hardly encouraging, because that "Woe to . . ." also applies to us. We should not forget that John here talks in generalities, even though he directs himself in particular to believers. It is especially they who are exposed to great pressure. Verse 17: "The dragon was enraged at the woman and went off to make war against the rest of her offspring—those who obey God's commandments and hold to the testimony of Jesus." Thus they are the ones who have to cope with the biggest blows, as especially at them is aimed the full impact of the demonic forces. There's little comfort here; on the contrary, it generates the scariest premonitions concerning what awaits us.

However is questionable if it is this that John wants to tell us. No doubt he intends to rouse the Christian church to greater vigilance and thoughtfulness. He likes to warn them that they should certainly not think that matters would become increasingly easier since Easter, because if they live under that illusion, they would be bitterly disappointed. On the contrary, now, more than ever, they should be on guard against that notion. Without letup they will have to guard against challenges of every sort because of the tireless efforts by the Satan to catch them in his tentacles. They will be despised and persecuted, stumble through fog and nasty storms, constantly be faced with injuries and death. The Easter morning is behind them, but ominous dark clouds lie ahead. The idea may rise up in them that Easter is nothing but a merciless illusion, a fata morgana, because this world does not show any signs at all of the resurrection. This fear may place such a burden on them that they would fear that there never would come an end to her worries and struggle. The celestial song of jubilation, extolling God's salvation, displaying his power, and the advent of his kingship, may all convey to them something akin to a very distant and rather unreal swan song. Yet this world doesn't show any of this: it is stronger and tighter in the grip of demons than ever before. Burdened and almost incapacitated, it is wading through the endless morasses of the daily occurring temptations, dangerous swamps from which poisonous, mind-altering vapors rise up, hypnotizing the mental and cognitive facilities. Also on the far horizon there still is not a ray of light visible, nowhere are shown the radiant beams of a victorious daybreak. All this can have a paralyzing and debilitating effect and the church is urged to be utterly vigilant here. She must be on guard all the time. She must be prepared for the worst, may not for a moment retreat when faced with the most terrible, but be fully aware that all this is the necessary consequence of the Easter morning, and, however strange this may seem, all this is the prelude of the coming kingdom. After all, the church is pitched between the mount of ascension and the glorious finale in which God will be all and in all. Between these two peaks lies the pitch-dark valley of a possessed world. There, totally in the dark, stands the church; there is her field of operation, there is where her task lies.

But is she really active there? Is it really there where she belongs? There is something in the song of jubilation that resounds through the heavens that throws this in doubt. "Therefore rejoice you heavens and you who dwell in them!" Who are they who live there? The angels? The redeemed? Of course, they too are included. And how about those who belong to Jesus? Aren't they part of this redemption, even though they still find themselves on earth? Paul in his letters, on more than one occasion, emphasizes that the believers, even though they live in this world, do in fact belong to the heavenly realm. "But our citizenship is in heaven," he says in Philippians 3:20. When he in his letter to the Ephesians recalls what Christ means for us, then he first says that "God made us alive with Christ when we were dead in transgressions" but then he does not hesitate to continue "and raised us up with Christ and seated us with him in the heavenly realms in Christ Jesus" (Eph 2:5-6). We do live on this earth, but our real place, our rightful position is elsewhere, we already now belong to another "age," a different world, a different kingdom. And John? John often makes a sharp distinction between the world and the believers. "We know that we are children of God, and that the whole world is under the control of the evil one. . . . We are in him who is true, even in his son Jesus Christ" (1 John 5:19-20). We no longer belong to the "world" in the sense in which John designates it. "They are not of the world," says Jesus in his high-priestly prayer (John

17:16). Therefore it can never be said only that the church resides under the "woe unto you." The church also participates in the "Rejoice you heavens and those who dwell therein." This rejoicing applies to the church in a far broader and more truthful manner than that ominous "woe unto you." Because, in spite of all signs to the contrary, the church, in the ultimate sense, must be counted as belonging to "the heavenly realms."

If that is the case then the essence of everything that John proclaims is bound to be in a different direction. That means that the very last thought in this chapter points not to anxiety but to ecstasy. That implies that there is every reason to be extremely excited over the ongoing victory of which the current darkness on the planet is a clear sign, because that darkness would not be so terrifying and horrible had there not have been the Easter morning. Softly in the background of the world's happenings murmurs the melody of Christ's victory song. It, at times, may be drowned out by the bangs of bombs and the cries of the persecuted, but this celestial song is more substantial and more indisputable than all the smart missiles in the world's arsenals. What John wants us above everything else to grasp, is that the victory has been won, that all threats and terrifying tactics must be seen against the background of this victorious event, and only when we see it in this way will we not be overwhelmed by all this.

In other words, we are between the "woe unto you" and "rejoice." We are part of both. We can only then fearlessly abide in the "woe unto you," when deep in our hearts resounds the indomitable song of jubilation expressed in "rejoice." In the same measure that the overwhelming joy over the victory of our Lord Jesus Christ fills the uttermost crevices of our existence, in that same way we will find ourselves more secure amidst all upheaval and disruption. The more we are taken in by the technological miracles of the present age, all parts of the unrestrained historic maelstrom, the more also will we inwardly become defenseless, discouraged, and desperate. On the other hand, the more we live a more insightful and sincere life, trusting the certainty of salvation in Jesus Christ and his glorious future, in that same way we can persist in our opposition until at last we have overcome. There exists an extremely delicate but nevertheless unbreakable connection between what the Bible calls "joy in the Lord" and the holy fearlessness that befits every Christian in the dark night of today's happenings.

That means that only then are we securely safeguarded today, when we have a vision of the history behind the history, when we can detect what has taken place in the totally different sphere of world history. Those who only stare at what appears in the newspapers and on television, slowly become blind, mesmerized, and confused. Only those who understand that what we daily read and view, is simply a tiny fragment of a far more elaborate happening, and only those who know that, in that comprehensive totality, Christ's glory is all-dominating, only they are not unduly anxious and can resist the demonic influences. Only they have found their basis in God and stand secure.

It is this concept that I would see as the focal point of the Revelation of Jesus Christ given to John. All other chapters are an elaboration of this theme. They show us in flowery language the fearsome figures arising from the human world and relate to us in somber words what awaits us thanks to abundant arrogance, to passion for power, to tyranny and terror, to disasters and disputes, to disintegration and deprivation. Without pulling punches they depict the harrowing perspective of the "woe unto you," but there is not a grain of despair inherent in all this, there is nothing of a disarming defeatism. Through the entire book resounds, at times very softly, at times almost inaudible, yet also swelling to a mighty choral, the jubilation song of the victory. Those who are tuned to the song of jubilation need not feel discouraged ever. This song stays with them, occupies all their thinking and living. They can look forward to the future without ever being afraid. "Now have come the salvation and the power and the kingdom of our God, and the authority of his Christ."

CHAPTER TWO

The Road More Troubled
(Revelation 2 and 3)

WHERE WE ARE NOW

We have asked ourselves what our own place is in that long and troubled period between the Easter morning and "the rebirth of all things." From John we have received the answer: we are caught between anxiety and ecstasy, between fear and feast. That sounds quite simple, given to us in one single phrase, but in reality the situation is far more complicated. The true state of affairs resembles a wide and deep stream in which it is difficult to separate the different elements from each other. The real situation has infinitely more variations, is chock full with nuances and side-issues, loaded with doubts and temptations. We can describe the life of the church of all ages, that period between Easter morning and the Last Day as hovering between anxiety and ecstasy, between fear and feast, but then we must not overlook that these two extremes appear time and again throughout the ages in new versions and come in new colors.

The Revelation of John shows that it is acutely aware of this. This is not a book that wants to mold the variegated reality into a preconceived framework. No, it is a book that has an open eye for all minute details and does not shrink to outline these in their totality. That is already quite plain in its first chapters, especially in the letters to the seven churches. Right from the beginning of the church it has been understood that the snapshots presented here depict the church of all ages. That implies that the peculiar difficulties encountered there, the exposure to temptations, the looming dangers, were certainly present there, but that they also resembled in many ways the church of all ages, including those today. These seven churches lived in a hostile world, they were threatened from within and were persecuted from without, they were dangerously susceptible to compromise and easily sucked in by paganism that then permeated all of life and constantly agitated all around them. They at times were exuberant in their joy and then again deeply disheartened in their despondency, then again decisive in their faith-witness in Jesus Christ, and then again affected by all sorts of doubts and insecurities. At times they rushed at the world around them in a radiant push, and then again they crawled away to the hide-outs of world-flight. They were tossed about to and fro, they failed and failed again, and time after time they had to be called to repentance and renewal. That's how the seven letters to the churches in Asia Minor come to us as a witness of what it means to be church in this confused world and what it means to dwell between anxiety and ecstasy.

That's the reason why life in these small cities of ancient Asia Minor shows us something that goes on far beyond those times. They contain something of the everlasting, something that is valid throughout the ages. It always involves the church, that mysterious church, the church that stands there, endowed with the sun and crowned with a garland of stars on her head, the church that holds the universe in place, and at the same time is persecuted, is deathly afraid, is hunted and is continually in mortal danger. It is this church that is displayed here in all her strength and frailty. Her royal lineage is not denied, her pitiful state fully acknowledged. Every one of these portraits painted here brings forth recollections of what we are ourselves and the struggles we endure in our own faith-life. We proceed past these letters to the seven churches as people who walk past a mirror and constantly see their own reflection. We do this but it does not invoke despair in us because with each step we are fully aware of the close proximity of Jesus Christ who always guards us and protects us.

LIFE IS DANGEROUS.

The first snapshot presented to us is that of the church in Ephesus. The letter starts out with some quite praiseworthy words about its conduct.

In the first place it mentions that this church has demonstrated great industriousness and tenacity, indicating an active group of people. They are constantly busy, and there is not a trace of tardiness or laxity evident. Their efforts are pursued with vigor. With these people we don't detect sudden bursts of enthusiasm but we do see a steady and quiet progress. All this is extremely favorable and praiseworthy.

How do we know about this persistence and effort? That is immediately shown in these words, "I know that you cannot tolerate wicked people, that you have tested those who claim to be apostles but are not and have found them false." That's where it is all about. It right away reveals to me what this church of Ephesus sees as the crux of the matter. They are a group of people who has mastered the most difficult job of saying "no." No chance there to be sucked in by crafty liars, by people who piously pretend to be apostles. They won't tolerate all sorts of wrong elements within their ranks just to keep peace and quietness. They have a keen nose for some deviation from the truth, they detect it right away when a speaker proclaims some sort of heresy. If need be, they are not afraid to intervene. They rather risk temporarily disturbing the peace than see the truth assaulted. They tirelessly guard the veracity of the holy word of God. They won't tolerate theories that seem nice and enticing, but in reality appear more like poisonous and overpowering vapors, confusing common sense and causing them to deviate from the only true way. In all this they will proceed very cautiously, they certainly will thoroughly investigate all relevant matters, but when it finally becomes clear that these so-called apostles really are pure self-seekers, that they only are out for self-promotion and not at all concerned with Jesus Christ, and that for them the truth is not the final criterion, then these people in Ephesus do not for a moment hesitate to expose them for what they really are. Yes, indeed, this congregation masters the art of saying "no."

This world goes to its demise because people are incapable of saying "no." They are either too polite, or too modest, or too cowardly, or too weak, or just lack character, or they don't grasp that a sharp "no" is at the same time the inescapable flip side of a true, sincerely meant "yes." Those who have said "yes" to God, "yes" to Jesus Christ, must, until death say "no" to oneself, "no" to every item, every thought, every spiritual movement, every desire, every friend or enemy who wants to undermine or even weaken the "yes." Those who cowardishly try to evade the inevitable consequences of a "yes" are people without convictions, in spite of calling themselves good-natured and broad-minded. In any case that's not what ails Ephesus. They are able to say '"no," and even when necessary they can do so emphatically in terms that unmistakably cannot be misunderstood. They find it difficult, they may not like it, but they do not shrink back. They know the priceless value of correct doctrine, of true orthodoxy. They detest the honeyed tongue of deceit, even when lie appears under the cloak of love for the truth.

All this is fine and dandy. A few other remarks are added which even more directly illuminate the condition there: the church there in Ephesus possesses "perseverance." Apparently this is such a striking characteristic of this group of people that this is mentioned twice. "You have persevered and have endured hardship for my name and have not grown weary." That they have endured sounds quite appropriate here. It says in the previous text that the church in Ephesus cannot tolerate wickedness, that she certainly could not do, but what she could tolerate, could endure, was the hardship, the pain and suffering that resulted from this perseverance. She was not afraid for affliction and that was also the reason why she could not tolerate evil. She had the inner strength, the moral fortitude to say "no" to evil because she had the courage to bravely face the difficult consequences resulting from that "no." And those consequences did come. It is not important how they did come: they revealed themselves as persecutions, as blackballing, as shame and poverty. But all that is unimportant compared to that one condition: the church of Ephesus has never shied away from these ills, and neither did she become discouraged. The subversive opposition by their enemies tired them out; there was no let-up in daily shunning by their neighbors and other city dwellers, but this opposition did not divert them from their allegiance to the church. There was depth in this congregation, latent power that was stronger than all trouble and inconvenience. It was this resilience that became more and more public, in direct proportion to the difficulties experienced and the evidence of the hostility. This congregation did not compromise: she did not budge.

And yet, this very same upright, courageous church lacked one great and decisive feature: "But I hold this against you: you have forsaken your first love." Losing one's first love, that is really something! Yet it can happen, almost without noticing it. It is possible that this tender love ever so gradually diminishes when daily confronted with the never ceasing struggle for survival. Yes, slowly love can flag somewhat. Actually the Bible uses stronger language, more direct: you have left that love behind, you have forsaken that first love. There's almost something like intent here. That love had become a bit of a burden. You have abandoned it, you have taken distance from it.

Extremely poignant here is that word *love*. The word *love* is used without mentioning an object. Love, for whom? It's logical to assume love for God, love for Jesus Christ, love for the eternal kingdom. I imagine this would be the case here, but it is not mentioned. There only is made mention of love without any further indication. Only the Bible can speak about love in this way. This reminds me of the line in Psalm 116: "I love the Lord, for he has heard my voice." Of course here also love indicates love for God, love for the Lord who hears my voice, but what is meant here is much more all-encompassing and all-inclusive. Yes, I love the Lord, but because of that, from him and in him I am able to love all people and through him I can love this great, glorious globe. In a word, it was that holy, all-embracing love that went AWOL in Ephesus. It went into hiding. It had faded away. "You have forsaken her, have abandoned her, have pushed it away."

The "no" remained, but the "yes," that positive, profound, enthusiastic "yes," which had its basis on the "no," which saw its culmination on that denial, that "yes'" was now diminished. That "no" against heresy, against all that wickedness, undoubtedly still resounded, but it has lost some of its conviction, because that "yes'" that backed it up, was now deprived of its true zeal. It became a "yes" against God, against Jesus and his work of salvation, even "yes" against his gracious love that has rescued us from the tentacles of death. In the heat of their struggles against evil influences, something totally essential had been sacrificed by these people. They had lost their focus on Jesus, and had refrained from fixing their eyes on the cross. Their prayer life had become impoverished, their tender contact with their savior had been curtailed, and their spiritual joy in him had languished. Something forced, almost something harsh had appeared in their eyes. They kept on staring at temptation, that heresy had crept into their consciousness, and it occupied them day and night. That robbed them of the moments of blessed assurance for the infinite marvel of God's grace in Jesus Christ. No longer were they able to burst out in joyful adoration of him, of whom and in whom and through whom all things are. All that had become almost absent in their lives, dangerously so. They still were people at the edge of salvation, and that was good, even necessary. But one thing threatened to slip away from them, because salvation is only possible when it involves the total person, when there is a constant struggle to be totally dependent on God. And because they no longer saw this clearly, their entire attitude toward life had assumed something artificial, even something pathetic.

All that had influenced them also in their attitude toward the heretics and their opponents. True, they hated the works of the Nicolaitans and that was good, even necessary. But had they started to hate them personally? Had they failed to see the human being behind that heresy, these miserable, led-astray human beings, speeding toward perdition? Paul speaks of people who go a different way, the enemies of the cross, but he does so "with tears in [his] eyes" (Phil 3:18). And about Jesus we read that he once looked at the Pharisees "in anger and deeply distresses at their stubborn hearts" (Mark 3:5). There too is that unbridgeable divide, in all its fullness, but it contains an element that lifts it to a higher level. There tears appear, there is sadness because it is backed up by love. Is that what is disappearing in Ephesus? They did not tolerate wickedness, which was good and necessary.

But it seems that something uncharitable was infiltrating their life and their thinking.

This letter to the Ephesians does not mention mission work, gives no hint that they proclaimed the good news outside their church in the world. These people were tirelessly busy with keeping themselves pure from dogmatic error and shunning all perilous influences. They saw the world around them as a danger, as a pitfall, as a temptation, and no longer saw it a possible field where God could work his wonders. They were equipped with the truth but they were far from ready and willing to bring the gospel of peace. That's why something fundamental was lacking in the "whole armor of God." All that could be traced back to that one factor that encompasses everything: a shortage of the only true love for the crucified one.

How did it come about that this congregation fell short in this so important matter? The Bible does not tell us that and it is foolishness to guess the reason. There is, however, one assertion we can make: the attitude of this group of people is one of escape. They have backed away from love because love is difficult, love is dangerous. Love makes that inevitable "no"—always an essential part of "yes"—not something to be hesitant about, not something of which we are not quite sure, but love changes the issues. Love has no trouble at all to very convincingly say "no" to heresies but it always does so in a particular way. These people in Ephesus were not able to combine these two ways, on the one hand being energetic and justified to reject any underhanded fraud, and on the other hand to live in the world childlike close to the savior of the world. In the heat of the battle something went amiss in them that caused them impoverishment and exhaustion. It sometimes seemed to them that the cross was so far away, so infinitely far, that the wide-open arms of the savior and redeemer could no longer be found, that there no longer was a refuge. It is true, the world is cruel, the pressure unbearable, life often bitterly difficult and people always disappoint. They no longer were able to truly rest in the surety of the constant presence of God's love that wipes away all tears and is the same yesterday, today, and into eternity. At times a searing pain touched their hearts, signaling the brokenness in their lives, but no longer were they able to completely surrender themselves to Jesus Christ in holy enthusiasm and in childlike joy, and so be embraced by his mercies.

And why were they unable to do so? I imagine that they were afraid. If real love would burn within them, they would attack the world with far greater abandon, and place themselves in Christ's service with much greater force, and with far deeper devotion. Then they would view with different eyes these wicked forces which they could not tolerate, then that outspoken "no" now so quickly uttered to forestall all temptation and to thwart all tempters, that "no" would have to be said with tears in their eyes. And by acting in such a way everything would become infinitely more difficult and dangerous because that would entail that for them new perils and new troubles. And it was just this prospect that kept them from doing this. They chose the road more accessible, the smoother way. In that they forgot that this would cause them irreparable damage. And so the light of Christ's love abandoned them, leaving them troubled and burdened.

And now Christ is facing them, the living lord and king himself. "Repent and do the things you did at first. If you do not repent I will come to you and remove your lampstand." Yes, there is a way out, but the road they travel on now leads to a dead end. These frightened people must turn back. To guard the truth, twenty-four–seven is important, is necessary and valuable, but it is only possible with love and in love. If love is absent then everything become bland, bitter, backbiting, bad. Then they become a movement, with a political agenda. Then they no longer are motivated by the joyful security of the cross. Then faith has lost its luster. Without love this small band of people live at the edge of the precipice. Drastic changes are needed, a totally different road must be taken, a route that goes back to the refuge of the only redeemer and savior, back to the intimacy of a daily communing with Jesus Christ and appearing before his face. If they do that then, indeed, the entire picture will change. Is that really the case? In his letter Christ's last words are a personal appeal to each of the people involved. That is how it must start. This is initially not a communal affair: no, it first is a matter of every person needing a new commitment, and starting with that, and only in this way, the life of the Christian community can be renewed and rejuvenated. "To him that overcomes I will give the right to eat from the tree of life which is in the paradise of God." There we have the crux of the matter: to eat from the tree of life, to eat from the cross, from the saving grace of Jesus Christ. To eat means to daily rejoice because we have a savior, because our sins are forgiven, because we are filled with the hope for life eternal. It is exactly these matters that we have to learn again and be open to receive again. When that happens they no longer will see themselves as a group of people constantly exposed to temptation and attack, feeling sorry for themselves in that hostile world and persecuted by demonic powers. Then, in their hearts something new shall resound: Rejoice you heavens and those who dwell therein. Then again undaunted they will sing out:

> The powers of death and hell
> Our Lord will surely quell
> Their rage we can endure
> For look their doom is sure.

One little word will fell them.

They will relearn these lines as soon as they eat again from the tree of life. Then again in the fatigued hearts of this little band of besieged disciples of Jesus Christ will dawn, as yet undefined and obscure, the greatest vision that they really are that woman, adorned with the sun and having a crown of starts on their heads. And that vision will expand and take root. Then too they will understand that very soon they will enter God's eternal paradise where they for ever and ever will eat from the tree of life.

But before all else, they must conquer, they must conquer themselves, they must conquer all temptation and danger. In all their disquiet and unease they must, as little children, return to the chief shepherd and allow him to guide them. Also for them beautiful prospects await them, provided they undergo another conversion, provided they see the looming dangers, provided they recognize these, turn away from them and rely on him who is the light of the world.

EVERYTHING IS DIFFERENT THAN IT SEEMS

The church in Smyrna was, in many aspects, totally different from the one in Ephesus. The situation there comes to us in only a few stark lines but even these few hints show us that Smyrna's spiritual life was undoubtedly much higher than was the case in Asia Minor's first city, Ephesus.

What is immediately striking in this short letter to Smyrna is the series of opposites we here read about. This is already evident in the first few words: "These are the words of him who is the first and the last, who died and came to life again." Here the first is also the last; he who was dead (dead in the fullest, most terrible meaning of the word, the way Scripture designates death), and has become alive again. And when we keep on reading then we notice that the poor also are the rich, that the Jews also are non-Jews, and that the Lord's synagogue at the same time is Satan's synagogue. And at the end of the letter we read that the congregation there is urged to be faithful unto death "and I shall give you the crown of life." Here we are confronted with a bewildered world, a world of blinding contrasts. When we go to the bottom of the matter, then we notice that everything here is completely different than we suspect at first sight. They who fail to pierce through that blinding sham cannot be a Christ's true disciples.

Actually, when we look more closely then we should really not be surprised with this depiction of Smyrna. Already before this we noticed the same phenomenon when we discussed "the woman, adorned with the sun and wearing a crown of stars," the woman who nevertheless, destitute and hunted, had to escape into the desert. The church in this world appears as something she cannot be; she possesses valuables that are not yet visible and tangible. Actually that is not strange at all. Paul, on more than one occasion, has explained the significance of all this. It only becomes strange when it is carried over into real life, when the church in fact becomes poor and persecuted and held in contempt, and chased away. We may organize conventions around this theme and listen to great speeches but they only hit us as puzzling and contradictory when the cruel reality confronts us from all directions. And that is exactly what surely happened in Smyrna. That was not a place for rousing oratory: there day in and day out they endured the bitter experience of being spat at, of being exposed to ridicule and enmity. There only was the mind-depleting and deadly tiring experience of being banned from society and cast out from the wider community. When a church finds itself in such a somber reality then much strength is required to remain standing. Then it may be easy to mention that "woman adorned with the sun" but that image resembles more a fairy tale or a deceptive fantasy. What the church in Smyrna needs above all is encouragement. She must be lifted up beyond the everyday picture of being oppressed and troubled and see beyond these to the glorious future that awaits them. The church was sorely in need of some sort of radar by means of which she could see through the fog surrounding faith so that the deepest realities in store for them could be observed. And it is exactly this perspective that the heavenly shepherd makes available to them.

The very beginning of this letter makes this clear to the understanding reader. "This says the first and the last, who has died and is alive again." That explains the entire letter. All the riddles contained in this world, caught in delusions and illusions are made clear in this one sentence. Jesus Christ himself, as *the* mystery beyond measure, stands at the center of the world's history. Even though the light of light, he yet penetrated into the deepest darkness of lonesomeness. God from God and yet hung on a cross. In him was life, and he was dragged into death. He was before all things and there was nothing that was not created by him, and yet he stood in the world as one of us. The first and the last, but it seems that the center has been surrendered to the demonic powers of darkness. Those who have seen him have also seen the mystery, because for them nothing in what is to come can surprise any longer. Of course, all this was well-known in Smyrna, but now she was, kicking and screaming so to say, dragged along the thorny road of defamation and slander, in order to really grasp the very nature and force of these matters.

It looks like the persecution of the Smyrna church primarily originated with the fanatic section of the Jewish population. These Jews were greatly upset by the inroads of the gospel, especially among the proselytes, those of the pagans who had gone over to the Jewish faith. Paul already, on his mission trips, had attracted among the proselytes many who with great interest had listened to his preaching. During the time John wrote his Revelation the number of these "proselytes" who had heard the gospel and had received the good news of Jesus Christ, must have been quite large. That this had caused the envy of the Jews was quite understandable. However the way in which this envy was revealed, by spreading all sorts of slander about these Christians to the pagans in order to rile them up against them, really was mean and undeserving. That's why we read in that letter this sharp condemnation: "they say they are Jews, but they are not." By ethnic origin they were Jews, but they completely lacked the highspiritedness so pronounced in the patriarchs and Moses and David. Especially they had abandoned the God of their forefathers and were in all respects solidly in the power of the prince of this perishable world. On the Sabbath days they congregated in their synagogues, the meeting place of the Lord as they called it, there to punctually and with great fervor hear the proclamation of the old law. But their hearts had become so dull and lackluster that the radiance of the holy writ could no longer penetrate into their soul. They had degenerated into a "synagogue of Satan" under the disguise of piety and strict observance of the law.

It is this group of jealous Jews that made life so difficult for that tiny Christian church. The persecution was even more difficult to bear because it originated with them. That exactly those who pondered the same pages of Moses and the prophets and who had so much in common with them, that precisely these people threatened and so painfully afflicted them, caused them much extra grief. It seems that the end was nowhere in sight. The Lord in heaven does not promise them any relief at all, on the contrary. He warns them that they must expect even more terrible things to happen. "I tell you the devil will throw some of you in prison to test you and you will suffer persecution for ten days." Apparently something will happen that will suddenly inflame the hate and anger of the pagan people. That will give the Jews the opportunity to incite the entire city against the adherents of the Nazarene. That will mean that some will become the victims, probably the pillars of the church. This severe persecution will also be a serious test for the church. People will be asked to escape the danger but that will come with certain conditions, meaning forsaking the confession of the only true Savior. However this persecution will be short-lived. After ten days the prison doors will be opened and those incarcerated will be set free. Who wrote that again? This writes he who "has been dead and has come alive." It is the same he who says that they will be imprisoned and set free again. Something of what has happened to him also will be duplicated in them. Death will also dangerously hover over them for a short time and then they will, "having been made alive again," return to their families.

It is a tremendous privilege that this congregation that had to endure so much hardship, had been prepared in this way to know what would happen to them: ten days of persecution. If we knew ahead of time that it would only be ten days, then that really does not pose a problem. If Christians anywhere now persecuted would know ahead of time that their plight would only be of a short duration then their struggles would not be so difficult. It is exactly the uncertainty, the interminability of the suffering, the lack of hope and perspective that can make the pain so unbearable. In that regard the church in Smyrna was certainly exceptional by having an advance notice concerning the duration of the coming suppression. But, come to think of it, is not this always the case? Do not all Christians, wherever in the world, know that when they are in deep trouble because of their confession, that liberation is always close? Even if that liberation means something we regard as the worst, that is when the prison doors open not for freedom but for being placed in front of a firing squad. That too is liberation. That assurance is anchored in the fact that our Lord and savior is nobody else but he who "has been dead and is alive again." Some of his suffering, but also the full force of his glorification, of his liberation will somehow reflect in the life of those who belong to him.

"Be faithful, even to the point of death, and I will give you the crown of life." Again that remarkable contrast. Death immediately followed by life! That means that worse is to come, perhaps not right away, not yet during the ten days of oppression, but later. It then could happen that somebody of the church, perhaps an elder or even "the angel," the shepherd himself, would be imprisoned, and then the doors won't open so quickly again. Then it is quite possible that this time it will become quite tense, quite dangerous. It is even possible, yes that cannot be excluded at all, that the moment will come in which the choice has to be made between suffering a cruel death for the sake of Christ, or being freed as a Christ-denier. Then the ultimate test is at hand, the dearest in our life lies in the balance. "All goods they can take, even our blood" as Luther said some 500 years ago, words even current today when the flashing sword of the executioner is seen again. These people in Smyrna must be steadfast until the point of death, these poor and oppressed people. Will in the very last anxious moments the haze fade away and the scales of the eyes be lifted? Will they then suddenly see that this so toilsome life is nothing else and has never be anything other than a tiresome and exhausting phase in our life's story until at the finishing line our poverty-prone existence is safely secured by him who will endow us with the victor's crown of life? Is then the spell of bewitchment severed and is then at last the woman crowned with the sun and will she receive the crown of stars on her head? Is it finally at that point that everything will be perfect, as it really always has been since that moment when we found Jesus Christ, or better, when we let Jesus find us?

"They who overcome, will not be hurt at all by the second death." The "second death" is the true, the terminal death, the sinking away in the pitch-darkness of God's absence. That is something that will not affect these faithful, these wretched, these insulted, these tortured people. Not for a moment need they be bothered by that. That "second death" will quickly shy away from them even when they are far away from it. That "second death" after all is the death Christ has suffered for our sake, the death through which he painfully pursued his perfect path, and from which he emerged as the eminent victor! It is remarkable that in this short letter the word *death* appears three times. The reason for this is that the letter to these people was not just a false alarm, but a daily occurring reality. Every day and every night death was at their doorsteps; their lives were in the fullest sense of the word "a continuous death." But they, with total and indisputable certainty see, that they, beyond any doubt, have nothing at all to do with that death, that is to say with death in the utmost sense of the word. If they only were not afraid to face death, not back away from perishing, if they dared to face death valiantly, then there would be no cause for anxiety and worry, then everything would fall into place, because they are securely settled in the arms of him who "has been dead and have come to life again." After all, that is decisive for everybody and for always!

CAESAR OR CHRIST

Persecution is a daily occurrence in the life of the young churches in Asia Minor, and in some way it also is a normal matter in the church of all ages. The reason for this is that the church here in this world is a foreign element, is an abnormal entity and for that reason is a dangerous matter. We should not forget that the world itself is still the domain where satanic powers reveal themselves to their full extent, and that's why "the woman, adorned with the sun" can only exist there as one hunted and banned. She does not proceed "according to the ways of the world" (Eph 2:2), as Paul expresses it so succinctly; her entire way of life collides with the normal course of events. That's the reason why we should be amazed not because the church is persecuted, but wonder why the church is not in that predicament. Not to be persecuted seems of necessity to include that either the church is no longer church in the fullest sense of the word, or the world around her no longer understands what the church is doing. In any case it is something that gives food for thought. The book of Revelation of John sees the issue most clearly.

There can be all sorts of reason for the church to be persecuted. At the Smyrna church the main reason was the Jews, and religion was the main motive. The Jews hated the Christians because they viewed this new "sect" as a serious threat to the moral teachings of the patriarchs. To glorify in grace, something they found among Christians, they interpreted as an abuse of the law. Of course there were other issues as well, motives of a more secular nature that steeled them in their opposition, but there definitely were clear religious motives that entered the picture. In some way the dispute between Jews and the Christian church centered on the question whether salvation was the result of observing the law or whether it was pure grace.

The situation was totally different in Pergamum. There too there is persecution, but this has a rather different background. Evidently its nature there is politically motivated and has a direct connection to the Roman Empire. In Pergamum the persecution had its focus on the contrast between the divine empire and the earth's kingdoms, between the kingdom of God and the human rule, between Christ and Caesar. This motif applies to all times and all eras and is the real reason why the letter to Pergamum is still very relevant today and so very meaningful.

In Pergamum Satan has his throne. The meaning of "the throne of Satan" is manifold but its particular significance here is that in that city there were several temples erected to honor the Roman Emperors. Already in the year 29 before Christ a temple was constructed dedicated to the honor of the Emperor Augustus. Behind the city rose a high hill about 300 meters high, some 1,000 feet. Situated on this were the impressive edifices in which the inhabitants of Pergamum paid homage to the global authorities. It is very likely that the expression "the throne of Satan" is connected to the holy hill where day in day out incense was offered to those who were venerated as gods. We don't have to argue that this emperor-cultus was not some innocent pastime but that this had the most serious consequences. This honoring of the rulers of the empire placed the lives of these people completely at the mercy of human beings. All religiousness, all obedience, all devotion was gouged out of the eternal God and transferred to mortal men. They, as mortal beings, were yet honored as gods: they ruled every act, every thought, and every desire that would well up in human hearts. The state, the empire, developed gradually into an absolute, all-encompassing authority, dominating the life of all underlings from cradle to grave.

Not a single person could escape this totalitarian grip. They'd lose their freedom, their responsibility, and their moral compass. Their conscience would be seen as totally irrelevant, they'd slavishly had to follow the state's instructions, obliged to do what the emperor commanded. It's simply impossible for a church to exist or breathe in such a climate. The church is not like a person in the sense that the church can place the rights of the individual in the center, but still the church must emphatically demand that every person in good conscience be able to serve and to worship his or her God and savior. It is this very feature that the totalitarian system refuses to grant.

It is striking that this grand letter-writer, Jesus Christ, in this epistle announces himself as the bearer of the sharp two-edged sword. Here he is not pictured as the Lamb that was slain, but here he announces himself as the lion out of the tribe of Judah. Here, in the midst of this demonic domination of the human empire, Jesus puts down his kingdom, and he does this not as a beggar appealing for a spot, but as the Lord who speaks his word with authority. His sword is two-edged so that it can serve both as a defense against the threatening powers that come from abroad, but at the same time also can function as a weapon of judgment, as a pruning tool, and as a cleansing ingredient for the church herself. In any case, the bearer of this sword is not a person whom we ever can regard as an entity easily eliminated, or as an authority of no account at all. Whoever is of that opinion will in the final stretch be exposed as an utter fool.

So, what about this church in Pergamum? It certainly appears that in general she was quite capable to withstand the strong political pressure to which she was exposed. Of course she cannot participate in the general festivities, the ceremonies connected to the emperor worship. Of course she cannot sprinkle grains of incense on the altar of the world's authorities. She refrains from all that even though this stubborn refusal is seen by the authorities as a public indictment. She now is regarded as a spoil-sport in the context of the overall, communal enterprise: she's no longer a participant, but is sidelined. No longer will its members be eligible for positions of honor. No longer are they on the lists for public contracts, because they have opted out of public ceremonies, because they have other priorities, because they despise the ceremonies so solemnly adhered to by all. In essence they are dangerous, because they regard their own fantastic ideas more important than the unity of the state. But the church in Pergamum is not distracted by these allegations, because she knows all too well that all this grandiosely concocted emperor worship is essentially nothing else than Satan service. "You did not renounce your faith in me." They do not cling to the names of the emperors, who are here today and gone tomorrow, they do not call on earthly rulers who receive the honorary title of "savior," because they know the only savior, the only Lord who is the same yesterday, today, and into eternity. And this costly confession they have maintained against all odds, even when the blood of their most dedicated members flowed as a sign of what is in store for the future.

And yet, for some in this congregation all this was too onerous. There were those who wondered whether all this abstaining was really necessary, was carrying matters too far. Was it absolutely obligatory to so strictly abstain from everything connected to divinely honoring these emperors? After all, the emperor is there as a ruler by the grace of God and in that capacity what is there against honoring as such? Was it really totally against all biblical commands to participate in these folk festivals honoring these divine rulers? Was it a sin to sprinkle a few grains of incense on the temple altars there, by which nothing more was meant than a sign of obeying the proper authorities? After all we are here in this world as Christians and we must participate as such in this world, and that involves, naturally, an inevitable compromise once in awhile. As Christians we must be on guard not to behave as wild fanatics, impossible to live with.

This so-called commonsense talk of these compromise seekers is not unusual. Actually it is centuries old, already bantered about when the old church, when Israel made their way through the desert en route to the promised land. Remember a certain Balaam who advised a certain man named Balak, king of the Moabites, not to engage Israel in a war but to induce these people to slowly introduce them to pagan rituals? (See Numbers 31:16.) Balaam's recipe was, "Invite them to participate in singing and dancing, let them have some innocuous fun, a bit of wine and spirits, and, of course the company of some young women, and pronto, the people of Israel will eat out of your hand." Once Israel has removed the barriers, once it has done away with being different, once it has joined the parade, then gone are the troubles. The result will be that Israel itself will be a victim of that two-edged sword. Then court proceedings and incarcerations will no longer be needed, then Israel itself will become an object of the wrath of its own God and he will have no mercy. And finally—following Balaam's advice—this same proud Israel will be hauled off to Babylon as a helpless loser. Then all resistance has ceased, and it has become a nothing. Yes, that old man Balaam was a crafty fellow, who understood God better than many an Israelite. No wonder that many centuries after him new Balaams have arisen with the same enchanting melodies. They were there too in Pergamum, smart operators, at home everywhere, also well regarded among the pagans there. It was easy to do business with them and they never confronted you at any moment with "Scripture says." Those Balaams were reasonable guys who saw no harm in cheerfully joining the crowd at these temple festivities. If all Christians were like that, hey, we too could join them.

But most of the Pergamum church was not like that. But yet they, as a body, were amiss by not dealing with these Balaams. They participated fully in their gatherings, they took part in the Lord's Supper, in a word, they were regarded as full-fledged members. In all that they courted a tremendous danger, especially for the younger generation. That church in Pergamum tolerated these Balaams far too much. It's quite peculiar, that the extreme difficulty to say "no" in Pergamum, proved quite easy to do in Ephesus. The church of Christ likes to say "yes," "yes" to Christ and his work, but woe to that church when she no longer understands that the "yes" to her Savior contains a radical "no" to everything that detracts from him. The great shepherd of his flock cannot tolerate this. He will come and battle these compromisers with "the sword of my mouth." Pergamum must understand that they must not be afraid for the emperor's sword, but the only sword we most certainly must fear is that two-edged sword in the hands of him who loves his people so much that he will not allow them to perish.

The letter ends with some with some deep symbolism. "To them who overcome I will give some of the hidden manna." These words go back many centuries to when Israel traveled through the desert to the promised land. Then there were Balaams who seduced them, but there also was manna, bread from heaven. After many generations, do these same matters come back, but in a different form? Does the church on her travels always encounter the same dangers and also always again the same blessings? The "hidden manna" must indicate Christ's riches. Christ once called himself the true manna, the "true bread from heaven" (John 6:32). The manna word here refers to that text, no doubt. During its troubled trek the church of Christ is threatened from all sides by the sword of their enemies and the tempters lurk everywhere, but "the hidden manna" gives them the sustaining power to proceed in hope.

But that is only allotted to those who overcome. They will receive the "white stone upon which is written a new name known only to them that receive them." Again memories go back to times immemorial. When Israel received the law from God, then also the type of clothes the priests had to wear during their service were prescribed. The high priest was commanded to wear a breast piece with twelve stones and in these stones the names of the twelve sons of Israel were grafted (Exod 2:15–21). But here, in the new covenant, the picture changes. Here on the day of the great victory all believers receive a white stone as sign of their justification, and on that white stone appears a name only he or she understands. The very essence of that very person, the most intimate feature, something that nobody knows, that nobody suspects, will be written on that stone in the form of a name. In the world's kingdoms, the human's very personality is obliterated, in the imperial state of Caesar every person become an object, a nameless entity, a number. The totalitarian regime swallows the individual responsibility and the individual conscience. The kingdom of Christ precisely enhances the most precious, the most particular in a person. Christ right away fashions us to the "I" we are in the fullest sense of the word. He does not degenerate us but he regenerates us. He does not reduce us to a number but he makes numbers into people. At a time in the future he will reveal the hidden secrets of each of those who belong to him and do that via that new name, a name written on a special white stone given to all his brothers and sisters.

The church in Pergamum has no reason to fear. As long as the Balaams fail to dominate the church nothing drastic will occur. But that means that this group of people must forcefully resist all laxity, all half-heartedness, all inclination for concessions and compromise, and courageously reveal her "being different" amidst a world that, exhausted and morally bankrupt as it is, has succumbed to the will of the Caesars. The point is to proceed on the way the Lord has outlined, in spite of all opposition, and do so as living people who have reverently learned to obediently listen to the word of the savior. They who do so, who are able, they will always enjoy the "hidden manna." They then will increasingly become themselves in the same measure they no longer serve themselves but him who has bought us with his precious blood.

IN THE GRIP OF MONEY

The letter to the church in Thyatira is the longest of all the letters to the seven churches. The reason for this is that the situation in this church was quite complicated.

Thyatira had the same great problem as the other churches in that it too operated in a pagan world. That was not unusual; actually it was perfectly natural and necessary. Of course this situation brought persecution, opposition, and false accusations. The church there had to endure the same pain as all the other ones.

Apart from this the problems of this church had some special features. The first difference was that it revealed itself especially as a sociological problem. Thyatira was a city of commerce and industry, a place well-known for her guilds or labor unions or business associations. Everyone who did business there or operated a company was automatically part of one of these social organizations. It even was compulsory to belong to one of these outfits on peril of being boycotted by all others. It simply was impossible to do business without them, but everywhere and all the time all were dependent on these powerful social organizations. It was simply impossible for an honorable Christian carpenter to ply his trade on his own, no matter how hard he worked. If he were not a member of the trade union then he simply was regarded as unqualified and ran the risk that nobody would call on him for work. In other words, in Thyatira persecution was not the result of political tensions generated by the way the church functioned, but in this city they were especially its social network, the entire structure of society that imperiled the existence of the church there. And the situation was so that the church of Thyatira consisted primarily of small businessmen, people who for their daily bread depended on the cooperation of their clients. That meant that they had no option but to seek contact with the existing social network. That was exactly the great question the church there was wrestling with.

Of course we can argue that the church there had to face reality, accept the consequences and simply venture out into the business world. This implied that the Christians there were to become part of these labor associations and join these existing social structures. But there was more to it than that. These bodies were outspokenly pagan. They had special high days involving solemn ceremonies, all of a pagan nature. Ostensibly they were connected to the name of some patron deity and that meant sacrifices to this idol. Also it involved large banquets accompanied by all sorts of pagan rituals. These meals as a rule degenerated into debaucheries, with strong drink and disorderly conduct creating additional havoc. To join all this was by no means an innocent affair. If these people would really get themselves involved in all this then they had to go whole hog, and that meant that they could possibly not escape all these ceremonies and festivities.

The problem also was that there simply was no alternative. If they did not join then they simply could not make a living, and thus were doomed to begging for bread. And if they did join, then, in essence, their entire Christian life was imperiled. Between these two perils they had to choose.

The cardinal question for the church in Thyatira is also one that still has the utmost relevance for the church of all ages. The church exists in a world which breathes a different spirit. The church cannot withdraw, cannot isolate itself, retreating to an island. No, it has to remain right in the center of the world. But to stay there means that it constantly encounters new conflicts. The congregation of Thyatira was too small to exist on its own and so be self-supporting, so to say: it was simply too small and too insignificant. She simply did not have the numbers, and couldn't possibly put up a fight. The real question was: on what basis should she build her modus operandi, her total life's goal? Were she to participate in the public domain, were she to throw herself head over heels into the general events out there, or should she consciously refrain from any of these civic activities?

Apparently there were those in Thyatira who emphatically proclaimed that, yes, join them, become members of these pagan organizations, because the alternative is destitution. Common sense must prevail. If these people had been motivated by pointing out that it was their irrefutable duty to renew these pagan labor unions from within, then there might have been some ground for discussion. But then their exhortation to join these pagan bodies had to immediately be followed by the cautionary cry: under no circumstances do anything that goes against the Lord's commands and the holy will of Jesus Christ. Always remain true to your savior! It is clear that in every mission field, in pagan surroundings, a young church is always involved in all sorts of social problems, because it often is simply impossible to sever all social ties. But it is imperative to emphatically state that they should never be seduced by pagan practices.

That however did these preachers in Thyatira fail to do. On the contrary, they concocted a new sort of theology, a set of religious rules that seem to justify cooperation with paganism. That is the theology of the Nicolaitans, already mentioned before, but pictured here more explicitly. This theology seems to be based especially on the premise that these heathen gods really do not exist at all, and that throwing a bit of incense on their altars posed no real problem at all. It's a useless act that does no harm because the recipients, those idols, don't even exist. If they, with this empty gesture can guarantee one's place in society, then, well, go ahead. They even went a step further: even these orgies and the subsequent sinful conduct were glossed over. It's not so bad, during these nocturnal guild celebrations, to give in to the "primeval nature." It does no harm to give full rein to the desires of the flesh because only then do you learn to know the depths of Satan. Imagine, that even sounds pious! You forget yourself in the filth of sensuous passions, and the next morning you wake up with a terrible hangover, but that is especially what you need because then you can, with full force, glorify in the grace of Christ. After all you really don't identify with the "old" flesh anymore. As a Christian you are above these sinful matters and no longer able to be sinful. There's no danger in descending into hell because Satan can no longer overpower you, and tomorrow you are back to the Lord's Supper as a person who stared down the Satan. However further you sink into hell, how more glorious will later the ascension into heaven be.

Isn't that a marvelous theology! A true marvel, because it's also very profitable. It allows you to be a carpenter, your pagan fellow citizens regard you as a congenial fellow, somebody who can join in the fun, and they order chairs and tables from you. Your business flourishes, and all is fine and dandy. And your Christian conscience is at rest. These theologians cherish the serious hope that Jesus will not see through this subterfuge of making money and that he takes the idea of exploring the "depths of Satan" as a valid excuse because it will lead to a greater understanding of the function of the Lord's Supper in the reception of greater grace. That sort of theology is thoroughly practical and enables us to have the cake and eat it too. You become a successful businessman, you are in no time rich, you have the occasional fun-filled evening and happy-go-lucky night, and to top it off you can discover "the depths of the Satan." It's a perfect set-up.

In Thyatira the instigator of this new theology appears to have been a woman who is only identified with the less flattering name of Jezebel. Some manuscripts (Rev 2: 20) mention "your woman Jezebel." If that is correct then this lady was the wife of the "angel," the leader of the church. That would have been almost the worst-case scenario if this dangerous teaching would find its origin in the pastoral family and so be promoted in the congregation. Perhaps it is preferable not to accept this reading, but discounting that possibility, the matter is serious enough. This anonymous woman presents herself as a "prophetess." So, supposedly, she has her theology straight from the Holy Spirit. That's a smart move because it wouldn't be easy to base her ideas on the Scriptures. It's, of course, much easier to appeal to prophetic inspiration. At the same time that part of the church that has not bought into the new theology is labeled as unspiritual. They are the literalists, those who adhere to the text of the Bible and are afraid to be swayed by power of the Spirit. But she, Jezebel, has no such compunction, and she openly proclaims her theology. She does have adherents. She also has children and they side with their mother. Together they constitute a dangerous group in the midst of the church in Thyatira.

How is it possible that the church there has so much trouble to rid itself of the proclaimers of this new theology? It seems that faithful believers often have called her on the carpet but she has refused to recant her errors. But why wasn't she banned from the Lord's Supper and why weren't her teachings rejected as an awful abomination? Was that the result of a general, misplaced tolerance, which makes it difficult, if not impossible to say "no" and mean it? Or were they afraid that a sharp protest would cause disunity and perhaps a split in the church? Did they feel that their church was too small and too vulnerable for such a drastic event? Or was there yet another reason: were they themselves not quite sure how to handle this situation? So Jezebel would be ejected, but that did not solve the problem. Did they have the guts to categorically say that it was against the will of Christ to join these pagan organizations? That decision would mean that they, of their own free will, would face a future of poverty and hardship. Was there really an alternative? Should they, however reluctantly, follow Jezebel's example? Isn't that the inevitable result of living in this sinful and totally polluted world? Those were the questions facing the church in Thyatira. Apparently she was unable to answer these questions or lacked the courage to do so without creating a lot of misunderstanding.

The letter the heavenly Father dispatched to this church is of remarkable power and majesty.

First there is the introduction: "These are the words of the Son of God, whose eyes are like blazing fire and whose feet are like burnished bronze." You can't fool around with Jesus, you can't deceive him. He is the ultimate king and ruler. His all-penetrating eyes emit a scorching fire. If we don't grasp that then we fail to understand the good news.

Jezebel and her followers receive a harsh but justified sentence. She will become seriously ill, her children will die, her adherents, the proclaimers of the "new theology" will suffer severe suppression. These misguided souls. They had embraced this new theology precisely to escape economic hardship and live a life of luxury, and now exactly the opposite is happening. The Bible provides no details how all this further unfolds. Do the pagan people at long last tire of these half-hearted people and is that the reason why precisely they suffer the most? It would not be the last time that exactly the un-committed must suffer disproportionately. Didn't Jesus say something about the lukewarm people? However it is possible that the suppression does not originate with the outsiders, but is a direct result of God afflicting them.

It is striking that Jesus calls himself one who searches the hearts and the minds. He exposes the "new theology" as being essentially nothing else but cowardice, greed, and despicable compromise. "Hold on to what you have until I come." That is the great requirement, extended to all churches, also to Thyatira. Hold on, embrace what they and we have received from Christ and those are not matters we can bargain with. How this church must deal with the entire pagan situation, how she must determine her place within that social structure, is not further defined. That too is always different depending on the circumstances and the locality. But one thing is clear: nothing that truly belongs to the gifts Christ blessed us with may ever be abandoned.

The last few verses of the letter to Thyatira forcefully speak of what is to come. "To those who overcome and do my will to the end, I will give authority over the nations." The sharp reversal of all conditions is striking here. That tiny band of believers, tirelessly trying to maintain themselves over against the overwhelming pagan society, that small group receives the promise that in the future it will receive authority over the pagans. All power structures are reversed when God judges the nations. The hunted become rulers, the persecuted become kings. I will not speculate whether this alludes to what later is realized under Emperor Constantine. The ultimate realization lies, no doubt, on the other side of that great dividing line that separates this contemporary dispensation from what is to come. In the end a new ray of light flashes: "I will give them the Morning Star." That "morning star" is meant to be nothing else but Christ himself. After all he is "the bright Morningstar" (Rev 22:16). I will be his. In this world it often seems that they who hold on what they have received from him commit themselves to poverty and want. Those who overcome will miraculously experience that they, in the end, will have it all, because they have Christ.

THE VERY ORDINARY LIFE

There is nothing more dangerous in the life of a believer than just the very ordinary, everyday, totally harmless matters. That already starts in the morning with the first cup of coffee, the demanding hours of work, the customary dessert after the evening meal, and all the myriads of events that constitute life. It may all be quite nice and even pious, but it also may slowly deteriorate into a sort of spiritual staleness. Biblical life should always have a close connection with some perspective, with a "vision," with élan, with progress, but the everyday, ordinary things of life often stifle progress. These run-of-the-mill activities dribble on like the tiny waves of a brook: they paralyze these persons, render them powerless, and prevent them from thinking and doing something grand and extraordinary. The sickness of stale complacency is one of the most devastating and most dangerous of all spiritual ills. In days of fierce opposition faith can assert itself, can let sparks fly, but the everyday routine kills these sparks and make them appear ridiculous and superfluous. In days of dangerous temptations faith can suddenly be roused from its drowsiness and be alerted to looming dangers, but in the commonly experienced events, in the dull atmosphere of cozily settled occurrences, the alarm clock is turned off. Praying too becomes a routine because we really have everything we need. Giving thanks . . . well, yes, we still do that, sort of. The no-nonsense directives of the Bible that speak of mortal battles and a determined wrestling with evil look somewhat like an exaggeration in a cozily arranged living room where a mute television screen shows a nice new car and where outside the suburban dwelling is neatly settled on an immaculate lawn. Such an everyday life does not know what to do with terms such as battling evil, because its decay has simply gone too far. Something of that sort of somberness has sickened Sardis, an infectious illness all the more dangerous because there is no antidote against it, while an operation is also not possible.

Sardis happens to be an ordinary provincial town with some textile industry, such as wool spinning and cloth-dying. It had invented a new procedure that had some surprising results. There also was a bit of commerce, and that was pretty well it. Nothing further to report, no earthshaking events. No persecutions, no social boycott of the believers. There was nothing, simply nothing, nothing more than the easy pace of every new day, nothing more than the orderly, quiet rhythm of mundane proceedings. You could in that placid place preach a powerful sermon, but the real danger is that it would only sound ridiculous. It's like a stone falling in a small pond: there are a few ripples, but then it sinks away and the former state returns. Every day there is like the day before.

Imagine, the church of Sardis had the reputation of being alive! True, she was busy in several fields: she looked after the poor, and did other useful work, but none of these activities were really inspired. Something was lacking, and it was difficult to pinpoint exactly what was missing. There was no sparkle, no spirit, no *joie de vivre*, no holy enthusiasm, no real surrender, no deep-felt love. It seems that every breath of love was right away smothered in a muggy, mindless moment of commonness. The conversations, of course, always centered around wool, around other textiles, around clothes. What else would you expect from a place that made its living from these fabrics? But that their own fabric of life had slowly and imperceptibly become soiled and shabby and monotonous, that fact failed to register with them. For that to be noticed life was far too placid and far too comatose.

When the living Lord addresses this worn-out community each word hits hard. It is right away noticeable that he uses trade talk. That's the language people there understand. Three times in that letter he mentions clothes. In the letter to Pergamum he used political jargon, because Pergamum's struggle centered around that topic, in the same way when writing to Sardis he speaks to them in the language familiar to them.

There's something else that is unusual, and that is the introduction. "These are the words of him who holds the seven spirits of God and the seven stars." Why is here so much emphasis on the seven spirits of God? Is this because a strong gale is needed to blow away all that lethargy that lingers in that valley? Is this because lots of inner spirit power is needed to start new sparks, to ignite fires that are inextinguishable? Are these seven spirits needed to engender in these dull folk something of a sensation of ecstasy about the marvels of God's greatness? And who is more capable to elicit brand new vibrations from that worn out instrument that is the church there, than from the hand of him who is the great magician, the life-inspiring Spirit of

God? Yes, there still is hope for Sardis because the Spirit is still present there. This church need not slowly sink away in immaterial insignificance because there still are sources of infinite treasures, the never fading, always penetrating power of Christ's Spirit. That is the hope this church may cherish, on that hope she can rely, unencumbered and unhesitatingly.

"Wake up." That's the loud cry here. No mention of "the throne of Satan" as was the case in Pergamum, or of the "synagogue of Satan," as in Smyrna. Here in Sardis even Satan seems to be asleep. Not here the terrible but fascinating figure of Jezebel who has concocted a new theology; also not here the Nicolaitans who play hide-and-go-seek with the world. Here in Sardis just the one overriding danger, a slow, choking death from lack of oxygen, the more dangerous because all windows are shut tight. No breeze can penetrate here, and no Spirit can infiltrate these unfeeling lives.

What happens when these windows stay shut, and when they successfully manage to keep the Spirit and its flaming power from entering? "But if you do not wake up, I will come like a thief, and you will not know at what time I will come." What then? Then an intruder will come, one who will smash the windows, shattering glass all over the place, and that same brigand will break that carefully installed door lock with one mighty blow. He then will thump with his balled fist on the door of the living room, causing these nice Bible texts to drop from the wall. That intruder will shake up these impassive lives, causing shudders so stunning, so thoroughly terrifying, that suddenly all drowsiness disappears and frightened eyes are fearfully fixed on him. But for some this moment will herald the arrival of a great feast. There were some in Sardis who could not cope with all that tardiness that had overpowered them all, who inwardly longed for the moment when at last the Lord himself would come to shake up everybody out of the nightmare of triviality. There were those who experienced the spiritual deterioration and the superficiality of faith life there as a terrible burden. They were those who time and again would pause and fervently pray: "Revive my soul and my soul shall live!" For these people in Sardis the arrival of the great intruder will be a moment of mounting amazement and overwhelming joy. Then the chains of the mortal routine will drop from their hands as so much shredded rope. "And they who overcome will walk with me dressed in white."

The Bible often speaks of the clothes we wear, and here, in the textile territory of Asia Minor this was quite applicable. Clothes, in the Bible, don't, as a rule, give an indication of our personality, or of our economic or social situation, but rather they tell us of our status or position in life. Of course, basically our condition is one of wretchedness, of being lost. Adam and Eve are filled with anxiety and horror because they are naked, and dare not appear before God in that condition, because their nakedness only emphasizes their pitiful misery. Paul mentions in 2 Corinthians 5:3 that "when we are clothed we will not be found naked." Because what is a person when he only is what he is? That's why clothing is such an elegant sign of Christ's redeeming power. As sinners we are clothed with righteousness, we are in him sanctified as the people of God. And when we are clothed with the wedding clothes of Christ's righteousness, then our situation also changes, then, through his creative powers, we become a different people. "Those he justified, those he also glorified" (Rom 8:30). That means that those of Sardis who walk with Christ will do so in white clothes, because they are worthy and have such a savior.

At the end of the letter there once again comes something totally different. "I will never blot out their names from the Book of Life." Were they really in such a dire situation? Was the narcotic of fence-sitting so dangerous that it could result in the name being scratched out of the Book of Life? Of course this is a matter of speech and so it does not indicate that there ever had been an instant where a name was omitted from the Book of Life. Once it is in there, it is in there forever. But what most certainly can happen is that a name we would assume were in that Book of Life, in the final analysis would have never been there. The church in Sardis, in her lax behavior, certainly travels along dangerous paths. The followers of Jezebel at least kept the church on its toes, and this resulted in them finding a new arsenal of weapons to combat these heretics. In some ways the easygoing spiritual life in Sardis is a far greater danger for the church than heresies and persecution. When a church realizes this, and when she receives such a jolt that she is shaken to the core, then the possibilities are endless. But if the slumbering remains, then there is the distinct possibility that the withering twilight will become solid darkness.

THE ONLY MISSION CHURCH

It's a shameful fact and also a really sorry situation that of all seven churches in Asia Minor, the church in Philadelphia is the only one pictured as a church on the offensive, not afraid to take her missionary calling in the world seriously. All other six churches are far too preoccupied with themselves, are so engaged in remaining solvent that they have no energy left to take on the task of bringing the good news to those who are not acquainted with Christ. This is especially disheartening because here we are at the cradle of Christianity, at the place where the church was born, here we deal with a time frame only a few years after Pentecost. Sorry to say, but it is true that the church in its infancy was all too inclined to have a high opinion of herself and was inclined to let the world go to destruction.

But Philadelphia was different. That is an encouraging sign in the midst of all worries that face us every day. Of course Philadelphia too had a daily battle with the stubborn obstinacy of the pagan world around them. This church too did not have an easy time remaining faithful to the gospel, but with immense determination it continued to bring the message to others. Just as in Smyrna they encountered the vicious hatred from "those who say they are Jews, but are not, and lie about it." They say that they represent the synagogue of God, but in reality it is the synagogue of Satan. But all this does not discourage this church: they do not lose their holy enthusiasm, they remain on the offensive. That's why it is remarkable how this entire letter uses the metaphor of the door or gate. It already starts in verse 7, where the glorified Christ presents himself as the "Holy and true, who holds the key of David. What he opens nobody can shut and what he shuts nobody can open." That is immediately followed by "See, I have placed before you an open door." Both these lines are later further explained.

When we more closely read this letter, and examine what this church actually had accomplished, then we see that, in reality, it doesn't look like an awful lot. True, she has held fast to the word of Christ and hasn't denied his name. In other words: in spite of fierce opposition by the Jews she quietly continued to confess her Lord and savior. She refused to be intimidated, she did not back down, and she was not at all inclined to deviate even one iota from the letter of faith. In spite of all difficulties and troubles, she quietly and confidently kept on proclaiming that she unconditionally confessed Jesus Christ as the only savior. And evidently she did so in a manner that was impressive.

The reason why the proclamation of the gospel was so effective there was due simply to the fact that these believers in Philadelphia never regarded the world around them with hostility, rejection, and bitterness. Even when that same world started to treat them harshly and threatened them, she kept on seeing the world as belonging to Christ, who, as the ultimate victor wanted to do his saving work. She never regarded herself as a fortified citadel but always had the remarkable notion that these high walls around her would have doors which would miraculously open when the great Christ would use a finger to push against them. For that reason there was no need to be afraid, not even from "the synagogue of Satan." On the contrary, there was every reason to feel compassion for those who stumbled around in such great darkness. Perhaps all this was somewhat naïve and childish, but it was exactly this motivation that made the work of these believers so irresistible in that city. They never became upset, never acted hostile, they never scolded: they quietly and simply kept on confessing what was so dear to them.

That's the reason why Jesus revealed himself to these people as the great bearer of the key. Evidently there is a clear connection here to what Isaiah in Isaiah 22:22 said about Eliakim, the property manager of the royal household. That same Eliakim too could open and nobody was able to close the door. For him this concerned the properties of the king, both the buildings and the contents. With Christ, the great Eliakim, this concerns the possessions of the great king, the elect of the Lord. And this Christ will indeed cause the iron doors of the stubborn opposition to open to accept the gospel. And then it will be revealed that these doors were not so difficult and impregnable as they first seemed. These unwieldy monsters will move at last. Even out of the synagogue of Satan people will come and prostrate themselves before the feet of these simple parishioners of Philadelphia. The act of prostrating may sound perhaps somewhat contrived. It is possible that here we must go back to what Isaiah has said Isaiah 60:14. There it says that the oppressors will come bowing before you, and "will bow down at your feet." The pagan enemies of God's people will approach Israel and prostrate themselves before Israel's God. Here the straying children of Israel who call themselves the synagogue of God while actually being the synagogue of Satan, they will come and bow down at the feet of the believers, the former pagans. These Jews will now prostrate at the feet of those believers who now claim to be the true Jews, the true synagogue of God. In God's book matters sometimes are reversed. He writes his holy will straight through all human obstinacy and apostasy.

I ask once again: how come these believers in Philadelphia may experience this mighty miracle? In Christ's description of this church there appears one very significant word: "I know that you have little strength." That must have meant that in that church there were few exceptional people, few great orators, few important figures. They were just common folk, and they were aware of that. They did not assume an unsuitable higher status. They were plain people and they were faithful, that's all. They had little influence. All that must indicate that this small band of believers did not even consider to start arguing against their philosophy and culture, against the magnificence of pagan life with its glorious temple celebrations. Not for a moment did it enter their minds that by putting pressure on these heavy fortifications they were able to push them down. They remained steadfast in their simple faith: but Christ can accomplish that! When one of the first missionaries to China was once asked whether he thought to make an impression on these people with their centuries-old culture, he simply replied: "I can't but God can." That is a reply that fits Philadelphia. That's why that "little strength" is not an impediment but the opposite, a powerful victory sign. Today, in our situation, it is dawning on us that, both in the East and in the West, the resistance of unbelief is so insurmountable, that no human power can overcome this. That's why we are slowly beginning to realize, by the grace of God, that we must use the approach that was the secret of the church in Philadelphia, the secret of "little strength."

There was another factor that evidently invigorated this congregation: the expectation that the end was near. "Since you have kept my command to endure patiently I will also keep you from the hour of trial that is going to come upon the whole world." That small circle of Philadelphia passionately expected the return of the great day of God. That gave her lasting power and an anchor. Temptations come and they will increase in severity but as long as the flame of hope burns in their hearts an answer to every need will be provided. The promise given to these people is of particular fondness. "They who overcome I will make pillars in the temple of my God. Never again will they leave it." This short letter talks about doors, by which are meant walls that open up on hinges. Here the letter maintains the images of architecture. It talks about pillars. These pillars in God's house do not turn, do not move back and forth, and they do not shift. They can't do that because they sustain the building. That's why there are fixed and unmovable. The believers in Philadelphia may seem small and helpless, but they belong to the co-carriers, to the pillars, and that means they are steadfast. On them names will be recorded. Not their own names because they are insignificant, but the name of God, the name of the city of God, the New Jerusalem, and the new name of Jesus Christ. They have been included in the mighty work of God, they are part of that great, divine plan, they are inhabitants of the New Jerusalem that will not crucify its king: they are firmly anchored in the accomplished work of him who lives in all eternity. That is royal lineage of Philadelphia by which all earthly greatness dwarves into insignificance.

THE MORTAL SELF-DECEIT

Gradually, imperceptibly slowly, matters can slip away. Love, desire, hope, happiness, devout dedication to a lifelong duty, passionate conviction, they all can fiercely burn, but they also can, quite unnoticed, lose some of their spark and finally end up as a poor smoldering mess. Is that what happened in Laodicea?

We know of Laodicea that it was rich and situated on an intersection of roads. It had textile industry, and also a medical university. Science, art, technical know-how were flourishing in this well-established Asia Minor center. In this atmosphere the church in Laodicea was born and grew up. Apparently she acquired a touch of the mood of the city, one of self-satisfaction, just not so much that it became a terrible nuisance. This city featured an aura of contentment, an aroma of having arrived, and the church there too was that way. We sometimes speak of conforming to the world and mean with that such matters as gambling or lotteries, or abandoning church altogether. But essentially conforming to the world goes much deeper, is much harder to measure and more difficult to weigh. It more resembles a mist that, unnoticed, waves through the open windows, infiltrates the clothes, the furniture and penetrates all the pores of one's personality without perception. Something of that kind of conformity had affected that church. The entire mood of the city, of the surrounding area where they lived, had acquired this prevailing, lighthearted, upbeat, satisfied disposition that had permeated all thinking like an all-pervasive poison.

Of course worship services went on as usual. Once in awhile there were festive gatherings in people's homes: they were well-off and could afford entertaining lavishly. The youth participated fully, because these feasts were quite lively. But no one of these good-humored people realized that their faith had started to wither, that almost no warm glow remained in their hearts. They had become unaware that such concepts as the living reality of Jesus Christ and the grandeur of his return had faded away, had become a fleeting and elusive entity. There still was something like the purple glow, lingering against the high clouds after sunset, but all warming effect had long gone.

This letter is nothing else but a radical exposure. As such it hits hard, while at the same time being infinitely affectionate and loving. Being faced with our own condition is something we all need from time to time. Once in awhile we need a thorough shaking so that all that is within us is turned upside down and inside out, if we really want to discover how utterly dangerously we really live. Fortunate that church that has a preacher who grasps the art of shaking up, who has the rare ability to expose our real selves, but that can only be done when he or she has first undergone this self-analysis. The heavenly writer does pull the mask away. He does that in a way which mirrors the entire life of that place. "You say I am rich; I have acquired wealth and do not need a thing." We can taste the self-satisfaction in these words. Did they really say it that way in Laodicea? Were they sunk that deeply that, in their pride, that expressed this so openly? I guess not. They most likely bravely sang of God's saving grace. Nevertheless, in the deep crevices of their hearts, so softly that they themselves could not hear it, that's exactly what they said. It was there more as something unconscious, as an elated feeling within them rather than something they openly dared to confess. "I am rich and I have done that all by myself." That fitted exactly the situation in Laodicea, a city that indeed was well off and lacked nothing. You can sense how the church ever so quietly has started to inhale the mood of the surroundings, has been totally sucked in by it. The church still speaks of "grace alone," but in the deepest sense she reasons differently.

"But you do not realize that you are wretched, pitiful, and poor." It is strange that we can get so confused about ourselves, that the picture we have of ourselves is totally distorted. Everything in our lives is different than it really is: we ourselves are never what we think we are. There play so many different feelings through our minds that we have all sorts of secret ideas of what we are, so that if we could only fathom our real self ever so little we would be scared stiff. That rich man in Laodicea with his profitable business, with his extensive commercial contacts, with his nice house, his male and female slaves, he sees himself the real McCoy, and, of course, an important contributor to the Christian church. If he only would know how the Lord of the church would see him! You have no idea what you really are!

"And blind." Laodicea was famous for her medical university and famous for the doctors there. But, in spite of all these medical facilities all these members of the church there were blind. "And naked." In spite of the flourishing wool industry, in spite of these spinning looms, you are naked. You really need deep insight into yourself to be able to cope with this sort of unmasking.

Over against this threefold accusation comes a threefold advice. I recommend, I counsel you to buy gold . . . white clothes . . . salve for your eyes. No price is mentioned here. The price must have been quite high. We can only buy these things when we sell all we have, all our secret self-satisfactions, all our pseudo-importance and pomposity, all our intelligence and brainpower. The prices are high, very high in God's kingdom, and they never decrease in value. "Gold," but then pure gold, that has proven itself through genuine struggle, through temptation and persecution as the real thing. "White clothes" that cover our own lostness and guilt through the grace of Jesus Christ. "Salve for the eyes," which right away makes us see things nobody else can see so that we can observe those unknown depths nobody suspects in us. And after these sharp words follow, so utterly tenderly, these moving words, "Those whom I love . . ." (here Jesus uses a word that expresses a special tenderness and deep love!) ". . . I rebuke and discipline." The great shepherd of all sheep has a serious conversation with the church in Laodicea. Difficult days are at hand, but they too are included as part of the faithful care with which he surrounds his children.

In the end there again appears the image of a door. This time it is not the door as an entrance to the world. It is that mysterious door through which Christ gains entrance to our heart. There are more doors in our lives, doors to the outside and doors going up. And through the latter we often fail to follow. With tears in our eyes we can pray for God to enter into our distorted lives while at the same time bolting the door to God. We can ask to "Let your teaching fall like rain and your words descend like dew" (Deut 32:2), and at the same time carefully make sure that not a drop of rain has a chance to penetrate into the fortress that is our life. We do that because we are sorely afraid that Jesus would really come in and enter our hearts, that he would create havoc there, upset the tables and the chairs and rip away our wall decorations, afraid that he would really focus his light on our decrepit lives and we would become fully aware that we constantly are sinking into the mud of our so-delicate complacency. And yet, if we can gather the radical courage to remove the bolts and open the door then all will be totally changed. Then, yes, Jesus will upset a lot in our lives, but the immense event that is the result will cause something totally different: "I will come and eat with them, and they with me." A meal, the Lord's Supper, you could say. "I with them, and they with me." That would give birth to a true mutuality, something that will cause life to become a neverending feast.

In the end this letter exults in expressing visions of impenetrable depth and grandeur. To these poor souls, those people who have so little insight into themselves and understand so terribly little of Jesus Christ, to these folk who do not realize that every day of their lives they keep their hands on the door bolts afraid to unlock them, to these blind and naked in Laodicea the Lord says something about sitting with him on thrones and sharing in the indescribable beauty of God reserved for those who are anchored in Christ.

THE ROAD MORE TROUBLED

We are once again asked to return to the image of that woman, adorned with the sun and a crown of stars on her head and on the run in the desert because she is cruelly and fiercely pursued by the dragon. That represents the church ever since Jesus Christ was victorious on the morning of Easter. But how does the church conduct herself in that perilous period, the time of "woe unto you" for those who inhabit the earth? All this is pictured for us in the letters to the churches in seven concise snapshots.

In some instances that church is steadfast, anchored in the truth. In those times she resists all heresies and temptations while forcefully embracing the banner of God's word. And yet, even then it is possible that exclaiming her valiant "no" against all spiritual temptation is not sufficiently strong to be compensated by the loving "yes" of the savior and redeemer of our souls. That typifies Ephesus.

In some cases that church experiences cruel persecution, is forced to wade through mists and morass, and is daily in mortal dangers. That applies to Smyrna.

In some cases the church is involved in the powerful political problem of Christ or Caesar, and the question is whether she possesses sufficient spiritual stamina to steadfastly refuse to sacrifice even a grain of incense on the altar of the totalitarian state. Pergamum is the example there.

In some cases she is situated in the midst of social developments to do with secular communal life and yet she must show that she is "different," unlike the other spiritual movements, unlike the other social institutions, because her foundation is different. Then the issue is to be in the world, to stand amidst the tensions of societal life and yet not to be of the world. That was the situation in Thyatira.

In some cases there is a life-and-death struggle with the danger of lack of imagination, of daily routine, of plain bourgeoisie, of becoming drab and superficial. That is the struggle in Sardis.

In some cases the church is allowed to be a hope-giving witness in spite of all opposition, fully convinced that the great bearer of keys can open gates usually regarded as impossible to overcome barriers. That is the blessing of Philadelphia.

In some case the church must allow the total uncovering of herself, by letting the Word of God penetrate to the core, so that all pure self-deceit is blown away as dust and the naked image of the poor reality is revealed for all to see. Then she must have the courage to let go of the door key and let Christ enter to devotedly wait the redemption he will prepare.

That's how the church travels in that long period between Easter and the grand finale. She is not always on the right path, and she is not everywhere correct. She has Sardis scenes, and she has Philadelphia days. She sometimes is suddenly called "not to tolerate the evil," to loudly and without hesitation say "no" against the sweet whistling of the heresy teachers. She sometimes can sense a shudder seeping through her soul as she becomes aware how elusive her expectation has become, how faded her faith, how weak her witness. The church experiences all that and more. In the hearts of every one of us we find the images of all these churches or at least we find the symptoms. But above all these churches rises the mighty figure of the child who was snatched away to the throne of God, who gave Michael the power to defeat the demonic armies, who will return one day to give his followers the crowns of eternal life.

"To them who overcome . . . !" With these words end all letters. And finally, every member of the church, every one of us must ponder these matters and wrestle with them. This ultimate Good cannot be obtained collectively: every one of us, in our own, personal lives must fight the battle, however much may be the support we receive from the communion of saints. That is why every one who overcomes will receive the mysterious stone with the new name, revealing his or her life's secret. And on them will also be written the name of God, the name of the New Jerusalem and the name of the great victor, our Lord Jesus Christ.

CHAPTER THREE

The Ban Is Broken
(Revelation 4 and 5)

ABOVE THE EARTH ARE THE VAULTING HEAVENS

In that long, scary period between the victory of Jesus Christ over death and Satan and the ultimate magnificence of the new creation, the church travels a burdened and problematic road. Every day she is called to forcefully resist all temptation and nice-sounding but error-prone slogans. She also must constantly and carefully examine herself to prevent slowly succumbing to a mortal routine, often disguised as piety. In addition she must always keep in touch with the world around her that dwells in darkness. Then there are the mood swings: at times she triumphantly marches to her glorious future, and then again she acts as if everything in the world is against her. If only she would clearly and fully see how she walks at the edge of triumph, how powerless the satanic forces really are now that they have been thrown out of heaven, and cast down to earth. If she kept all this clearly in mind then she would not become so downcast and surrender herself to all sorts of anxieties and lack of faith. But, let's face it, it is part of her being in the world that the presence of the visible matters seem much more threatening than the fundamental, ultimate reality of the victory of Jesus Christ. That's the reason she often feels lonely and abandoned, stuck in the mud, wandering in mist and haze, lacking perspective and expectation. At times it seems as if she is ready to let go of her glory and royalty, just as those in Laodicea who suffered from self-satisfaction causing their faith to go cold, were robbed of its essence and so fell back to unbelief and godlessness. The church is always on the firing line, always in mortal danger, and that will be the case till the very end.

But after the somber picture of Laodicea follows the mighty vision described in Revelation 4. God does not want us to remain caught in a perspective seen only from an earthly point of view. He wants us to learn to look through that haze and to understand that we are only an arm's length away from the indescribable majesty of him who carries the scepter of the world in his hands. That vision of Revelation 4 may seem utterly strange for a people who with bent backs and heavy hearts, slowly and hesitantly make their way through the wilderness of history, but that does not detract from the truth and comfort of this vision. As a matter of fact it is the only truth, it is the only matter that counts, even if the entire world is upside down, even when floods and hurricanes and typhoons sweep through seaside regions. That's why it has been of the utmost importance throughout the ages to reverently listen to what John tells us in sober words about that grand vision.

THE GRAND VISION

I imagine that John, when he envisioned these tableaux must have been standing at the shore of the small island of Patmos, to which enemy powers had exiled him. It is evening and the sun is about to set. Before him, the Aegean Sea is becalmed, the water surface as smooth as a mirror, stretches out before him, alive with light and reflecting all the different shades of the fading rays. In the west some cloud formations loom large, high cirrus clouds are like burning candles in the evening sky. The entire celestial expanse is illuminated by the orangy-red, gold-fingered glow of the sinking sun. The tower-like clouds resemble old fortresses, constructed from crystal and flickering jewels, with illustrious light bundles shooting from every opening that, like shootings stars, explore the entire expanse. The scene out there resembles a fairy tale feature, so grandiose and so brilliant and glorious that all earthly thinking and imagination pale in comparison.

While John speechlessly takes in this overwhelming scenery, he suddenly notices as if "a door is opening in the heavens." Again a door! We already have noticed how a door was opened for the church in Philadelphia, a door nobody could close: the door to the world. We also saw how the savior himself had said to the church in Laodicea that he stands "at the door" and knocks. Here for the third time a door is involved. In this case the door indicates how it separates the temporal from the eternal, the visible from the invisible, and how this door splits this world from the mysterious world of the divine majesty. This door is perhaps better regarded as a wall against which we are dashed to pieces. But somehow this wall opens up on hinges and there is the One who can push it away. It is that door that opens up for John, and at that same moment everything changes. Those majestic-looking cloud formations, rising up in the heavens as purple-colored fortifications with impressive gates, are miraculously mirrored in the sea, smooth as glass. They slide away, opening up a perspective of infinite magnificence. This entire world with all its strife and tension disappears from under his feet, and there he stands, somewhere far away, as one lost in the impenetrable beauty of God's eternal palace.

At the same time he hears a voice. Rising above the never-resting rustling of the sea suddenly sounds something as a trumpet. John recognizes the voice as one that had spoken to him in earlier times, the voice of the glorified king and mediator Jesus Christ. He it is who invites him to enter the holy halls of the house of God. And because of the mysterious quality emanating from these words, this becomes possible. John is able to transcend the boundaries separating the two worlds, he is able to leave this deeply agitated world far behind and rises up to the highly elevated summits of God's majestic dwelling. There he can leave behind Laodicea and the synagogue of Satan, and the Nicolaitans, and the too numerous cares and temptations afflicting the life of the believers on earth, and enter the serene silence of the eternal temple.

It is immediately clear that there is a remarkable similarity between what John may witness here and what Isaiah was able to experience some centuries before. When we draw a parallel between Revelation 4 and Isaiah 6 then we notice many of the same points. But there are also some very noticeable differences.

The first difference that is immediately noticeable is that in Isaiah the entire vision is full of angels, singing while they are approaching Isaiah. Isaiah just stands there as a creature of a different order, not at all at ease between these angel choirs, so uncomfortable that he does not join in with the singing of the "holy, holy" that continuously rises up to heaven. In Revelation 4 we don't see any angels. There is the singing of the "holy, holy" but not by the angels. This is sung mostly by the "four animals" and by "the elders." This difference already indicates that the entire intent is something else. Isaiah receives a vision from God where the entire emphasis is on the immeasurable difference, the unbridgeable distance between the divine world where the holy angels praise God and the damned earth languishing under the curse of sin. Isaiah has to furiously fight against the worshiping of false images, against the arrogant attempts by the human race to reproduce

God according to their imperfect criteria and so visualize him. For Isaiah the priority is to show that God is "totally different," that he is so far above all earthly endeavors that every attempt to reproduce him will turn out to be a miserable failure and will mean an assault on his majesty. But with John the entire matter is different. John, in his vision, obtains a totally other picture, and this is that this God, this great and high God, who lives in the high heavens, is still very much concerned with this world and has made it part of his plan for salvation. This vision affirms that he, out of this world, will gather a people for life eternal. That's the reason why with John there are no angels and instead there are "four animals" and the "twenty-four elders."

The second difference is that Isaiah, when he enters the heavenly palace, is overwhelmed by an inexpressible anguish. At the same time he realizes how insignificant he is, his earthiness, his connectedness to sin, the impurity of his lips. He is unable to sing with the angels because his lips have continually expressed angry and sinful words. He realizes that he feels as a foreigner in this celestial gathering because he "lives in the midst of a people whose lips are unclean." The immense distance between the angels and him has a devastating influence on him.

Not so with John. Yes, he observes the hidden matters with increasing surprise, but his description lacks any hint of being upset. With him there is nothing like the "woe to me, for I am ruined." No, with him there is nothing else but the devout approach to the secret. The vision of John also makes no mention of an altar, of live coals that take away the sin. All that is absent here or, better, it is no longer needed. The reason why it is no longer needed is that John is conducted in the everlasting holiness by the hand of him who himself has carried all sins and has taken them away. It is Jesus Christ who dominates this vision. In his presence there is no mention of anguish, no mention of a scared urge to flee from the glorious crown radiating the light of God's face. We can also put it this way: John enters here the hallowed grounds as one who is not a stranger there, who has come to a place where he belongs, whose citizenship is in the heavens (Phil 3:20). He is deeply moved by this marvelous panorama unfolding before his eyes, but it does not crush him.

And yet John here stands face to face before God. "And there before me was a throne in heaven with someone sitting on it." That "someone" was further described in words that reveal deep reverence. His appearance was jasper and carnelian. A rainbow, resembling an emerald, encircles the throne. There ceases the description of the particulars. In other words: every attempt to describe his features is lacking. It is as if John did not dare to cast his eye to see the sublime face of him who rules all worlds, or perhaps he was unable because of the radiance reflecting from his face, impossible to see by mortal eyes. The only description is one of the quality of the light radiating from him who was seated on the throne of the world, totally at rest in his all-encompassing holiness.

Totally at rest. Yes, that is indeed the most striking in the depiction we receive. In that heavenly palace there is constant motion, constant activity. The throne emits thunderclaps, there are the choirs of the four animals and the twenty-four elders, and there is worship and homage. But he who sits on the throne, he is the totally unchangeable. With him there is no anxiety, no disquiet, no wondering, no tension, no apprehension, and no consternation. The very center of the universe is pure restfulness, displays a supra-human majestic silence. He sits on his throne; he who summons all worlds before his throne, he never, not even for a single instant, has surrendered his scepter, he who is, who was, and who is to come.

All this is of immense importance for understanding the entire book of Revelation. In the following chapters a lot of puzzling happenings will be described. Bitter cries of anguish will rise up, the tension will be unbearable, and distress will drive people to the edge of suicide. Time and again people will wonder, What about God, Where is God, What is God doing? Then a quick thought given to the grand vision is sufficient to understand that there is no reason at all to assume that God himself is perturbed by this, no reason to assume that it is beyond his control. When we have understood this, when we've seen that quiet light that radiates from that unfathomable figure on that elevated throne, when we've seen all this in faith, then we can never again be shook up to the core of our being because we know that behind all mysterious happenings in the history of the world there lies, deeply hidden, the ultimate rest and majesty of him who never is surprised by anything, who never is taken off guard by any happening. He is who he is, he is the eternal being, the faithful One who never will abandon the works of his hands.

It is regrettable that we don't quite understand what is meant by these precious stones mentioned here. The word "jasper" may mean a diamond. It may indicate that it is a green transparent jaspis, which, Greek writers assure us, was quite popular in those days. The carnelian is often equated with the Hebrew *odēm*, a word that means being red. But even if that were to be true, we still don't know the deeper meaning of all this. No doubt these stones and those colors have a special significance in biblical thinking. It would, however, be incorrect to guess their meaning because we don't know enough about them. If with emerald indeed the emerald is meant then that points out that the rainbow around the throne has a wonderful green hue, a hue that sort of corresponds with the green of jasper in the center. On the one hand the rainbow itself represents a radiating crown brilliantly sparking from the royal stature sitting on the throne, a radiating crown of infinite size and beauty. Within this rainbow is he who sits on the throne, present in his entire world, in the entire cosmic palace he has constructed. On the other hand the rainbow, by its very nature, is a reminder of the covenant that God made with Noah and a sign of his faithfulness and his graciousness.

This is what John observes: light, nothing else but light, in wonderful, ecstatic colors. He does not see the setting sun, which, with her very last brilliant rays, illuminates the cloud formations and miraculously transforms the entire heavens into a fairy-tale castle. Well, yes, he sees all that, but his eyes see through them, he sees how all these entities express an explanation for the deepest realities, the reality of God who sits on his throne and who fills this entire world with his splendor. He does not see God. That is impossible. Paul's words come to mind, "Who alone is immortal, who lives in inapproachable light, who nobody can see and nobody has seen" (1 Tim 6:6).

"And before the throne there was what looked like a sea of glass, clear as crystal . . . Before the throne seven lamps were blazing. These are the seven Spirits of God." The vision offers more and more details, so ever more new appearances become clear to the seer. It is almost impossible to explain what the crystal sea in this context indicates. Initially I am inclined to think that we must remind ourselves that the prophet here stands at the seashore where the placid sea extends before him. And at the distant horizon it looks as if the sea itself melts away into the serene perspicuity of the infinitely expanding celestial sea and finally fading away into the mysterious magnitude of the divine palace. It is quite possible that memories of the ancient world picture play a role here that alluded to "waters above the skies" (Ps 148:4), where God stores "the upper chambers" (Ps 104:3). This heavenly ocean is in some ways the counterpart of the earthly ocean, except that, while the earthly ocean in the Bible continuously represents the demonic powers dominating this cursed earth, the heavenly ocean is exactly the opposite. The earthly ocean is always menacing, replete with satanic forces out of which emerge the monsters that make the earth unsafe and conspire to destroy the Lord's holy place. Daniel already saw it this way and John too, as we shall see in Revelation 13:1. This earthly ocean therefore is the symbol of the combined forces of everything that has conspired to obstruct God and his kingdom. The heavenly ocean, on the other hand, is the symbol of the larger-than-life loftiness of God. This ocean mirrors his faithfulness and his majesty. Smooth as ice, motionless, the ocean stretches out before John's eyes similar to crystal. No misshapen monstrosities are concealed in her, and no powers of disruption and destruction are erupting from her innards. Her transparent clarity reflects the face of the eternal. At this point that's how John observes the mystery of the heavenly ocean. Later in his revelations he will again see this same sea, but then she is different, then she is "like a sea of glass mixed with fire" (Rev 15:2). But then we are in the center of the last things when God's ire has been unleashed over the "beast" and his image. After all, that heavenly ocean may be clear as crystal, but this does not at all mean that she lacks power and terror. She also can reflect the fiery force of God's terrible wrath "from which earth and sky fled from his presence" (Rev 20:11). However all this lies far into the future. Here John stands at the outset of these awesome events which will herald the new age, the age of the kingdom of the Lord.

Above the limitless expanse of the heavenly ocean John sees seven blazing lights. Just as in the holy place in the old temple a golden lampstand is found with her seven lights, so too in the heavenly sacred place are lamps fully alight. They are not joined together as one lampstand. Instead they are somewhat strangely suspended there, mysterious in their infinity. Are they the first stars that, now that the sky slowly is turning dark, can be seen sparkling above the waters? In isolation this is not entirely implausible. We often see in Scripture that what is shown in a prophetic vision is closely connected with what happens in the ordinary, day-to-day events. However we must not forget that the vision gets behind the truth of the matter, sees more than the physical parts only, sees matters of a higher order. That's how it is here as well. Those seven mysterious lights floating out there in the infinite space could be stars, made visible in the evening sky, but in John's vision they indicate something else completely. They are the lamps burning before the throne, the prayers rising up before the throne, as "the seven spirits of God."

There is no further explanation of the meaning of these seven spirits in this vision. It is plain that they are the one, unique, Holy Spirit of God, revealing itself in the life of the church on earth. Just before, we have learned about them as the seven churches in Asia Minor, each one involved in her own particular struggle, her own special temptation, her own perils and her own opportunities. In all of them the Spirit is at work. It is clear that in the one church the work of the Spirit is much more clearly expressed and is more intimately at work than in the other, but in all of them the quiet flame of his sustaining power is still alive. Purely seen from the point of view of down-to-earth reality these seven churches are but a tiny flock of confused people who, in a totally hostile world, wage a grim fight. They are but a small-minded and bickering bunch, occasionally celebrating communion and for the rest are just as jealous and just as egoistic and just as ordinary as all other people. But they possess a spark that changes them altogether. They possess something that all others lack. Occasionally this spark lights up in them and when this happens it always is a wonderful surprise. These people possess something that enables them to valiantly face death. They have something that gives them the courage to respond to all bitterness and all persecution with a loving compassion. It is that secret, evident in these seven churches, that is in a few words revealed here. It is the secret of the seven spirits of God, suspended as silent lights in the infinity of the heavenly immensity, situated directly above the crystal sea in which the face of the eternal is reflected.

Seen from this perspective the earthly reality is indeed totally bizarre and confused. Out there is the violently agitated sea of the earth's inhabitants from where cruel monsters arise, in which demonic powers are concentrated. Yet here lies smooth and boundless the crystal sea displaying the infinite magnitude of God's works in which the radiant reflection of his presence is displayed. In the earthly hemisphere there are these tiny churches who, with great difficulty, try to battle the different expressions of the spirits of the age that pursue and confuse humanity everywhere. Here are the seven lamps of God's spirits still visible, never to be extinguished, suspended in plain sight as a hymn of devoted adoration. In the earthly reality everything is always disguised, everything is under pressure, everything is terrifying. That is why we now approach the ultimate meaning of all things, coming closer and closer to discover what lies hidden behind the true state of affairs as a secret that will bare it all. Those who have seen through all this can never again be captured and frightened by what's going on here upon earth. They have understood something of what Psalm 93 so courageously and humbly has confessed:

> The Lord reigns, he is robed in majesty;
> His throne was established long ago
> You are from all eternity.
> The seas have lifted up, O Lord,
> The seas have lifted up their pounding waves.
> Mightier than the thunder of the great waters,
> Mightier than the breakers of the sea
> The Lord on high is mighty.

THE FIRST RUSTLING OF THE COMING THINGS

Everything we looked at until now inspired restfulness, unimaginable serenity. The mighty throne with the radiating rainbow, the crystal sea, those mysterious lampstands, they all conveyed an element of immense silence.

Yet there was some movement. "From the throne came flashes of lightning, rumbling and peals of thunder." They originate from the throne, the throne is at the center, even though this throne itself is securely fastened. Are these flashes of lightning the first indications of what is to come? Because, let's face it, matters must change because of the deeply penetrating difference between the serene heavenly quiet and the turmoil on earth. It simply cannot go on like this when out from the world's seas all these demonic kingdoms arise and the church of God is squeezed to dust by hostile powers. The situation must change now that this helpless woman who has given birth to the child is pursued by the dragon and must flee to the most desolate place. Sometime soon something decisive must happen, matters must move at last to a denouement, come to the goal God always has had in mind. When John was there in the island of Patmos, there was in him that feeling of a deep longing for that final moment, because he was so burdened by the confusion and the disorientation of this world. Now that the great Christ has gained the victory, now it seemed to him, the power of the demonic forces on earth could not exist much longer. They have been condemned, they already have been vanquished there and expelled from heaven, and now all their pride and their domination have become null and void. That's why now matters must move, the grand finale must arrive soon. For the time being John notices as yet nothing else than the lightning flashes and thunder claps from the throne. But soon he will observe that these thunderclaps in the high heaven will vibrate all the way to earth where they will result in a long series of overwhelming events.

That is the first sign that indicates what is coming.

The second apparition that draws our attention is the mysterious action of the "four animals." It is exceedingly difficult, almost impossible, to grasp what the meaning is of these four "animals" or "living beings." Right away we notice that there is a great similarity between these "four living creatures" and the mysterious figures Ezekiel in his vision has observed around God's throne (Ezek 1:5 and 10:2, 20). Still it is not difficult to show some real differences. In Ezekiel the four animals or "living beings" each have four faces, one of a human, one of a lion, one of an ox, and one of an eagle. In John's vision each animal only has one face. In Ezekiel the four living beings carry the throne, while with John the throne is not carried at all. Also the number of wings is different. In the Ezekiel prophecy it is clearly outlined that these four living creatures are angels, cherubim, guardians and bearers of God's throne. Should we assume that the four living creatures John sees are angels? It is remarkable that that is not indicated at all.

It could well be that these four mysterious figures represent a multitude of possibilities. Some, for instance, have thought that they reminded them of the four images from the Zodiac, the Taurus, the Leo, the Scorpio, and the Aquarius. The Scorpion would then represent the figure of a human being, while the Aquarius would be replaced by the image of an Eagle, because the star formation of the Eagle is close to the Aquarius. Because the signs of the Zodiac mark the course which the sun takes every year, people in antiquity paid a lot of attention to these signs. The Taurus (Ox), the Leo (Lion), the Scorpion, and the Aquarius indicate the four important stations of the course of the sun, pointing to the four seasons of the year. So, in this way, the four living creatures would signify nothing else but the annual course of the sun, the four wind directions, and at the same time the four seasons of the year. Thus together they would indicate the totality of the grand, cosmic course of events, summer and winter, life and death, in short all that what takes place in the course of nature.

How far this idea can be accepted is not easily determined. Seen in isolation there is nothing really wrong to assume that the Bible describing heavenly happenings makes use of symbols and signs current then with the people around the area, in particular with those living in Babylon. The Bible often uses material borrowed from other cultures, and then gives it a totally new and authentic meaning. However we don't have enough backing for this theory to totally rely on this direction.

It does make sense to assume that the four living creatures John observes have a connection to the cosmos in its totality. The number four is already an indication of this because that is the number that is preferred in indicating the world in its completeness, with its four wind directions and its total variety. Also it is a point of interest that in the Old Testament the cherubim have a connection to the wind. "He mounted the cherubim and flew; he soared on the wings of the wind" (Ps 18:10).

So we can't go far wrong when we assume that these living creatures here represent creation in her totality, the stars, the wind directions, the different seasons, plants, animals, in short all of nature that provides the background to history.

Of these four living beings we read that they sing night and day, "Holy, holy, holy, is the Lord God Almighty, who was, and is, and is to come." There again is a striking similarity between this song and that is sung in Isaiah 6 by the seraphim. And yet here too there is a pointed difference. The seraphim in Isaiah 6 praise God as "The Lord of armies," and then add "the entire earth is full of his glory." They praise God as the almighty who fills the entire world with his glory. The striking feature of the song the four living creatures sing in Revelation 4 is that they glorify God as the One "who was and who is and who is to come." In other words they praise God as the God who dominates history. He is there now also as the almighty, the king who rules over all, and comes as the finisher who shall at one time guide that mighty process we call history to a successful finish.

This song, actually, is not an unusual one. It contains words that repeatedly appear in the Bible and that dominate the entire book of the Revelation of John. The really remarkable thing here is that here are the four living creatures who are singing. The four living creatures, as we have seen, represent nature in its fullest sense of the word. Nature itself is the background against which history is depicted, the history of all her high and low points, her bloody wars and glorious discoveries. That in the song John hears it is the existence of the four living creatures, the beings of nature glorifying God as the God who was, who is, and who is to come. In our way of thinking nature is very little interested in what goes on in history: she every year causes the buds to swell, the flowers to bloom, even when humanity at large suffers from the most devastating disasters. We look up and see the splendid starry sky, we look down and see burning cities and villages; we look up and see the shiny, sunny skies, we look down and see horrendous battlefields. It is as if nature pokes fun at all human efforts and searching and suffering of the human race; she goes her own way and doesn't seem to care that her magnificence so often contrasts with our poverty, her ebullient joy is so often different from our misery. But, apparently, we are wrong when we think that nature doesn't care about what happens in the world out there. On the contrary, she is deeply interested in what God's deeds accomplish in the world. A shining star illuminates the Christmas night, and "creation waits in eager expectation for God's children to be revealed" (Rom 8:19). Seen in that light it is not so strange that these four living creatures glorify God as "he who is to come." This song has the undertone of a longing for the ultimate finish. With bated breath the entire world looks forward to the great day of the Lord.

The song of praise of the four living creature is also taken up by the twenty-four elders who John sees, sitting on thrones with golden crowns on their heads. They don't come first, they are not the initiators, but when the four living creatures have begun to sing their songs of adoration, they too can no longer hold themselves back. Then they rise up from their thrones, and throw their crowns before God's throne. They synchronize their song of praise with the devout words of the living creatures: "You are worthy, our Lord and God, to receive glory and honor and power, for you have created all things, and by your will they were created and have their being."

The meaning of the twenty-four elders is not difficult to guess. They represent the church of all ages, the church both of the old and new covenant. In other words they represent God's powerful plan for salvation realized in history, in the gathering of his people, which he has known before the foundation of the world. In the hymn of praise of these elders we recognize therefore the hymn that the church sings in the heavens and on earth.

They are the people of God who cannot cease to glorify him, to whom we owe everything without exception.

Here again the words of the song are significant. The four living creatures adored God as the God of history, the king "who is, who was and is to come." In this they demonstrate that they too are involved in the developing of salvation that God makes real in his unfathomable plan in history, and will soon bring to fruition. The elders, though, they praise God as the God of creation, the God of nature, who has made it all, by whose will it all came into being. It is as if nature sees God in history from the aspect of "he who comes," while the church, the fruit of God's acts in the history of the ages, lets her eyes more focus on nature. The living creatures look forward to the end, to perfection, while the church through her heavenly representatives worships God as the Almighty ruler who carries the entire creation by his totally, all-encompassing power. The church has already been lifted beyond history, forgets about the tears and misery she has suffered, and sees as her only real calling to prayerfully devote to God all that she has received, and that's the reason why these elders place their crowns before his throne.

With this display of devotion the first vision ends. For a moment it transposed us to heaven, far above the jungle this world has become and far above the temptations it presents. No unholy, no uncouth sound rises up that far, nothing that resembles balled fists, bloody hands, cries of anguish or ugly curses are heard here or seen. The heart of the universe is synonymous with rest. There stands the throne, high and exalted; there is the radiating crown of God's faithfulness and majesty. There only penetrates the sound of worship and the pious profession of one's own unworthiness.

But the heaven is not so distant from the earth that it does not notice what is happening down below. Thunder and lightning emit from the throne as a sign of the approaching threat of the terrible judgment. The four living creatures look forward to the moment when God will subject everything under his feet. And the twenty-four elders see it as if everything has happened already, as if God has already displayed his kingdom in this world in its full magnificence, and they worship him who is the creator of all.

In all this we hear the first rustling of the grand finale. Here down below the church is still persecuted, still succumbing to temptation, still dragged along in its staleness, in its colorlessness, in the chilliness of loveless life. Here still stands "the throne of Satan," and the synagogue of Satan still sows sedition. Here down upon the earth, the woman still dwells, hunted and haunted by the dragon, in her agony stretching out her hands to heaven. It seems as if heaven doesn't care what happens down below. But that is not true. There is a soft rustling that soon powerfully will increase in volume. The great moment of liberation is at hand and the first signs begin to show.

THE BEGINNING OF THE LAST THINGS

When John looks up he notices that he who sits on the throne carries a sealed book in his hands. It is right away clear what the meaning of the book is. The Bible, on many occasions, mentions the presence of such a book in the heavens. The poet of Psalm 139 says that all the days of his life were written in God's book "before one of them came to be" (verse 16). Also the prophet Daniel received an indication that what was revealed to him was recorded in "the Book of Truth," the writings in which God's plan are noted (Dan 19:21). Here in Revelation 5 also is the roll of the book discussed, obviously the synopsis of the great, all-decisive happenings that will announce the coming of the kingdom. This book-roll contains the description of the final battle, the great victory over the demonic powers and the light that will break through. But this book has a totally different content than the history books on earth. The earthly history books contemplate the happenings of the past, they record what has happened before, but this heavenly book has been written in such a way that reading it sets the events in motion, stimulates them. So it does not say what already took place, but it records what is about to happen and, as soon as it is read, it starts to come into being. It is with this book the same as with creation. God calls the things that are not yet, as if they are there already, and the moment he calls them they are there. That's why this book contains the events that are here not yet, as if they are here already, and the instant the book is opened and read, the events are here too.

That alone explains the troubling mood that apparently has settled there, because there was nobody in heaven or on earth found capable to open the book and read it. It seems that John himself experienced this lack of capability so profoundly that he was moved to the depth of this soul.

What really does this mean that this book with its seven seals, remains closed in the hands of him who sat upon the throne? It means nothing else than that the history of the world cannot yet come to an end, and thus cannot yet reach her fulfillment. Matters stagnate, and there really is no progress. On the earth a certain balanced state comes into being: the dragon is not able to destroy the woman on the run, but neither is there escape possible for the woman. Those churches in Ephesus, Sardis, and Laodicea continue to exist, celebrate communion, and carry on their struggle in the midst of a hostile world. They are still tempted, are still occasionally persecuted, and are still finding out how difficult it is to keep focused day-in-day-out, and barely managing to do so. In short, they are not swept away, but neither do they really succeed. They still continue their cumbersome course through history tiresomely, slowly and disheartened. They still have their occasional festive days but also times of depression when everything is too much. At times it seems that they are completely submerged in the morass of this world, as if nothing of their royal status counts anymore, and then suddenly they soar proud and courageous and capable of great accomplishments. But then again there is no progress, no pattern of growth, and nothing really has a finishing touch. It's all these things that make everything on earth so tiring. Never is there a decisive battle, a definite victory. There are reformations but they routinely are followed by days of new deformation, by world conformity and new contaminations. There are in the church times of revival, of great spiritual growth, but these are often immediately followed by times of dullness and chill. There never is a reformation that lasts, never a revival that doesn't wane. There never is a day where, when we get up we can say: This is it! Today we will see it! Everything is up and down, everything moves in the monotonous dance of rise and fall.

And just as it is with the church so it also is with the efforts of Satan. He too sees no definitive victory. He can destroy churches, he can cause believers to be bloodily persecuted, but he never manages to totally annihilate them. He with his deadly venom of temptation may for a long time paralyze the church as she sinks away in a spiral of death but he never succeeds to deliver the final coup de grâce. He can sweep up entire nations into a frenzied hate against everything that carries the name of Jesus Christ, but he can never manage to eradicate that name. He too discovers that history moves in cycles, goes up and goes down. Sometimes irrational hate subsides bringing in days when the message of the cross celebrates new triumphs. The devil too is unable to force decisions, he too must cope with the fundamental failure to open the seals. He too can never deliver a decisive blow.

John displays acute and deep insight here. This situation may not and cannot continue, because it can drive a person to despair. To stand in history becomes a nightmare when no end is in sight, when there never is a point in time in which matters converge to its final disposition. That's why he is emotionally touched, cries his heart out when he so concretely sees that fatal powerlessness before him, when he notices that nobody is able to respond to the loud challenge of the angel. Nobody on earth or in the heavens is capable to break the seals of the book and to read its content. Nobody is able to cause the last things to happen because there are obstructions that cause all efforts to result in failure.

We are inclined to wonder why it is that nobody either in heaven or on earth is capable to open the book. Why is world history during all these many centuries doomed to dwell under the curse of indecisiveness? Why is it impossible to break the ban of that monotony, of that deadly, tiring to and fro?

It would be foolish to presume that we can answer these questions. There are hidden questions there that we can only guess at with great precipitancy but that we under no circumstances can grasp. We do have reason, based on Scripture, to assume that the entire problem of world history is more than a question of balances of power. We simply cannot state that God is the almighty and that there is no doubt that he in one swoop can eliminate Satan's rule. It is not that simple. We cannot say that, if God so desires, he can lead his church to a definite, decisive victory, in spite of all attacks by the devil. Again: it's not that simple. Satan is more than a daredevil, a pirate, a criminal brigand. He occupies a rightful place in this world, as to some extent, this world has been transferred to him. It is not for nothing that he is called "the prince of this world" (John 12:31; 14:20; 16:11), and also "the god of this age" (2 Cor 4:4). There is in his mysterious power something that is frightening, something totally flabbergasting. No powerful angels are capable to expel him or cast him down. He has cast a spell over this world that nobody can break. That's why what takes place in the world is far more than a simple game of a balancing of power: there is something here that is beyond the understanding of our sharpest minds. And that is precisely the reason why nobody is able to open the book. Opening the book implies the definite conclusion of world development, implies the victory of the church over all opposing forces, and implies that the enchantment is ended, that the bewitchment is forever broken. The opening of the book entails that at last everything in this world has finally become what it really is, that all delusion and pretense has forever vanished. And that is not a small matter. That is not simply a matter of a heroic struggle; that is not a matter of an energetic eruption of enthusiasm. That totally fatiguing feature of the world's history is the necessary consequence of that single fact there is something more, that there is something that goes beyond the simple clashing of powers. We are so inclined to talk in terms of war potential and balances of power. God reasons differently, in ways we simply cannot fathom. That lies behind that stupendous secret that is obscured by the fact that no angel, no archangel, no hero, no saint can come forward and state: give me the book! I will break the seals!

Is there really nobody who can do that? Yes, there is One who can. But that One does not step forward right away. He does not at once volunteer. It is as if he waits awhile to see whether one of all the numerous powers in heaven and on earth will advance to the throne. It is as if he only wants to assume this task when it has been shown beyond the shadow of doubt before the face of heaven and earth that only he is capable. "Do not weep," one of the elders speaks. "See the Lion of the tribe of Judah, the root of David, has triumphed. He is able to open the scroll and its seven seals." It had to be an elder who spoke these words to John. The angels could not give him this assurance, and neither could the four animals, the representatives of the cosmic powers, whisper this into his ears. Only a person who himself or herself belonged to the church of Jesus Christ, a colleague of John, could inform him of the solution of the world's great secret. At that critical moment John must been reminded of the communion of saints. Here too he is not there as a loner, but is included in the global connection of God's people that has received God's Word and that, based on that Word, may obtain the answer to the untold many problems that daily confront us.

Beautiful is the name the elder gives the Christ: the "lion out of the tribe of Judah." Are there still whispers in heaven murmuring the words Jacob spoke on his deathbed many centuries ago when he compared Judah to a lion cub? That this elder uses the word *lion* here indicates that an enormous exertion of power is involved here. The Christ of God is a lion but not in a sense that he has pushed his way in the world by means of sheer force. He is not a formidable field marshal who fires up his army to go to war. His power lies in radical surrender; he is a lion because he is a lamb, because he allowed to be offered like a lamb. That he is called "the Root David" is clearly indicated in Isaiah 11:1. In Revelation 22:16 Christ calls himself "the root and the offspring of David," the patriarch and at the same time the descendant. Here he is only pictured as the "root." David is only David through him, David refers to his power and his accomplishments. David is what he is because he is foreshadowing Christ's royal power. It is as if this elder clearly wants to indicate that, when we very carefully read the Old Testament, then there alread6y we can detect the secret that only here is revealed in its complete clarity.

Almost immediately after this elder has recalled these old, very distant memories, is there movement in the heavenly armies. Only now the Christ steps forward, but not as a lion, not as a warrior in full armor, but as the "Lamb that has been slain with seven horns and seven eyes."

These sober words are deeply moving. Here enters the only person who can bring the world history to its fulfillment and can break that ban. Here the One who has been announced as the lion from the tribe of Judah approaches the throne, and he appears in the form of a lamb. Here the giant, the greatest of all powers in heaven and on earth, who alone can bring about the final decision, here the most powerful steps forward with his pierced hands, a clear reference to the cross, on which he once wrestled the most bitter battle with death. Here a new light shines on the concepts of greatness and power, giving them a totally different slant, a new interpretation found only in heaven. To be great, a giant, does not mean being a fiery fighter, an invincible hero, but truly great is he who appears capable of the most total self-surrender in order to save others. Truly great is he who is prepared to die on the cross. Truly great is he who is placed in the heart of the universe as the only one who can bring salvation. He is not the fully armed warrior, but the great carrier of the cross. He is the one who has deleted the word self-preservation and has surrendered himself to death, and because of this has become the cornerstone of the coming kingdom. The history of the world does not come to its meaningful finish by submarines and subterfuge, by missiles and machine guns, but because there has been one who "being in very nature God, did not consider equality with God something to be grasped but made himself nothing, taking the very nature of a servant, being made in human likeness" (Phil 2:6–7). This coming forward by the Lamb reveals something of the indescribable impotence of all violence when the real issue is to truly accomplish healing and salvation. This lion is lion only because he does not for one moment hesitate to be the Lamb. This hero is only a hero because the total surrender to love is written in his deepest essence, with his pierced hands as proof. All heroism and bravery not expressed through Christ's secret is in its essence hubris, results in cruelty, torture, and tyranny. A lion which is just a lion and does not carry the signs of "The Lamb that was slain," is not a lion. In this place, before God's very throne, now that the moment has arrived where the great Book will be transferred, only one person can take that place: the king with the pierced hands. That Book is only safe there, nowhere else—every other hand will make it into an idol. Only in the hands of him who allowed himself to be crushed so that the world can live, only in those hands can the Book be given without any misgivings whatsoever.

As soon as this decision has been made, John hears all powers in heaven burst out in loud jubilation. The four living creatures, representing all that moves in the universe, and the twenty-four elders, symbolizing the church of the old and new covenant, they all sing a new song: "You are worthy to take the scroll and to open the seals, because you were slain and with your blood you purchased God's people from every tribe and language and people and nation. You have made them to be a kingdom and priests to serve our God, and they will reign on the earth."

After that this hymn of praise is taken over by the multitudinous choirs of angels: "Worthy is the Lamb, who was slain, to receive power and wealth and wisdom and strength, and honor and glory and praise."

A grand moment is this when all spheres of creation devotedly arrange themselves around that unique moment in history when, dark and threatening, on Calvary the cross was erected. Now, at this moment, now that the great mystery is beginning to be revealed, now all are becoming deeply aware that this certain day, the day of Calvary, has been the very center of all that ever happened, that on that special day all powers in heaven and on earth were concentrated in that single point in time, and that in that one moment the great victory has been achieved. Every section of creation harbors its own recollections of that day and has experienced these terrible moments in its own way.

The four living creatures, symbolizing nature's powers, remember how on that day a horrible darkness covered the earth, how the sun went into mourning, how a sickening, scary stillness succumbed over this doomed world. They remember how the birds ceased to sing, and frightened, retreated into the density of the trees, because it was so unnatural, so incomprehensible. They remember that unique moment when the Son of Man surrendered his spirit to the Father, and the rocks split and the earth shook. They remember the wonderful glory of the Easter morning when indescribable joy jolted through the trees and the flowers, and when the entire creation arose to a new life. Nature itself experienced all this as something unknown. It never fully understood what was really involved, and never really saw that what happened on Calvary was something totally different from any other experience in the past. But now, now in the light of God's throne, she suddenly sees the significance. Now she fully realizes that also her destiny, her history, was determined on that one day, because on that great day of Calvary, when the Lamb of God was slain, the people of God were "bought," and that in the glorification of those children of God, all of nature too will be "liberated from its bondage to decay" (Rom 8:21).

And the twenty-four elders remember how already in the days of the former temple service each sacrifice that was brought, each lamb that we slaughtered, was a prophecy of what later would happen on Calvary. They remember how the prophets had already an understanding of this when they in veiled terms spoke of the mysterious "Servant of the Lord," who, "like a lamb was brought to the slaughter," and "who was crushed for our iniquities" (Isa 53:7, 5). These elders themselves were there on Calvary, all shook up, with remorse in their hearts, not understanding, not in the least suspecting how grand and overwhelmingly beautiful that cross was in reality. But now, with the scales fallen from their eyes, now that they can see through this happening as clearly as glass, now it fully dawns on them, and now they can do nothing else than in the bottom of their hearts glorify the Lamb of God who from every tribe and language and people and nations has obtained salvation for the people of God. And while they sing this they see before them the splendid panorama of the nations of the world. Chinese appear before them and Japanese; they see the nations of the North where cold winters are severe; they look at the sons and daughters of Africa and Indonesia, and those who live on the islands in the Pacific. In one glimpse the world opens up before them. Their songs of praise proceed from rich palaces and poor ghettos, from dry deserts and grassy steppes, from mountainous regions and fertile meadows: from everywhere in the whole wide world the hymns rise up to honor him who embraces the entire world in his unfathomable love.

And don't forget the angels! They too have memories of Calvary. They strengthened him when he in the darkness of Gethsemane wrestled with God (Luke 22: 43). In great consternation they saw the unspeakable agony of the death of the righteous man, but they too, with pure pleasure rolled away the stone on Easter morning and opened the door, the door of life for him who lives and has been dead and behold, he lives into all eternity. With loud hosannas they greeted him when he, as king of glory, entered the beauty of heaven. At first, when the night of extreme suffering descended upon him, the savior of the world, they did not fathom its universal significance, but in all humility they bowed down "eager to see" the message of salvation entrusted to the community of the redeemed (1 Pet 1:12). But now, in the radiant light of the new day, there, before the throne of God, they understand it as the unique grand plan of the God of infinite wisdom, and they combine their praises in total harmony with those of hymns of adoration that now rise up from all spheres of creation. It must be noted that these angels do not address the Lamb directly with "You are worthy," but that they say it in the third person, "The Lamb is worthy." Is that because the angels, in the overall work of redemption, occupy a different place than the people in the natural world? Is that because they, as the holy angels, who have remained steadfast in their loyalty to God, cannot completely conceive the immensity of salvation that Christ has wrought for the lost? They have not known the darkness of the night in the same intense way as we have experienced it. Of course that does not mean that they stand outside the blessing of Calvary. Paul says somewhere that it has pleased "the great Totality" to make peace through Jesus Christ and through the blood of the cross "to reconcile all things with him, whether on earth or whether in heaven." Due to the nature of things, the word *reconcile*, when applied to the things in heaven—referring to angels—has a different meaning than when applied to us. They are not reconciled in the same way we are, because they were not lost in the same way we were lost. Yet, in the existence of angels, there too a sort of vacuum occurred through the sinful rupture that affected the entire universe. The world of angels too has been saved through the cross, be it in a different way than our salvation. As soon as the singing of the two hymns of praise have stopped, the one song by the voices of nature and the elders, the other by the angels, this service in honor of the Lamb ends with a hymn sung by all: "To him who sits on the throne and to the Lamb be praise and honor and glory and power for ever and ever!"

This last hymn of praise is more general. It does not come from a special part of the creation but rises up in unison from all spheres and layers of the cosmos. The angels participate, but so do all people, and also the sea, the stormy winds, the plants, and the infinitely varied riches of the animal world. The atom and the solar system, great and small alike, they all unite in that one, mighty song of praise honoring him who sits on the throne, and honoring the Lamb who has saved the world out of the clutches of defeat.

ETERNITY AND TIME

When we first read chapter 4 of the Revelation of John and right thereafter chapter 5, then there are a few points that draw our attention.

In chapter 4 we listen to the hymns in praise of God, but these are more or less timeless. They have a touch of eternity in them: they rise far above the daily global events. They breathe something of the imperishability of the measureless majesty of heaven. In the fifth chapter the songs show a stronger historical content, they concentrate on that singular, dominating event that took place on Calvary. And because of this they also offer a greater perspective on the new heaven and the new earth. They are full of promise, full of the radiant joy that awaits us in the kingdom. In the fourth chapter history is not seen as important while in the fifth chapter we are in the midst of it, opening up for our elated eyes the perspective of the end times.

That does not mean that in the first part of the great vision, described in that chapter, that point of view is not present. We receive a hint of that in the rumbling of the thunder and the flashes of lightning that originate from the throne. There already we see announced the great happening that is about to happen. In the hymn of the four living creatures this is reinforced again when God is addressed as "the Almighty who was, who is and who is to come." In the expectation of "what is to come" is already indicated the beginning of the very last things.

And yet that perspective in that first part wasn't very clearly spelled out, but only very vaguely indicated. There was a reason for this: it was not yet possible to come to a clear definition, because the cross had not yet entered into the picture, because the Lamb had not yet been mentioned. That first part still breathed the serene silence of eternity elevated far above all the change and turmoil of historical happenings.

In the second part the Lamb becomes the focal point. It is totally centered on the Christ. The hymns there are directed at the Lamb and contain Christ's great sacrifice. The entire second part is totally dominated by the incomparable greatness of the Christ of God and his holy work of redemption. From the very first there's where the focus of the second part is aimed at. At stake here is what's going on in the world, the all-pervading, deep problem of the completion of history. Christ alone can break the seals, only he can destroy the ban, only he can push matters toward their decisive end.

In other words: in the two parts of that great vision time and eternity meet. First time proceeds slowly, is gradually depicted in more detail, and then takes on a clearer and sharper form. And in the end everything flows together into eternity, in the serenity of the everlasting greatness of God.

This last hymn is now no longer completely centered on Christ. The focus there is no longer exclusively on the glorification of the Lamb. Now all praise and adoration is in on "him who sits upon the throne and on the Lamb." The last hymn is more theocentric, God himself is the focus, but in this case the God who has revealed himself to us in the sending of his Son, in the offering of the Lamb, in the accomplished work of the only mediator, the shepherd and savior of our souls.

When we hear the words of the last hymn fade away, we raise our heads in complete attention. Now the seals are about to be broken, now the Book is about to be opened and read, the Book that, when it is being read, at once becomes reality. As of that moment the history of the world is gaspingly gyrating to the end. The end is near. The enchantment has forever faded away.

CHAPTER FOUR

God's Great Disruption
(Revelation 6)

THE THREAD IS UNWINDING

In his great vision John has witnessed that Christ was given the Book with the seven seals because he had the right and possessed the power to break the seals and so set in motion the course of events, leading to the last things.

We cannot call this event a prophecy, at least not a prophecy in the sense of a prediction, because these matters are pure reality. Christ, through his suffering, his death, and his resurrection has removed all impediments, all obstacles, as he had received "all power in heaven and on earth," and so he has the authority to read the hidden content of the Book. Nothing else was necessary, no new suffering, no new struggle: everything was ready for the implementation of the ultimate outcome. And that's why an immediate start is made. There is no delay, the seals are immediately broken one after the other. That's why the period now commencing is a time of a speedy succession of enormous events.

In other words, this means that John is very much aware that he does not talk about matters that are far into the future, but that it involves realities that have already started to become visible. From now on the history of the world assumes an apocalyptic character, which means that the world's happenings are projected in wars, in tensions, in natural disasters, in economic anguish, in famines, in enormous forced migrations, all due to the breaking of the seven seals. We no longer can regard world history as standing on its own, having a momentum that is predictable, but we must see it against the backdrop of what starts to happen in the heavens. And what is occurring there is nothing else but the unwinding of the last thread. The all-encompassing victory by the Lamb must now take on form, must now slowly penetrate the reluctant and unbelieving human consciousness, must now step for step become an accepted fact until the day when this victory will be visible to all.

In the meantime we will soon find out that the event of Christ's victory becoming a generally accepted fact will prove to be far more complicated and a much more difficult task than we initially had expected. The main cause for this is that we are used to thinking in terms of power. Of course now that Christ has full authority, he can exercise that too, but things are not that simple. The Bible sees these matters right from the start as being much more involved, because there are other factors at work than merely those of power. Later on we must give some special attention to the important matter of deceleration, something that plays an enormous role in Revelation. The entire situation is not as cut and dried as we had thought because there is a host of different powers at work that act as brakes. Everything has to reach a certain stage of maturity. It is simply impossible to cut the thread without further ado because severing it can only be done when everything is ready for it. It is true that certain influences will originate from heaven that will enhance the onset of maturity. But everything needs its own momentum and a sudden, radical break in simply impossible.

It is this thinking process that gives the entire book of Revelation such a surprising character. On every page there are clear indications that there is a definite propelling force toward the end, but as soon as the end seems near, some sort of delay interferes and new restraining factors come to the fore. It resembles climbing a mountain, where at every moment it feels that this is the last stretch before the summit, but that when that point is reached, there still is the discouraging prospect that yet another, even higher top must be conquered. The book depicts this situation in far-flung flowery language. First there is the breaking of the seven seals. Then the opening of each seal results in a series of happenings of which each one carries clear signs of the end. And yet, when the last seal is finally broken, we discover to our great surprise that the end does not burst upon us like an overripe tomato but that a new series of powers comes into force. The opening of the seventh seal results in seven new events: angels emerge with trumpets and when they blow these, the sound vibrates throughout the universe. The blowing of these trumpets causes rising tension. Again there is a strong desire for an overwhelming conclusion, an all-dominating finale. But once again we are disappointed, because after the trumpet-bearing angels, new angels appear, this time carrying golden bowls. And they empty these bowls, one after the other, over the world. Every time we assume that the end is there it is pushed back; every time when it seems that the coming glorious perfection is within our grasp, it fades away again. That is the ever-changing format in which this unfathomable phenomenon of the delaying feature is presented to us in this book.

In other words, there clearly are two opposing tendencies at work here. There is an outspoken push toward a definite grand finale. Objectively speaking everything is ready, the Lamb has been slain, he has received authority to open the Book, so nothing else is needed now, and the victory is there. And yet it becomes more and more evident that still all sorts of other events must take place. There still are opposing forces, there still are mysterious factors preventing a rapid realization. That confrontation, the meeting of these two tendencies, is the theme of this book.

THE RIDER WITH A CROWN

The image of the steady development starts with the depiction of the four apocalyptic horsemen. With the opening of the first seal a white horse appears, with the second seal a fiery red one, with the third seal a black horse, and a pale one with the breaking of the fourth seal.

It is right away striking that John here closely follows the prophecy of Zechariah. In chapter 6 of that book there also is mention of four horses, seen by the prophet in a vision. These horses too have different colors: red, black, white, and dappled. However, there these different colors directly relate to the four wind directions. "The one with the black horses is going to the north, the one with the white horses is going to the west, the one with the dappled horses toward the south, and the red horses go to the land of the east" (Zech 6:6–7). Just as it is the case with many nations, the wind directions are associated with the different colors. Black is typically the color of the dark and cold North, white is the color of the West where the sea with her white-topping waves delineates the inhabited world. Red in this context is characteristic for the East, where each morning the sun as a fiery red ball rises up. And finally, the dapple color is seen as belonging to the South.

In the Revelation of John horses appear with a somewhat similar color code, but there is no indication pointing them to the wind directions. The similarity in form is there, but the meaning is completely different. In John's vision the four horses evidently point to something not at all similar to the vision Zechariah had.

"I watched as the Lamb opened the first of the seven seals. Then I heard one of the four living creatures say in a loud voice like thunder, 'Come!' I looked and there before me was a white horse. Its rider held a bow, and he was given a crown, and he rode out as a conqueror bent on conquest." There is a difference of opinion concerning the meaning of the white horse. There are some who think that this means war because the rider who appears on the scene carries a bow. The depiction of the archer would then convey a memory of the invasion by the Parthians who in the year 62 forced a Roman legion to surrender. These Parthians were experienced archers and exceedingly quick and valiant. The invasion of these barbarians would be felt as a prelude to the approaching fall of the Roman Empire.

Others, however, are inclined to see the bowman on the white horse as the triumphant march of the good news in the world. This means that the glad tidings of Jesus Christ, preached first in the entire world, precedes the series of arrival of these destructive forces.

It seems to us that the last explanation is indeed preferable. It is quite possible that the image of the archer has been derived from the invasion of the Parthians and that the memories of this invasion play a role in the totality of this picture, but still this makes the scenario depicted here totally different. It is not the cruel war that is sketched here but the peaceful war of the gospel proclamation. That same proclamation of the good news will soon approach the gates of pagan Rome, she also will topple mighty forces, but she will accomplish that in a totally different way and with totally different objectives. The Parthians on their tiny, fast horses came storming in as a whirlwind, and poured an avalanche of death and destruction over the people. Here follows a new force, the counterpart of the Parthian archers, who likewise as a tsunami overwhelms the mighty Roman Empire. But this new archer on his white horse is very different. His work is different, his goal is different, and his result is different. No burning cities and villages, no fearfully fleeing flocks of people, no male or female slaves, no captured enemies, no plunder, robbery, rape, tyranny. On the contrary: blessings, peace, joy, expectation of eternal life.

The reasons why we are of the opinion that this explanation is preferred can easily be stated. In the first place it must be noted that when that second horse appears it is said that its rider has the mandate to "take peace from the earth." That indicates that the red horse is the symbol of the wasting war, which makes it highly unlikely that this white horse also would represent this, making the two horses essentially identical. The white horse may perhaps symbolize the invasions of the barbarians who from the endless steppes of Asia penetrated the Roman Empire, and that the red horse would point more to the civil wars, but in both cases the issue is identical:

the peace on earth is shattered. In all it seems much more likely that the white horse means something very different from the red horse.

A second consideration is that the rider on the white horse receives a different description than the other horses and riders. Of the rider of the white horse it is said that "he was given a crown, and he rode out as a conqueror bent on conquest." None of these other riders receives such great and honorable mention. That indicates that this first rider occupies a very particular place. In that regard there is some resemblance with the rider on his white horse as described in Revelation 19:11–16, and there is called faithful and true, the Word of God. That in Revelation 19 the rider on the white horse is depicted in that way is another reason why also here in Revelation 6 we must connect this to the way the gospel was preached throughout the world. And finally, this portrayal also completely fits with the indications we find in other places in the Bible. Matthew 24 gives a terrifying description of the approaching last days. In the midst of this vivid depiction between the mentioning of wars, famines, earthquakes, there suddenly appears the prophecy: "the Gospel of the Kingdom will be preached in the whole world as a testimony to all nations, and then the end will come." This preaching of the gospel of the kingdom in the entire world fits right into the events of the last days. It is predicted next to many other signs of the coming end. Would it therefore be so strange when here, with the reading from the Book of the "very last things," as the first sign is given the triumphant course of the rider on the white horse? Doesn't that fit in exactly with the picture that the Lord himself has painted of these same last things?

In the meantime many other questions pop up. We could well imagine that the image of the archer is a fitting one for the preaching of the gospel. The bow is a weapon that finds its target from afar while the preaching of the gospel must much more be seen as a wrestling match. Preaching much more resembles the image of a sword fight and not so much the shooting of an arrow to a goal far away. It much rather is a fight where the blows fall in the immediate vicinity. That's why in the Scriptures the image of the sword is used much more frequently where it concerns the proclamation of the good news. Christ himself is described as one out of whose mouth came a sharp double-edged sword (Rev 1:16). When Paul in Ephesians 6 described the spiritual armor there is mention of the "word of the Spirit that is the Word of God" but there is no mention of a bow and arrows. On the other hand we find the expression of the "burning arrows of the Evil one." Apparently the devil uses bow and arrow but the Christian is only concerned with weapons for close contact, a good way to describe its armor. So again we must consider whether the image of an archer is a fitting one when we deal with the preaching of the good news.

The first comment that can be made is that the image of the arrow is not completely foreign in the Scriptures. In Isaiah 49:2 Christ himself is compared to "a sharp sword" and at the same time "a polished [pointed] arrow." The meaning here must be that Christ through his word hits the heart and in that way saves the person. He is the arrow that afflicts healing wounds, wounds that bring salvation. In that same spirit we too can speak of the archer as one who proceeds as a victor.

It is both intriguing and surprising that in this chapter—and only here—there is mention of a bow and arrow. Perhaps it is possible that here an allusion is made to a phenomenon that especially will occur in "the last days." The preaching of the word can work two ways: it can be close contact, in a duel between two persons, or it can work from a distance. In the first case it resembles a sword fight, in the second an arrow encounter. The arrow character is represented by the written word in whatever form is conveyed through the air, lands at places where the preacher never has been before, and remains effective long after the author has passed away. The arrow simile makes conveying the message possible through any type of electronic means, is listened to or read in places where no preacher ever comes or can come and be heard or read by people who may never have entered or will enter a church. So it cannot be denied that the preaching at times can have a striking likeness with an arrow that can hit a target far away. In our times when the bow and arrow has gone into retirement and this replaced by guided missiles and smart bombs operated from thousands of kilometers away, this image has even more relevance, because the spreading of the Word too has far wider possibilities and can now be heard and read throughout the entire world and influence people everywhere.

So if we wondered whether there was any reason why the preaching is portrayed through this arrow character and why it is so strikingly emphasized, here is an explanation. It is now very likely that, in the framework of the last things, this has been done intentionally. There may come times in which the Word can no longer be proclaimed via the sword character, in close personal contact, in public gatherings, or even on a door-to-door manner. There may come a time in which the Word can no longer function that way. There may come a time when the only possibility remains to spread the Word through quiet, perhaps secret, handing out of literature or furtively slipping a tract into a mailbox, which then become the arrows this chapter is referring to. No matter what, the Word will be spread somehow, somewhere, and will hit the targets it is supposed to hit. Perhaps there is a particular reason why, amidst the riders on a red, a black, and a pale horse, amidst war, famine, and death, the rider of the white horse is described as an archer and not as a warrior with shield and sword. And, I must add, that the

Bible has been translated into more than eleven hundred languages, which can be seen as definite fulfillment of what here in the rider of the white horse is being described for us.

In general it strikes us that this strong emphasis on the preaching of the good news is an integral part of the last things. That preaching then totally becomes a matter of eschatology, surrounded as the proclamation is by events that proclaim the end of the world. What is actually amazing is that normally this sort of preaching is the ongoing function of the church all the time. The church is always mission-minded, or should be. As has been noted many times previously, mission makes up the essence of the church. It is not something that also must be done, not a sort of extra that the church does on special occasions, but it is an essential element in the existence of the people of God. It is not difficult to show that the Scriptures see it that way. When Paul describes the spiritual armor, which we quoted earlier, then he enumerates a long list of weapons, but as first of the necessary ingredients he mentions "the feet fitted with the readiness that comes from the gospel of peace." That is a much needed part. And when Paul addresses the church in Colosse he admonishes them to "be wise in the way you act toward outsiders" and to "make the most of every opportunity." That, of course, means the opportunity to proclaim the gospel. Thus the church must always be alert and conscious of bringing to message to everyone. She must use every opportunity, grab every chance. After all that is the hallmark of a living church. Peter expresses it in even stronger terms when he calls the church "a chosen people, a royal priesthood, a holy nation, a people belonging to God," and then right away adds, "that you may declare the praises of him who called you out of darkness into his wonderful light" (1 Pet 2:9). Especially the little words "that you may" are especially significant. It seems that all the other words serve that one goal. To be a "chosen" people only means one thing: to serve that one overriding goal, that we proclaim the praises, the great deeds, of God. There the call to missions is given such a central position that it overshadows every other facet of the Christian faith. So, if the proclamation of the good news is such an essential hallmark of the church of all ages, is it then not remarkable that this archer on his white horse is marked here as belonging to the events that herald the end of the world?

This question can only be answered in the affirmative. Something else that is peculiar is that the preaching of the good news is totally counted here as belonging to the events of the last days. However, two things must be taken into consideration here. In the first place it should be pointed out that this thought regularly appears in Scripture. Already in the Old Testament, when the people of the world are going to an Israel that has been redeemed by the Messiah, that is seen as one of the very last events before the great day of the Lord. Time and again it is striking in the prophecy that the matter of missions is closely associated with the coming grand finale and the ensuing reign of peace, covering the entire world. The Old Testament sees the universal proclamation of God's message always at the horizon of history. And behind that horizon lies the new kingdom, where "the mountains will bring prosperity to the people and the hills the fruit of righteousness" (Ps 72:3). We saw that already in the word of the savior in Matthew 24:14, where mission is placed in the context of the events that will precede the end of the world.

In the second place, all this does not exclude that this entire mission effort will have a long gestation period. It need not be that the rider on the white horse makes a quick tour around the world just before that great day of the Lord. The reason is that this entire ending episode does not run its course with the speed we initially assumed. Everywhere there is the factor of delay that we mentioned before, and with which we will deal again in the next chapter. That may mean that this rider on his white horse and with a crown on his head may not accomplish his mission in the sudden and speedy manner as we would expect. His going too is slowed down and falls apart in a multitude of happenings. That facet of the final events takes much longer and may not be seen as a "quick as a flash" sort of conquest. However we cannot discount that toward the end there would indeed by something like a formidable revelation of the triumphant power of the good news. Just as the disasters will accumulate and toward the end will manifest themselves in an unheard-of severity, so too the course of the white horse will be seen only in its full glory toward the end.

In all this we must not forget that the history of missions teaches us that it is exactly the knowledge and insight that the day of the Lord is near that has always driven the church to extra missionary activity. The overwhelming zeal in the first centuries to bring the gospel was possible only because the church lived so strongly in the expectation of the speedy coming of the Lord. All early writings express this belief as a joyful witness that gave them power to valiantly pursue the struggle in spite of all persecution. In the following centuries the church also has done missionary work driven by other motives. At times the missionary activities were shaped by the desire to subject the people to the spiritual and political authority of the pope. However we keep on noticing how the awareness of the approaching end keeps playing a role and how it is exactly that notion that gives the work of missions its greatest impact. All other considerations simply melt away in the heat of history, but that singular insight withstands all threats. Every time the church becomes aware that her place in the world is one of being a stranger there, and she looks forward to a better fatherland than that the history of the world may prepare for her, then she becomes enthused, full of fire with the desire to acquaint far away people with the message of the cross. Indeed, there is an intimate and extremely subtle connection between missionary preparedness and the knowledge that we are faced with the final battle. It is therefore quite logical that the rider on the white horse is seen as one of the signs of the coming kingdom.

THE THREE GREAT DISASTERS

When the Lamb that was slain, the victorious Christ, opens the other seals, horses appear with red, black, and pale colors. These horses have riders who pour out these great disasters over the world.

In the rider of the red horse we right away recognize the terror of war. To him was given power "to take peace from the earth and to make men slay each other." I don't have to elaborate that the terrors of war are a regular feature in the prophecies of the future as one of the signs of the approaching end. "When you hear of war and rumors of war," says the savior, "do not be alarmed. Such things must happen, but the end is still to come. Nation will rise against nation and kingdom against kingdom" (Mark 13:7-8). We could object here that wars have been a regular occurrence already from the earliest years, that history is one long series of continuous wars, so how can the war be a sign of the approaching end? The answer here is that each war, waged no matter when and where, is proof of the people's appalling powerlessness to build a state of true peace and prosperity. That implies that each war is an indication of the demise of the world and thus points to the new kingdom God will bring. That's why every war is an eschatological sign and points to the end.

That answer is no doubt correct, but it is not sufficient. The intent is, I am sure, that, when the end is nigh, the by now so common occurrence of war that as a red thread is woven through all the centuries of history, war will grow in intensity, will become more common and more cruel, to such an extent that all previous wars will look quite insignificant. Peace will disappear from the earth, which means that war will involve even the most remote regions, the farthest away islands. Nowhere in the world will there be spot left untouched. "And that people should slay each other." War will degenerate into massive destruction, so total, so terrible, that all previous wars would seem mere skirmishes. Today we slowly come to understand the explanation of this text. We suspect that the wars of antiquity would more resemble picnics when we compare them to the conditions we begin to call war today.

It may not escape our attention that again in this entire picture there is something unusual. We are talking here about the breaking of the seven seals. By now we would expect that God would start doing something, that it's time for heaven to respond. The terrible script of history will now be interrupted because God himself will take the initiative. Now we will witness intervention from above; now powers will appear in history that are out of the ordinary and no longer belong to the normal order of things. But no, as soon as the seals are broken, events take place that are completely "normal," matters instigated by people and implemented by them. Humans retain their voice, keep on talking, and nobody interrupts. The course of history retains its earthly character, remains tied to the worldly spheres of things. There's no supernatural intervention, nothing extraordinary emerges. It is almost disappointing that now in the development of the last things it still always is humanity that takes the initiative. Nowhere is the God-factor visible. History remains a monologue, people speaking to themselves.

And yet this is obviously not true. The book of Revelation quite clearly does not see the rider on his red horse as a normal phenomenon, not as something that belongs to the usual course of events. On the contrary here God is definitely involved, here God directly intervenes. It may seem that this rider is a product of history, but that is certainly not the case. It is God himself who dispatches this rider; it is God who hops here into history and speaks his word. How this happens and how this unfolds remains a secret, and is not disclosed to us. But that God himself is present here is made quite clear. The rider on the red horse has been sent by heaven to earth.

Of course by this is not meant that God is behind these wars and that he is the cause. Actually the Bible says the opposite: "He makes wars cease to the ends of the earth" (Ps 46:9). But nowhere do we find that God instigates them. What does become plain to us is that the king of the ages, the Lord and ruler of world history, in his unfathomable mercy and long-suffering has until now curtailed the ineradicable urge for war and radical self-destruction that as a mortal danger lives in sinful human hearts. But now, in the end of days he has loosened the brakes and has opened the sluice gates of warfare. That would mean that he has left humanity to its own devices, allowing it free play to deploy all evil powers that always are present and so permit to open the way to chaos that he before has so prudently blocked. Wars always originate with people; they have their root in the human desire to dominate, originate from their pride, greed, insanity, and folly. However it is undeniable that the danger of war will accelerate in history to such an extent that the possibility for total disruption and complete destruction will become a reality. All this is reinforced by the cessation of God's restraining powers that hastens the moment when he surrenders the human race to the annihilating forces so deeply ingrained in them. That's the reason why the rider on the red horse starts his journey from the heavens, even though the powers that he represents in symbolic form are actually inherent in sinful humanity and so become effective. God's judgment over the rebellious human race begins in that God no longer restrains the hand by which humanity will destroy itself.

In many ways we can already notice this ongoing destruction today. God has given our generation a power over creation that borders on the unbelievable, endangering the entire human race. Also secrets that were hidden for centuries from the human eyes are one after the other in our time being revealed, even in the very heights of heaven. It is as if God has now removed the blindfolds that prevented us from discovering the secrets of the universe. But also this fabulous force now in the hands of us small humans is increasingly becoming a factor of horrific threat. Isn't that too a sign that God has released the brakes that now allow us to employ the unlimited evil that dwells in all of us? However this all may be, there is one fact that is true beyond dispute and that is that the Bible bases the tremendous acceleration of planetary peril on theological grounds. It cannot be simply understood as based on human thinking but can only explained when we grasp something of the riddle of the rider on the red horse. The American general MacArthur has seen this correctly when, on the day the Japanese delegation signed the conditions of surrender, he spoke the remarkable words: "If we do not devise some greater and more equitable system, Armageddon will be at our door. The problem basically is theological."

Immediately after the second horse, right after the breaking of the third seal, the rider of the black horse arrives. About his intention we too need not dwell in ignorance. Its rider carries in his hands a scale, and while he proceeds, there is a voice that says: "A quart of wheat for a day's wages and three quarts of barley for a day's wages." Both that scale and these words signify poverty, hunger, and inflation. Money loses its value and the costs of daily needs become more and more expensive. A quart of wheat was about what one person needed to stay alive, which meant that a laborer by working could only earn enough to keep himself from starving, but not his family. Were he to use barley, instead of wheat, the situation would be more manageable, but even then it would be impossible to maintain a family. The prices mentioned here are about eight times the prices normal in those days.

This is in not unusual at all. After the red horse always comes the black horse. After a war we always experience scarcity, prices always go up. A war sucks out so much raw materials for destructive purposes that want is the inevitable result. We always throughout the ages have experienced famines and poverty but it is self-evident that in the context of the universal wars connected to the last things, these both scourges of humanity will affect the world population with much greater force. Even today's tremendous technical developments, the never-imagined possibilities modern science is offering us, will not be able to avoid these dangers of misery and want. A constant process of impoverishment—now already evident everywhere—will close the door to greater improvements in happiness and living standards. And, inevitably, there follows the sinister rider on the pale horse, signifying death. He has the authority to freely roam the killing fields of the world. In the wake of war and famine his task will naturally be an easy one. His prey even approaches him: all he has to do is open his arms to have them embrace death.

Again it is striking that even the immense medical advances will not prevent these dangers. Now that war is so terrifyingly present and famine so widespread, death has an easy time. There are not enough hospitals, not enough doctors to stop this irresistible force. Death goes it way, a grim smile on his face. In the past years we have heard the footsteps of this rider so loud and clear that we don't need to spend much time on his appearance to understand what he looks like.

All this is unlocked, is opened wide when the first four seals are broken. When we once more look back what had been shown here, then one question remains unanswered: is there an interlocking connection between these four seals? We have already pointed out that the last three horses are closely intertwined. The red horse of war is automatically and logically succeeded by the black horse of famine and misery, and both of them are completely understandably followed by the pale horse of death. A child could easily predict the kind of perils resulting from war. The last three verdicts are so intimately connected that it is unnecessary to dwell upon them. In that context the question arises whether that first horse, the white one, is part of this total picture. Can we put it this way, that just as the war inevitably causes hunger, does that also mean that the spread of the good news causes wars? In other words, is there between the different travel routes of these four horses not only a chronological connection but also a logical tie?

This important question warrants some elaboration. Is it really true that the spread of the good news enhances the danger of war? Is it logical that, after the rider of the white horse with a crown on his head, the red horse arrives? Is there between the proclamation of the good news and war a closer connection than we usually assume?

It seems to me that this question must also be answered in the affirmative and that first of all on theological grounds. The proclamation of the gospel is a call by God to all people, a call to turn from their vain pursuit and to serve the living God. As such this call is extended as a witness to all people. When this call is not heeded, when it is rejected, when it is purposely resisted, then such a nation has assumed a terrible liability. The sin is the more awesome because it constitutes a conscious and intentional act. No longer is there the excuse of ignorance (even though that excuse never had any validity! See Romans 1:20), because there is the greater accountability. God's sentence is based on such matters, also in the sense that God has loosened the brakes and has allowed life to proceed in its own ways. When that happens then one deluge follows after another, then no longer are there brakes that can slow down the increasing deterioration. Thus, in a theological sense, there is indeed a connection between the white and the red horse. Because of the proclamation of the gospel the responsibility of the nations becomes greater and the judgment heavier.

Beside the theological connection, or rather as a result of this, there also is a relationship of another order, something that can more or less be seen in history. The preaching of the gospel awakes in people a strong desire for liberty and independence. There where the gospel is proclaimed, people in general are no longer inclined to be treated as a mass product, as was the case before. Conversion gives people a deeper insight, a sharper notion, of their personal responsibility and also the certainty of the rightfulness of the convictions that rule their moral lives. They no longer allow others to sweep them along into some mass deception because they now have a greater insight into their own self-worth. Also their outlook on nature undergoes a change. The pagan nations, in their approach to nature, have always been constrained by their fear for demons, caused by superstition and reluctance to further investigation. That prevented them from vigorously exploring the world around them because they were afraid for unleashing dangerous forces. The proclamation of the gospel takes this fear away and replaces this with the knowledge that we, in obedience to the order of the Creator, are allowed to develop the earth and cultivate it. This proclamation also tells us that we are kings of this world, while at the same time also servants of the Lord who has granted us this authority. However when this desire for independence, freedom, self-realization, and the mastery over creation is separated from the framework of humble and childlike subjection to God's will, in other words, when we become a law to ourselves, then the danger for degeneration and deterioration grows from day to day. Then all religious constraints are gone, then the fear of catastrophic outcomes disappears and in their place emerge something like unfettered lawlessness and normlessness. The proclamation of the gospel in a nation entails a very serious crisis, a crisis that may spell its demise. The proclamation causes old defenses to disappear, causes the yoke of old moral traditions to be lifted, and causes new forces to come to life. However, these forces can bring disaster as soon as they are severed from the affiliation to God's Word and from the context of a humble belief in his mercy in Jesus Christ. Then the humans proclaim themselves as "free," as independent, capable to conquer nature and subject her, allowed to do everything.

All this on closer examination bears out that the four horses that succeed each other, not only follow each other in the order of time, but also that their connections to each other are much closer than previously assumed. The mysterious Book with the seven seals, which may only be broken by Christ, is a book with seven chapters, but these chapters themselves form one inseparable whole. It has been written from the point of view of one spirit and expresses one single topic.

When we, from this point of view, look at the situation in our Western world, we are overcome with fear. The four riders are relentlessly advancing right where we find ourselves. The forces they are unleashing are becoming evident in our lives in their full ferocity. Over our modern life appear, like the dark clouds of thunder, all the threats implied in the breaking of these first seals. When our current society fails to embrace anew the seeking after God and fails to engage in a vivid and true conversion for God, then the picture of these four riders point to what is recorded in Daniel 5:25: "God has numbered the days of your reign and brought it to an end. You have been weighed on the scales and found wanting."

THE HIDDENNESS OF THE LAST SEALS

When we take into consideration that the breaking of the seventh seal involves a new series of happenings and thus does not fit into this category, this means that there are still two seals to be discussed. Both of them have their own peculiar character.

First a few words about the breaking of the fifth seal. When John saw this he noticed under the heavenly altar the souls of those who had been killed because of the Word of God and the witness they proclaimed. It is clear here that the scene suddenly switches from the earth to heaven. No rider here who gallops into the earth to do his important work, no, here John describes what goes on up there, in heaven, but what takes place there is very closely related to what first has happened on the earth. So we have to see through this heavenly happening and it then cannot escape us that here matters of a very ominous nature are shown.

What then had happened here on earth? There have been people, believing folk, who have been "butchered" because they testified about the Word of God. This all sounds quite straightforward. It does not say that they were killed because of the witness they spoke but because the way their lives show this. Apparently they did not openly give testimony on the street corners. They did not stand at the entrance of the temple with a tract to persuade people to become adherents of the Way. They were not that provocative. But on the other hand neither did they fearfully avoid all confrontation. Where it was called for they undoubtedly brought witness without any hesitation. And that witness could hardly be different than the confession what Jesus Christ meant for them in their lives. Jesus Christ in this world gave witness of his divine mandate and that same witness has been accepted by many and confessed as the truth. The people who have accepted this testimony of Jesus Christ in faith, have held on to this and carried it in their lives as a precious possession. It was this treasure that was now their own, and of which they never again wanted to be deprived. In a word, it is because of this witness that these people were imprisoned, dragged before judges, and finally executed as criminals. With the word *butchered* John wants to indicate on the one hand that this could not be called a proper judicial process even though it took place in a courthouse, and on the other hand he expresses hereby that there is a striking similarity between what these people experienced, and what their Lord Jesus Christ had to suffer. (See Rev 5:12.)

This court-sanctioned murder did, of course, take place on earth. It is there where the blood of the martyrs flowed. John now observes, however, that the souls of these martyrs are hidden under the heavenly altar. The Scriptures often mention an altar in the heavens. Already Isaiah in his vision saw such an altar (Isa 6:6). Often this heavenly altar is an altar for incense where the incense of the prayers are offered, but here this altar also functions as the altar of burnt offerings whereby blood flows. The blood that drips into the ground reflects the soul of those who have been sacrificed there. Every time when on earth a martyr is killed by the executioner, it is as if on the altar in heaven another person offers himself or herself as a sacrifice to God, and as if their blood streams from the altar. That is the thought that serves as the basis of this depiction.

John notices that these souls, under that altar, cry out to God. They ask that their blood be revenged upon those who have afflicted them with these deadly deeds. They ask for justice. Where the earthly judge has committed them to death contrary all rules of justice, there they appeal to the ultimate Judge that he would exercise his verdict. However, this appeal to the highest court cannot be heard, even though these blood-witnesses do receive a white robe, a symbol of Christ's righteousness—their request for justice can, as yet, not be granted. They were instructed to wait patiently "until the number of their fellow servants and brothers and sisters who were to be killed as they have been was completed." With these last words we will deal later again when we pay particular attention to the factor of "delay" that plays such an important role in the totality of the Revelation of John.

The picture that is painted for us here is therefore quite basic. Nothing is revealed about the nature of the persecution these people suffered. Not a word either about the motives, why these earthly authorities condemned them to such a severe punishment. Also we are not allowed to look from heaven to the earth, to the anti-Christian world powers in the midst of which the church must exist and where she must be on guard every step of the way. Later in this book of Revelation all this is further described in much more detail, but at this stage all this is merely very carefully indicated. Only the heavenly reflection of what happens on earth is briefly indicated.

Right away after the brief mention of the persecution of the church follows the breaking of the sixth seal. This opening introduces the immense cosmic disasters the entire world is to undergo. An enormous earthquake took place, the sun was darkened as if a balaclava had been slipped over it, while the moon turned blood red, and the stars fell to the earth.

All this involves a series of tremendous natural disasters. It need not be mentioned that the mentioning of these disasters appears in all prophecies in the Bible concerning the future.

An earthquake. Amos already speaks of it: "the whole land will rise like the river it will be stirred up and then sink." Ezekiel 38:19: "In my zeal and fiery wrath I declare that at that time there will be a great earthquake in the land of Israel," and Joel 2:10: "Before them the earth quakes." The savior himself says: "There will be here and then there earthquakes."

Eclipse of the sun. Amos mentions that too. "I will make the sun go down at noon and darken the earth in broad daylight." And Isaiah, speaking about the day of the Lord, says: "The stars of heaven and their constellations will not show their light, and the rising sun will be darkened (13:10). Also in Matthew 24, in the great forecast of the future, Jesus (verse 29) says that the darkening of the sun is one of the signs of the coming end. Also that the moon shall be as blood is a well-known thought in the prophecy. Joel speaks of this in the promise of the coming of the Spirit (2:31): "The sun will be turned to darkness and the moon to blood before the coming of the great and dreadful day of the Lord."

Concerning *the rain of stars,* it too has been repeatedly foretold. Isaiah speaks about this announcing his judgment over the pagans. "All the stars of the heavens will be dissolved and the sky rolled up like a scroll; all the starry host will fall like withered leaves from the vine" (34:4). So it comes as no surprise that also this element finds a place in the words by Jesus Christ concerning the future (Matt 24:29): "The stars will fall from the heavens."

So there is nothing unusual in what is announced here. On the contrary they are simply phenomena that are mentioned in all the predictions of the approaching "day of the Lord." It is worth noting that in the description of the opening of the sixth seal very little is mentioned about the damage suffered through all these calamities. That is done later on in the book of Revelation. Then it is foretold that, as a result of God's judgments, "a third part of the people will be killed" (9:18). These are, indeed, indications of the terrible outcome of these judgments that will burst over the world. However this is not yet the case here. This here shows that we must see these signs announced more as a last warning, as a severe threat, as predictions of the tremendous terror that is coming.

We must not lose sight of the fact that all these signs come straight from God. The wars and the subsequent famine and death were also God's judgments, but they originate from the human world. God bounced back what came forth from humans themselves. It's a different picture, however, with the very last frightening portents, the eclipse of the sun, the blood-red moon, the falling of the stars, and these earthquakes. These are not the works of human hands, and not the result of human interference. They come straight from above, as God starts to interrupt the frightening playing out of the history of the world. He invades the works and doings of the human race: over against all the works of human hands he posits his own mighty deeds. The intent of these signs is to inform people how really powerless they are. The human race has through its science and enormous energy expenditure and tremendous tenacity attained incredible results. They have penetrated into the very deepest of the universe, have entered into the treasuries of creation, and have taken possession of the indomitable powers hidden in nature: indeed humanity was and still is great and strong, and increasingly powerful. These very same men and women, recognizing no boundaries, having treated as their playground almost all of nature, of which they are part, as their toy, these same people are here in one instant, confronted with the proofs of their own radical powerlessness and helplessness. Their microscopes and other scientific tools are now totally useless, their hydro dams and nuclear power stations now dangerous liabilities, their military force now a total farce, their proud boast of might that emboldened them to embark on empire expansion, now as deflated as an empty tire. Their earlier sense of superiority is now replaced with feelings of indescribable inferiority and insecurity. When this devastating darkness descends over the earth, when these scary star-showers show up and these menacing meteor particles pound into the planet, when the ground erratically vibrates, when an alien and menacing moon blood-red hangs in the heaven, that's when humanity starts to become sorely scared. It's not that their own lives are in immediate mortal danger. It would be quite a coincidence if a meteor fragment would hit them and it's possible to evade the dangers of an earthquake because they can pretty well pinpoint its epicenter in advance. They can flee from the factories and get out of the cities to seek safety in the wide open fields. And even a darkened sun poses no threat, according to the explanation by the weather office. They explain its darkening being due to an ash rain originating from a tremendous eruption somewhere. The newspapers write reassuring articles and state that all this will be over is a few days. Already some enterprising photographers have made some striking pictures of that blood-red moon right above the ruins of a destroyed city. Nevertheless, in spite of these tabloids reporting this as being a completely normal occurrence, and in spite of the list of casualties being rather small, a sense of pure panic has gripped the population. It seems as if humanity suddenly finds itself in the center of a hostile world, as if all forces of nature are conspiring against them. Self-assurance no longer serves; a rational explanation remains evasive, lacks any comfort. No single explanation offers satisfaction and fails to quiet the dawning despair that now conquers them, and causes them to tremble from top to toe.

John here gives a brief but totally characteristic description of what is about to happen. "The kings of the earth, the princes, the generals. The rich, the mighty and every slave and every free man hid in the caves and along the rocks of the mountains." That's how it starts: the massive move to safety. Out of the high rise condos and the townhouses, out of the packed cities, out of the rural retreats and cottages, as far as possible away to the safe hiding places hewn out in the mountain caves. Just as when a city is threatened by bombs and people seek refuge in their underground bunkers, deep into the earth, so now too people flee away, far from the horror-provoking terror that confronts them from all directions, running away from themselves, from their own conscience, from their own God.

Yes, away also from their God, because all these stalwart souls, inescapably somehow, are suddenly reminded of God. Of course there are affirmed atheists among them, people who never have believed in God and who have denied his existence based on convincing scientific arguments. There are among them people who always have regarded religion as an infantile folly, and who have spoken about God only in scornful and mocking ways. But in that fateful instant, now that these strange phenomena are starting to appear, now that nature herself is starting to turn against them, now that everything has turned hostile, now that even the sun stubbornly refuses to cast its illuminating rays, now that they must escape from the universe like fugitives, like outcasts, like pariahs, now, in the deepest depth of their being, the overwhelming evidence of the certainty that there is a God dawns on them.

So God lives after all! That scorned God! That God long ago pushed away, that God who by now should have been buried under mountains of scientific arguments, yet it is that same despicable deity who, as the sole reality, as the heart of all certainty, now stands before them. God, in whom they never have believed, and in whom they, in the depth of their soul always have known to have existed, God, whom they every day, every hour have evaded, and whom they yet experienced as one who always was close, as one whose grasp was inescapable. God, the object of an occasional thought, perhaps on a sleepless night, but, when daylight dawned, was quickly pushed away again. God, who fortunately never uninvited entered the living room or the office, or the bedroom, who never forced the locks and said, "Here I am, you no longer can chase me out!" Because God can easily be banned; it is ridiculously easy to push him away, to forget about him, to let go of the nightmare of his existence, to joke about him, and with a quick smart remark write him off. God, you can turn him off like you do a TV so that nothing is visible on the screen and the voice is silent. That's how we can turn off God and say, no God today. That God who always was the weakest, who always was the least, whom we could use as a butt, that same God now rises up high as a mountain, now stands before the human race in all his awesome majesty. It's impossible to ignore him at this point: no longer can we dismiss him with a witty remark. No longer is our intelligent reasoning about evolution any use, nor does a stiff drink help us over the impasse. Here the TV is silent, the radio totally off the air: the only electricity is in the divine air: all other wires are dead. Humans here stand before God as they are: there's nothing now between them and God. So what happens? These big shots, these once so influential people, they crawl away as small children, they hide away in the caves and crevasses of the earth, just as Adam did in those very ancient times when he hid himself between the trees.

A long series of different groups of people and population classes are shown to us here in this chapter. Consider first "the Kings of the earth." That means all those who have been the rulers of the nations, joined by their most trusted officers, the ministers, those who had positions of authority in various departments, including the generals and other high officers. Also the bank directors, those ruling the large corporations as well as the leading scientists, the heroes in their fields, these ultra-smart people who opened new perspectives in science and research. There are those who had great following, whose words captivated the attention of thousands. All these self-assured people, always so composed and confident, that no one could ever detect the slightest moment of hesitation in their presentations, they were there too. And so were those who dared to make big decisions, affecting the fate of thousands, exceptional people always so successful, always so intimidating and dominating, they too stood before the Lord. All these proud people, ruling with an iron fist, as well as those smooth-talking politicians, plus the leading thinkers, and celebrated artists, the cream of the crop, the so-called One Percent, the financial emperors, all these stand there, now suddenly reduced to their radical nothingness, they stand shoulder to shoulder with "the slaves and the free." In other words: the horror now haunting humanity affects all layers of society. Here the beggar stands next to the billionaire; in the darkness of a cave a CEO hides behind a cleaning lady. All these numerous class distinctions which rule society melt away like ice on a summer day and what comes instead is humanity itself, the human being in its total existential tininess and anguish. In the languishing last rays of the frightening twilight they slink away as a vanquished army in long rows, toward the mountains rising up in the distance as the sole secure spot in a world falling apart.

In a heartrending way their desperate cry echoes from the chill of their hideouts, from their caves and crevasses: "Fall on us and hide us from the face of him who sits on the throne and from the wrath of the Lamb. For the great day of their wrath has come, and who can stand?"

From the face of him! They dare not even mention the name of God, the word gets stuck in their throat. But it is all horrifyingly clear to them who the "he" is. He is the one always left out, the one always denied. "He who sits upon the throne," he "whose wrath has come. The wrath of the Lamb." There is something contradictory in these words, something that strikes as being out of place. The Lamb is an example of meekness and surrender, an image of him who accepts death without a murmur. That Lamb here is pictured as the wrathful, whose anger so astonishes all sections of creation that an unimaginable anguish overcomes everybody. Indeed, this is outspokenly a matter of unfathomable contradiction: the meekest and the strongest are next to each other. The humblest is simultaneously the exalted above everything else. He who allowed himself to be destroyed and assumed the condition of a slave, he has become the mightiest, the king of kings and the lord of lords. The full mystery of the Christ in contained in these few words. They were allowed to nail him to the cross, but even in his defeat he is the victor, in death he is alive. Those who try to beat him get beaten themselves and will eventually succumb dead-tired and physically maimed. Those who oppose him hurt themselves, deprive themselves of peace and goodness. We can do anything to him, we can say anything about him, but whatever we do to him boomerangs, it bounces back on us and the hurt we do to him hurts us even more. In these few words "the wrath of the Lamb" is expressed everything that gives our life on earth such a fearful responsibility.

THE EMERGENCY SIGNAL

With this the opening of the first six seals has been concluded. When we survey its totality then we notice that the grand process of the last things has its start here on earth: wars and its aftermath. But these wars only begin to reach their utmost intensity after the message of the kingdom of God has been brought to all nations and people as a witness.

That is the start. It is rooted in life on earth. It's there where matters obtain their earthly form. Initially we might assume that God has ceased to be interested in the human lot, that humanity has been left to its own devices, but that is really not the case. In reality God is very directly and concretely engaged in guiding the development of history to its final destination. That completion, however, is not something that is imposed from above, is not an unexpected event that suddenly interrupts our cozy life. The divine action consists of the removal of all brakes; it is more than ever before evident in the growing awareness of an increasing intensity in our world and the unveiling of the true face of things. Sin will show itself in its most hideous and most horrid form. Egoism and power hunger will spread out like fast moving fires, scorching and torching all that is still left of a vulnerable and fragile humanity.

Only then God interrupts. Not even right away in his overwhelming majesty. At first only as a threat rather than as judgment, more as an admonition than as an annihilation. But it comes. The universe now refuses to protect the human race, refuses to feed it and to provide food and light and blessing and act as if nothing has happened. Humanity becomes isolated, a lonesome figure in an unpredictable world, more lonely than it has ever been. It can scream to high heaven, and the sound will simply bounce back. The light fades, the blessing disappears. There it stands and for the first time it becomes aware how infinitely small and defenseless it is. There it stands all shook up in a totally unhinged world. And in its final fatal fear it flashes through its body that, yes, there is a God, and that it, this insignificant, impotent human being who in his impertinence, has all its life, all through the ages, kicked against God with its tiny feet. That is the great SOS that gloomily and ominously resounds throughout this slowly perishing planet.

Is that really the road we must travel in order to reach the eternal kingdom of God? As yet not a single ray of light has come our way. Neither is there a single glimpse noticeable of the magnificence of the new kingdom that surpasses all thinking and imagination, the city where God will be all and in all. Are these really the first steps on the way to the New Jerusalem? It really looks as if we are on the wrong road, going away from it; it really looks as if the kingdom of the demons is now securely established. It is as if precisely now the entire universe, the whole world, humanity with all its infinite possibilities and powers, is thrown into the pitch-dark night of utter destruction. There is not a single indication that beyond that night there is a different panorama, that behind that horizon there still beckons a new future. That woman that gave birth to the child, now escaped into the desert, pursued by the dragon, is gripped by panic. Now being in the world is really becoming an unfathomable fright. Now those who live upon the earth for the very first time feel the full brunt of the universal woe. The woman—the church—is in the midst of it. With every sinew of her being she is connected to the world's history. And with her anxious eyes opened wide she looks ahead to the end, but nowhere is there any sign that can give hope or comfort. On the contrary: everything signals that there is worse to come, that it will become a thousand times worse. Because all these wars will only have one result, something will come out of it, and one thing is already clear, that the all-powerful global rule that will be born out of all this strife will carry the hallmarks of an insane hatred against God and his anointed. This famine and this misery will result in increasing poverty, and dissatisfaction, in insurrection, in bitterness and hate. And these first victims, killed because of their "witness for God" will be followed by others, by many, many others. And these threatening signs in the heavens, the eclipses of the sun and the raining of stars, and these earthquakes, all these are only a prelude of what is to come. When the powers of history arrive at their ultimate revelation then too the power of nature will be unchained against the human race in spite of its greatness, its wisdom and power. And what will become of the persecuted human race? Where will this anguish push it? There is no way we can even start to speculate here.

The only consolation that makes all these things bearable is the knowledge that in the highest heaven there is the Lamb and that it is this lamb who has opened the seals. The only consolation is that this is not some sinister, some mad destructive power now starting to play her role in this frightening world. The only consolation is that there is not some sort of bad fate that threatens this terrified human race. But the very same person who, when dying, prayed for his followers, who offered himself up to death and so in his suffering and death saved the world, it is he who is behind all these happenings. It is that he who opens the seals and reads the Book, the Book that once read immediately becomes reality. It is that faith alone that, amidst all seeming senselessness and confusion, gives us the strength to keep our heads high. It is that faith alone that enables us, in spite of all the terror, to confess that the kingdom has come near. It is that faith alone that can give us the courage to withstand the ugliest persecution. They cannot fool around with us; we are not left to the capricious fate of chaotic powers. Neither are we ground up like meat, hacked to pieces, caught up in the millstones of history by our own stupidity, pride, and hostility. Neither is it the case that there is no way out. In the night of doubt there always remains the only way out, the way of conversion.

> Kiss the Son lest he be angry
> And you be destroyed in your way.
> For his wrath can flame up in a moment.
> Blessed are all who take refuge in him.
>
> (Ps 2:12)

CHAPTER FIVE

The World Advances toward Chaos
(Revelation 8, 9, 10, 11)

THE BACKGROUND OF THE GREAT DELAY

At this point we'll have to elaborate about the great delay that plays such an important role in the totality of the book of Revelation.

We have been confronted with this great delay already. Right in the first chapter, where we dealt with Revelation 12, we found it remarkable that in the picture we read about there, something unusual was happening. There the woman is already clothed with the sun and carries a crown of stars on her head. The child has already been born, and, in spite of all attacks by the evil one, has been carried off to God. All this resulted in a tremendous struggle in the heavenly regions. Michael was the winner there while the dragon suffered a great and decisive defeat. Everything now indicated that the final triumph is at hand because now the attacks on God's church are prevented, and everything is ready for the crowning event. And yet, at the end of the chapter it is shown that this woman must flee into the desert and as a miserably persecuted being must seek safety in lonely isolation. In this entire scene there is something that is totally unusual and, in utter amazement, we wondered why it is not possible for this great liberation to start now.

The same thing happened when we later on investigated the opening of the scroll of the book more thoroughly. This scroll was closed, which meant that the last things could not yet happen. But when heaven and earth remained silent, because nobody was able to come forward, or dared to do so, it was the Christ of God, the lamb that was slain who, undaunted, approached the throne, and then it was he to whom the scroll was given. And in holy ecstasy both the church and the entire cosmos started to sing that the Christ "was worthy to take the scroll and to break open the seals." And again we were ready to say: at last it will happen, now finally the great redemption is about the happen! Seen from an objective point of view everything is ready for the final decision. Christ's great offer has been accomplished, his victory over death and devil has become a fact, he has shown to be the victorious hero against which no evil power could prevail. Now the end is near and now we are confronted with the last things, now the thread is unwinding finally. But instead of a victory song we experience disasters, instead of the liberation of God's people, we have persecution. The blood of the martyrs started to flow, and anguish and dread overwhelmed the world. In retrospect the breaking of the seals proved to be a great disappointment. Nothing of what we had expected had come to pass. Instead many other matters happened, happenings that filled us with anxiety and worry. The end was there but the final end lingered and lingered. Everything was in place and yet nothing happened of what we had looked forward to with such great anticipation.

So there we have it: the question of the great delay is before us as one of the crucial elements of the book. And now it is equally clear that it not only touches upon the heart of this book, but it is also for the church of all ages the greatest problem it has to wrestle with. The church of Ephesus valiantly opposes all infection involving scriptural error and other foolishness, but she falls for the danger of forsaking her first love. The church of Smyrna fights a desperate battle against the synagogue of Satan, and the church of Pergamum becomes involved in all sorts of conflicts and is tempted to arrive at a compromise with the world. The church of Thyatira is in daily danger to deny their faith, while those in Sardis slowly sink away into a dull shoddiness. The church in Philadelphia courageously tries to confess the good news, but those in Laodicea become more and more the victims of internal degeneration. All these churches plod on, wading through dirt and difficulty, and nowhere do we see a ray of light on the horizon. Perhaps it is not true that now that the seven seals are broken, the last day will come speedily. Is all this merely an illusion? Is it then not true that the great Christ for ever has triumphed over all powers of evil? Are we, after all, not in the final stretch of the last things?

Before we elaborate on the manner in which this entire problem is explained in the rest of the book of Revelation, we do well to mention that this same problem is also touched upon in other places of the Bible. We will have to listen to the answer given to us in other Bible books, where people also anxiously question this, and, based on what God tells us there, apply this to the last Bible book.

In the prophecies of the Old Testament this delay is, in general, not a burning issue. There the believers of those days eagerly look forward to the coming of the Messiah, to the appearance of "the servant of the Lord," and they were convinced that his coming would simultaneously herald the new day, making an end to all suppression and want. Isaiah speaks admiringly and devotedly of the birth of the child, whose name will be Wonderful Counselor, Mighty God, Everlasting Father, Prince of Peace, and he continues to assure us that there will be no end to his government and his reign of David's throne (Isa 9:5, 6). In beautiful colors he paints for us the new age that then is to come when the wolf will dwell with the lamb and "they will neither harm nor destroy on all my holy mountain, for the earth will be full of the knowledge of the Lord as the waters cover the seas" (Isa 9:6, 9). The book of Isaiah does see something of the great riddle when it also points out that this same Messiah who would bring such everlasting joy would appear "having no beauty or majesty" and would be "cut off from the land of the living" (Isa 53:8). But the total problem of delay is not sharply delineated here, which also is the case in the other books of the prophets. Daniel sees the succession of different world empires arising from the stormy seas of life on earth and immediately after this he observes the coming of one "like the son of man," and "he was given authority, glory and sovereign power" (Dan 7:13, 14). When Malachi prophesies that "this Lord you are seeking" will speedily come to the temple then he sees him at once sitting on his judgment seat "as a refiner and purifier of silver" (Mal 3:1–3). In short, the Old Testament's prophecies look with great joy forward to the day of the coming of the Christ of God, but they are not fully conscious of the delay which will happen after his coming.

In the Gospels, however, this delay is soon noticed. Herman Ridderbos, in his book *The Coming of the Kingdom,* focuses his attention on this delay, pointing out that this question is often the central point of Jesus' teaching. On the one hand the Gospels strongly emphasize that "the time has come, the Kingdom of God is near" (Mark 1:15), and Jesus himself, in the synagogue of Nazareth, after he had read the Old Testament prophecies, said "Today this scripture is fulfilled in your hearing" (Luke 4:20). On the other hand, however, it becomes more and more evident that a sort of shift has taken place, and that the kingdom *is* here but that it also is in the future, that it is still coming. That is the reason that Jesus' preaching can be characterized "that he proclaims the Kingdom in both its fulfilling and eschatological meaning as well as in the present and the future reality" (Ridderbos). The significance of Jesus' historic self-revelation is "that he identifies himself both in the form of the Son of man as in Daniel 7, and also as the Servant of the Lord as in Isaiah" (also Ridderbos). There are clearly in Jesus' teachings two lines of thinking to be detected, one which points to his death and resurrection, and another which indicates his great glorification. Throughout Jesus' teaching we see that the question of delay is more and more gaining prominence and is regarded as one of the greatest problems both the disciples and the future church has to wrestle with.

That delay itself is approached in the Gospels in different ways. In the parable of the Tenants Christ's suffering is the central theme but based on that it is clearly shown that "the Kingdom of God" will be taken from the obstinate section of Israel and given to "a people who will produce its fruit" (Matt 21:43). That means that a new era will arrive, a time when "God's people" will be gathered. This same thought is clearly evident in the parable of the Wedding Banquet. There it plainly says that "The wedding banquet is ready but those I invited did not deserve to come" (Matt 22:8). In other words: essentially everything is ready, nothing now stands in the way because "it is accomplished," but the fact that Israel itself, in its unbelief, has rejected the blessing of the Messiah, this can only mean that others are to be invited to the banquet. The Lord's future is assured but the time has not yet come for its glorious deployment, because a congregation must be gathered to be participants of that future.

The parable of the Talents (Luke 19:11–27) deals with a "man of noble birth" who traveled to a faraway country "to have himself appointed king." Everything is prepared, the "man of noble birth," Christ himself, clearly has a well-founded claim on the throne, but there is a time lapse before he can really reveal himself as king. In the meantime the disciples, the church really, must be on their guard and make the most of the treasures in their safe-keeping.

Time and again we encounter that same phenomenon: the time is full, the kingdom is near, the last things are about to appear, and everything is speeding up on the way to glory of the future of the Lord that brings delight to all hearts and minds. God "soon" will brings justice for his chosen ones (Luke 19:7). All the signs are there, demons are on the run where Jesus approaches, and, quite surprised must abandon their prey. The blind see, the lepers are healed, the dead raised. The kingdom arises, sturdy and strong, amidst this confused world, wedded to sin. And yet nothing can really come to its total development. Yes, there is movement, yes the disciples are sent into the world to go quietly and confidently about their task and they many not even have an inkling of "the times or dates the Father has set by his own authority" (Acts 1:7). There still is some respite, and a certain room to maneuver. How long this will last is nowhere disclosed. Often in the Gospels we receive the impression as if the timespan is short such as in Matthew 10:23 and Mark 9:1, but in other passages it looks as if the waiting time is much longer. In the parable of the Wise and Foolish Maidens the full emphasis is on the waiting (Matt 25:1–13). "Because of the increase of wickedness, the love of most will grow old but they who stand firm to the end will be saved" (Matt 24:12). It becomes more and more evident that in the interim period, whether this is long or short, the church of Jesus Christ has one overarching assignment to fulfill: it will have to look for and seek out in the alleys of the town and bring in the poor, the crippled, the blind, and the lame and make them come into the wedding hall (Luke 14:21). "This gospel of the Kingdom will be preached in the whole world as a testimony to all nations, and then the end will come" (Matt 24:14). In essence everything is in place, but one thing has to happen: from every nation those who God has ordained to be part of his glory must be alerted to the message. In other words, the interim period must be used by the church to bring the gospel message to the entire world. Once this is completely done, then nothing can stop the coming of the last things.

This great delay is often the topic of discussion in the letters of the apostles. Paul, in his Letter to the Ephesians, clearly shows that in God's great plan the most important part is that in Jesus Christ the entire building of the church of all ages is joined together and rises to become a holy temple in the Lord (Eph 2:21). That same thought is also expressed in Hebrews 11: 39–40. The great question why the believers in the Old Testament have not obtained the fulfillment of the promise is explained in this way: "so that only together with us would they be made perfect." God is at work to gather a church out of all the nations of the earth. As long as this process is still going on, as long as the last member of the church has not yet been added to the universal church, only when these conditions have been met, can the glory of the Lord be revealed. The believers of the old covenant are singled out here, but in some ways all this most certainly also applies to those of the New Testament. They too have to wait for the moment when the building will be completed. Only when that happens can the hiddenness of Christ be unveiled.

In his second letter to the Thessalonians Paul gives a somewhat more extensive explanation of the riddle involving the delay. He refers to their way of life where the believers in Thessalonica were inclined to focus their thoughts so much on the immediate coming of the Lord that they started to neglect their normal earthly duties. They began to live disorderly and this became their way of life because, after all, the return of the Lord could happen any moment. In that context, so says the apostle, the coming of the Lord will not happen until the great falling away has taken place and "the person of the lawlessness" has appeared "who rises up against everything that is called God or is an object for worshiping him." Paul assumes that the church in Thessalonica is sufficiently acquainted with "what holds him back, so that he may be revealed at the proper time." It is for us extremely difficult to determine what the apostle has in mind when he writes "what holds him back." In the total context of the Scriptures it is not entirely unwarranted that this refers to the missionary task of the church. Only when the good news has been preached throughout the entire world, when from all the nations those called to the royal wedding have come together, can the last things take their course. That also means that the antichrist and his reign can come only then. "What holds him back" could then also be applied to the fact that the task has not yet been completed, and the good news has not yet been preached to all people so that "the lawless one" cannot yet appear. But all this remains guess work.

It is, however, remarkable that this same Apostle Paul in his letters gives hints that we should not discount the possibility that the return of the Lord could take place in his lifetime. "We will not all sleep," says he in 1 Corinthians 15:51, "but we will all be changed." In the first letter to the Thessalonians he assures the believers that "We who are still alive, who are left till the coming of the Lord, will certainly not precede those who have fallen asleep" (1 Thess 4:15). Paul sees the coming of the Lord as being close, "for this world in its present form is passing away" (1 Cor 7: 31). That same feeling must have lived in the ancient church. When the savior said to Peter, "If I want him to remain alive till I return, what is that to you?" right away the rumor circulated "that this disciple would not die" (John 21:22). This is certainly proof how alive the expectation was and how close people thought that the glory of the Lord was at hand. In the second letter of Peter the people express their frustration that affected that entire church there when the interim time of delay lasted so much longer than they had expected. They started to doubt the fulfilling of the promise and wondered whether the time of trouble and suppression would never end. Peter really had no answer here except that he in the name of the Lord gave them the assurance that "with the Lord a day is as a thousand years, and a thousand years is like one day" (2 Pet 3:8). Of course that is not a solution to the problem, but it is an important indication that we in our thinking about these matters easily fall victim to foolish pride. We think in small, human terms and forget that we deal with God, whose thoughts are at a much higher niveau.

Those who carefully read the New Testament will clearly notice that the riddle of the delay occupied the first church very much. That first church had stood at Calvary and had seen the open grave. For these people it was totally undeniable that, looked at objectively, everything was accomplished, the wedding meal was "prepared," the time was full, so every day again they were surprised anew that this world kept on functioning as if Jesus Christ never had existed. The devil had not lost any of his audacity and cunning, he still was about "like a roaring lion" (1 Pet 5:8), and nothing suggested that he in fact had been defeated. People still had to struggle against "the powers of the darkness, against the spiritual forces of evil in the heavenly realms," without ever noticing that these "world rulers" had been defeated (Eph 6:12). Even though Paul was convinced that "the God of peace will soon crush Satan under your feet" (Rom 16:20), the fact remained that in the meantime the church still had to plod along on her obstacle-obstructed road. Everything turned out to be more difficult than they, on good grounds, had assumed to be the case. Christ had accomplished his great work, but there was not a hint of it anywhere, nothing in the world had noticeably changed at all. If anything whatsoever had changed, it had changed for the worse: everything looked even darker than before.

What is certain is that the riddle of the delay or its shift to a later date is, in the New Testament, looked at from different points of view. Sometimes it emphasizes that this delay is needed because the primary task of the church is to preach the gospel to the entire world. At other times people are reminded that the opposing forces which now stall the coming of the antichrist have to be removed. That thought is based on the belief that Christ can only bring his work to a successful finish after first Satan himself has been enabled to create the greatest havoc. Only after the demonic powers have been employed to their fullest extent can the light of the new day dawn. A third possibility often stated in this connection, is that first the number of those who are saved must be added to the church. The edifice can only then be finished, and the end cannot come a day sooner. And the last consideration of which we were reminded is that we must refrain from expressing any judgment regarding the duration of the delay. We count matters in days, but God thinks in totally different terms than we. Humbly and patiently we must wait for what God wants to do. In the meantime we must always be alert because we do not know the day and the hour upon which the Lord of the house will return. These are some of the considerations that we find scattered in the several books of the New Testament, all referring to the riddle of the delay.

THE HORIZON RETREATS

We must now return to the description offered us regarding this delay in the Revelation of John. Earlier we remarked how this delay was shown through colorful scenarios by constantly divulging a bit more through a series of happenings, with the latest of these series resulting in a new chain of events so that continuously the end appears to be further removed than first is assumed. Apart from this remarkable phenomenon, which will be expanded upon a bit later, there are still a few more angles that need to be explored.

In the first place there is the aforementioned rider on his white horse, wearing a crown and the question where he is going. If it is true that the meaning of this rider indicates the way the gospel spreads throughout the entire world, then this indicates that quite a number of years are needed. To preach the gospel over the entire earth cannot possibly be accomplished in only a few years. Unknown nations need to be visited, long trips to far away continents must be organized, foreign languages must be learned and the good news must be brought to all peoples and nations in such a way that they can understand it. That's why it is very unlikely that with this course of the white horse a short period of some few years are meant. History has made it clear that this course of events was one of immense struggle and intense difficulty. If this is the case with this particular rider then there is no reason to assume that the others would fare differently. Their way over the wide extent of the earth too would require not days, nor even years, but centuries. In John's vision these events pass by as fast as lightning, as in a flash, but when we start considering the immense implications of what is involved, then it becomes clear that factors here are at play which can only be realized over a long period of time.

Another indication of delay can be found in the first verses of chapter 8. There we find: "When he opened the seventh seal there was silence in heaven for about half an hour." This silence is the more remarkable because evidently everything was ready for a new series of powerful events that were to happen before the final hour. Seven angels stood poised with seven trumpets and it was clear that these angels would soon be sent out to proclaim mighty matters all over the world. But before all this is about to happen, there suddenly is that silence for about half an hour. What is its purpose? What does it mean?

The explanation for this silence is found in the subsequent verses. There another angel advances, carrying a golden censer. He respectfully advances to the altar situated before the throne. Clearly that altar is the altar of incense that in the earthly temple was placed before the curtain which gave entrance to the holy of holies. As soon as the angel arrived there "he was given much incense to offer with the prayer of all the saints on the golden altar before the throne." We have to assume that the incense here indicates that these prayers before they are placed before the face of God have to be cleansed of all unholy matter so that they can be presented to God holy and without blemish.

That, then, is the holdup. The last things cannot take their course as long as that one angel has not returned from his trip to the earth. The huge events preceding the coming of the glorious kingdom cannot proceed as long as the prayers of the holy have not been placed upon the altar. The heaven is not able to reveal its full authority and majesty as long as the earth has not yet prayed for it. Everything has its prescribed time and so also the last happening can only begin when the proper time for it has arrived. And one of the factors that determine that the time has come is that the church on earth must have sent up her prayers to God.

We need not argue that this touches upon an extremely important matter. In the development of the great final happenings the church upon earth has a very particular and important assignment. It is true also that this development has its own time frame because the Book with the seven seals has been given in the hands of the great Christ of God. But this development also has another aspect, and in connection with this the church, as she lives and struggles on earth, has to fulfill an important task. The great finale can only be revealed in its totality when the reality in heaven completely corresponds with the reality on earth. Only in a true concordance can we look forward to the grand finale.

Seen from that perspective it becomes clear what is meant by the half hour of silence. The church on earth is not yet ready. Her prayer lacks power, is not sufficiently intimate, not mature enough. The church on earth, Sardis and Laodicea, Ephesus and Smyrna, they all are far too preoccupied with worldly affairs, far too much involved with what ferments and foments here in the goings on in the world. The church of all ages is too tied in with her present plight, and not sufficiently geared to the final ending, not enough yearning for the completion. Her clock is slower than the heavenly timepiece. Everything is in place, the seventh seal has been broken already, and still there is no start. The waiting is for the earth, is waiting for the church that amidst this world has her place and calling. There's where that mighty element of delay is to be found. The delay does not lie in lack of power of Jesus Christ, because that power is sufficient to make the end come speedily. Neither does the delay come because the world itself is not yet ripe for the judgment. By itself that is true, but there the church has a task. If she were to confess more ardently, were to pray more fervently, were to look forward to the coming of the king more eagerly, then it all would fall into place because then God is capable to make all other matters come to pass. But first the church has to look inward and know where she stands and what is in store for her. Her primary task is to fully prepare herself to enter the last oppressions in complete surrender, and in the midst of this great emergency, which as a dark thunder cloud starts to appear above the earth, look forward to the coming of the savior with head held high. That's the reason why heaven cannot proceed. That's the reason why those seven angels with their trumpets are waiting. That's the reason why there is a breathless silence in the heavenly palace. That's the reason why in the infinite majesty of God's holy temple there is that almost unbearable tension.

John describes that pause as a silence lasting a "half hour." We don't have the slightest idea of what that means. Is that "half hour" of a long duration? Is it, as soon as it is projected on the screen of the world's history, a period of many centuries? Who can state this with any certainty, but then who can deny it? Actually the duration is really not that important. The real significance lies in the fact itself, that is to say that the development of the last things depends on how the church on earth experiences her spiritual life. Her prayer-life, her surrender to God, her faithfulness all are part of the process of the grand finale. And John, really upset, observes that in this important moment, when everything is ready to go, the church herself is lagging behind. She has not kept up with God, she has clung to her old customs and modes of life, has failed to grasp God's unfathomable majesty and refused to undergo a true conversion. While being fully exposed to the grand revelation of the last things, she remained stuck in the small, everyday events of her earthly existence. Above her, while the loud thunderclaps of God's threats are cascading through the skies, she, with eyes wide open in horror, has become mesmerized while around her all human riches and powers are visibly collapsing. Amidst all these cries of anguish escalating exponentially she has not learned to think differently. She has remained mired in the immorally routine rest of her everyday existence. Now that the very last happenings are knocking at the door, she is not ready. She no longer knows how to pray. She can't keep up with what God is doing. The Bible time and again tells us to wait on the Lord. But now the roles are reversed. It used to be that God's clock ran slower than ours and we had to pause for a while for God to catch up. God always had a much slower pace than we. But now it appears to be the other way around. Now God has to wait for us. Now he is way ahead of us, now our clock is slow, now we no longer can catch up to him. Is all this happening because of what we with growing intensity see happening all around us today? Is it true that, looking back to the twentieth century with its devastating wars and its aftermath of displaced persons, famine, chaos, and today with the mayhem in the Middle

East, and environmental deterioration everywhere, God wants to remind us that the seventh seal is being broken now? Could it be that the breathtaking speed in which events overwhelm us today with tsunami force is a sign that the seven angels with their trumpets are poised to blow their instruments? And would all this be a sign to remind us that ours is the next move? Could it be true that heaven is in a holding pattern because the church on earth has failed to keep pace with God and his mighty deeds?

We are not prepared. We are still far behind. We have been slow in fulfilling our mission task. The crowned rider on his white horse is not yet done with his work. Let's be honest, for many centuries we have terribly neglected this mission task. It is true that the Bible has been translated in practically all the world's spoken languages. It is true that there now are churches in all parts of the world, among all nations. It is true that the young churches more and more bear witness in the midst of the world within which she has to wage her battle. It is true that we in the last century in that regard have seen immense progress. But in spite of all that, in today's so mind-boggling, frightful time, it pains us to accuse the church of not being ready, of having been too slow, too shortsighted, too confined in her thinking, and so she has lagged too far behind of God's majestic march through the world's history.

And then there is a second accusation: we also have been slow in our prayer life and slow in our contact with God and in our glad expectation of God's works of salvation. God works mightily but we cling to our small, earthly interests, and fail to acknowledge the peace of God that surpasses all, which would make it possible to face the future without any fear. We feel threatened, haunted, fearful, and have the notion that all security is being undermined, while we do possess the rock-sure security that God is there and that we are in his hands. We have been secularized in our thinking, we have been wide open to false teaching, we have in our daily life become far too much used to a daily grind of stereotype religion, and we have not allowed the living two-edged sword of God's Word to push us out of our easy routine. In short, we have grown slow, superficial, and colorless, and find ourselves thoroughly ill at ease and frightened now that the last things start to happen and everything around us becomes shaky. The entire church as she lives and struggles everywhere is far too little geared to the grand finale that begins to deploy itself before our eyes. She has become far too indolent and far too small-minded for this to happen. She's become unable to reach the level from which she can view God's perspectives. That is her severe sin now in this moment of such an unprecedented crisis.

Its logical consequence is that we are not the least impatient now that the grand finale is slow in coming. After all we are totally responsible for our own tardiness. It is not Jesus Christ who is to blame: we are the clear culprits. It is not that Jesus Christ has slackened the pace: we have done so. And that simple sign posed here by John that we have prayed too little, is deeply shameful for all of us. The book of Revelation strongly emphasizes two things: we'll have to become more missionary-minded, and we must learn to pray more frequently and more fervently.

THE GREAT PANORAMA

We will now take a bird's eye view about what is said about the course of the last things in the book of Revelation. For this we have to differentiate between the several sections of signs described here. When we once more go back to the happenings that occurred when the seven seals were opened, we can easily detect in these happenings a few different groups. We are first shown the triumphant journey of the rider on his white horse. We learned that by this course of action was meant the spread of the gospel over the entire world as an introductory sign to the final events.

This was followed by three signs all closely connected: war (the red horse), famine (the black horse), and death (the pale horse). Famine and the alarming rise in deaths must be seen as the results of war. God, as yet, does not directly and visibly intervene in the role humanity plays, but God leaves humanity to face the consequences. This implies that humanity by means of its superior technical culture (all dependent on fossil fuels) and its moral decadence causes the coming of numerous catastrophes. We could describe these signs as coming from the bottom up, as arising from humanity itself.

The fifth sign involved the persecution of the church of Christ. This sign, when that seal was opened, was not very clearly described, but there were hints that this involved the prayer of the martyrs in heaven. This prayer indicated that there had been victims on earth, and that this continued to be the case. The believers had in various ways been persecuted and tortured, because, after all, they were strangers upon the earth and therefore were not tolerated. This persecution evidently took place amidst all sorts of conflicts and disasters, but hard facts were not provided. The suspicion is growing that an anti-divine world power had started to develop on earth, which saw the church as a threat and therefore would not tolerate its existence. But that world power itself is not identified by any means. That means that everything remains rather vague. Yet we do well to also include, beside the signs mentioned before, the emergence of an anti-divine world power. This would be the logical outcome of all these wars and the consequent evils flowing from it. These violent wars on earth and against the earth result in one overarching world power and this world power is by nature dead set against the believers.

And finally, as last sign, God himself follows with his answer which involves earthquakes, eclipse of the sun, meteor showers, etc. All these signs are from above, that is to say, God intervenes in human endeavors. God interrupts the human monologue and enters in with his full powers.

When we then give a schematic overview then we arrive at the following summation:

(1) Preparatory sign: the spreading of the gospel;
(2) Signs on the earth: wars, famine, deaths;
(3) Emergence of the anti-divine world power;
(4) Divine intervention.

When we continue reading then it strikes us that in the remainder of the book of Revelation the same motifs return, but that the colors become more pronounced and the details more visible. When describing what happens after the seven angels blow their trumpets we notice that what stands out here is that the heart of the matter is totally situated in what we designated as the fourth group. A quick look at the eighth and ninth chapters will show this convincingly.

By the blowing of the first trumpet: hail and fire.

By the blowing of the second trumpet: the collapse of a burning mountain into the sea, turning the water into blood (see Exod 7:20).

By the blowing of the fourth trumpet: cosmic disasters, sun, moon, stars are affected.

By the blowing of the fifth trumpet: Satanic forces unleashed; a terrible locust plague.

By the blowing of the sixth trumpet: the release of the four angels who unleash demonic riders beyond count onto humanity.

In the first four of these signs the emphasis is on God's intervention into the lives of humans by means of his judgments. He casts his verdicts down to earth. Every one of these judgments is an act of God, descending from above. The two last ones are of a very particular nature. In these the satanic forces are released against humanity. In the first of these two they are depicted as locusts swarming in innumerable numbers. In the second they are compared to riders who bring fire and smoke and sulfur. It is very difficult (in the years before climate change, I might add) to understand what is meant by these last two judgments. There are those who by the first of these two, the locusts plague, are reminded of satanic influences on human life, whereby men and women are robbed of all *joie de vivre* and lose all common sense. This last thought would lead to new wars induced by devilish designs and so carry a total satanic character. John, by these armies of riders rushing in, may have been reminded of the invasions by the Parthians that took place in his lifetime. It indeed has merit to see these locusts plagues as resembling the satanic influences on human spiritual life expressed in radical despair, boundless degeneration, and disruption of all moral norms, completely discarding all generally accepted standards and notions concerning the meaning of human life. This all-encompassing nihilism would also reveal itself in a frightening increase in the death wish. This desire for death would push people to become immune to common sense and rob them of all certainties in their lives. This all sounds the more plausible as an explanation of this very difficult passage because it expressly states that those who carry the seal of God on their foreheads will not be harmed (Rev 9:4). However, as far as the riders are concerned this limitation does not apply. Apparently the believers also will suffer from their malicious acts.

However this may be we clearly see that, when the trumpets sound two different influential forces are called into being. In the first place the heavenly powers are activated, being expressed in immense catastrophes, cosmic disasters making life on earth a constant threat. And in the second place, the earthly powers come into play, originating from the world of demons, expressed in madness, unlimited alienation, doubt, despair, chaos, and killing. We can't be far wrong when we suppose that these last powers are the consequence of the first. When God with his frightening verdicts intrudes into the protected areas of human self-assuredness and safety zone, then humanity garners its last resistance and generates its utmost opposition. Then the satanic powers will exploit this opportunity to induce the terrified and witless people to engage in gigantic expressions of hate. Then a hurricane of sheer madness will rage over the harried humanity as people lose their self-confidence and their trust in others. Everybody is bewildered but there is no conversion. The oceans of despair that threaten to drown people and pull down all pillars of human happiness are not capable to bring about a change of mind. None of these poor creatures suddenly becomes aware that they have sinned against heaven and against God. None of them will say: "I will get up and go to my father," as the prodigal son did. If somewhere, here or there, something in that line would germinate in a person's deepest thoughts then it would right away be suppressed, drowned out by the shrieking of that massive madness that has hypnotized the entire society.

For a moment we are wondering how all this is connected to Jesus Christ's victory and the coming of his kingdom. Until now it seems as if whatever God does, the devil offers even more opportunity. It looks as if the woman who has fled and given birth to the child is still being pursued and gets in bigger trouble than ever before, as if the dragon is the only one who is successful. He is allowed hitherto unknown opportunities, enjoys a period of his greatest triumphs. For us it's not an advance but a retreat. We fail to see a single ray of light on the horizon announcing the new day, the great day of the Lord. No morning star is visible on the firmament: on the contrary, the twilight that was still hanging over the world is more and more replaced with pitch-black darkness. And in this gloomy blackness that disheartens minds and spirits, there the church lives, there she fight her last battle. And yet all this somehow seems to fit into God's unfathomable plan; and yet all this seems written in that mysterious Book that contains the key to the secret of the history of the world.

With the blowing of the seventh trumpet we are almost at the very end. That is apparent from what we read in Revelation 10:5–7: "There will be no more delay!," but that now "the mystery of God will be accomplished, just as he announced it to his servants, the prophets." There will be no more delay. That can only mean that at last there is an end to all deferral. Matters now in breathtaking speed rush to their fulfillment; all the brakes are off; there's nothing now that stands in the way of God's actions. The stream can no longer be diverted because all dams have been swept away.

In the meantime there is humanity caught up in that stormy world, tossed about like a ship that has been wrenched away from her anchors. All values and morals that, throughout all the centuries of the world's history, have kept the life of the nations within certain checks and bounds, now in these fatal moments, appear hollow, moldered, and useless. Conscience has gone, decency has ceased to be. The varnish of what for centuries was seen as civilization and recognized and celebrated as such, proves not capable to withstand the fierce onslaught of the last judgments. Humanity degenerates into an animal, a tortured animal, a driven-to-despair animal, but then worse, far worse. That's the great chaos, that's how history ends. Bands of brigands plunder the land, burn whatever they cannot take, strip the store. There's no more central authority that keeps order. These are the days of King *Madness*. Gone are the days of common sense that, in spite of its ultimate inability to really set humanity free, was still an immense factor to keep humanity from going berserk. All that is left now is a multilateral malignity, is threats that come from everywhere, is despair that expresses that all is permitted, that no norms are valid anymore. Now the general opinion is that life is a senseless game, and history is nothing else but a big joke, and all morals and values are nothing else but an empty fantasy. The only thing that is still lived to the full is the danse macabre associated with the day of doom. Emanating above the wild jeering of this very last ring-dance there occasionally emerges a heartrending cri de coeur, an all-penetrating cry of lament of some doomed character, a hoarse heaven-directed shout that sounds like a curse.

These human beings, who have accomplished so indescribably much, who have erected beautiful cities with grand palaces, these same persons so impressed by their own accomplishments, who managed to uncover all the secrets of nature's powers, they now have taken possession of them, stating that "now they are mine." These same persons, who drilled tunnels through the highest mountains and major highways through the hottest deserts, these same persons have transformed the wilderness into fertile fields, and have dug up its hidden treasures from the depths of the earth for their own enrichment. These humans who with their pens and brush have recreated all the beauty of God's marvelous world, they also have, from the dark corners of their own souls, poetically expressed the secrets of their own selves and exposed the tragedy of their own lost existence. These same people, afraid for nothing, valiantly storming every obstacle, and overcoming them all, these same people, so powerful, so immune to failure, so relentless in attaining success, so capable to achieve amazing results, and never having suffered the shame of defeat, these same people now experience the desperation of life on earth, now see the claim on nature fade away, now lose the power to engage their oh-so-clever tools. That same nature, once so cruelly exploited, now turns against them and as a wounded animal is set to crush them. All levels of security, within and without, fail to function. No longer can they rely on their own brainpower, or are able to cope with the daily problems of life. Everything around them becomes hollow, empty, hostile, pushing out all traces of joy from their innermost selves. They, always insisting on thinking and creating order, now personify chaos. They no longer can control themselves and no longer can control society. They have become like a ship that is adrift, that no longer obeys the steering wheel, that like a plaything is tossed to and fro at the mercy of forces beyond their control. That is the frightening picture this great prophet paints for us about the final days of history.

THE TWO WITNESSES

In the midst of this so very sad situation we suddenly see the appearance of two witnesses as described in chapter 11.

It is right away clear that their entering has a dual meaning. In the first place they appear to reinvigorate the so traumatized church of Christ. The believers in those days of complete confusion will often be totally at a loss what to do and what to say. They will feel depressed, without energy and courage. These two witnesses will come into the church and be able to encourage these so discouraged faithful. Their word will firmly and reassuringly reverberate within the church walls. They will resist any inclination to come to an easy compromise with the spirit of the age. They will firmly fight any deviation from the truth, which, in essence is nothing else but a cowardly concession to unbelief. They will also under no circumstances tolerate any form of waffling, or accommodation, or dullness or half-heartedness. Instead they will unhesitatingly point to the all-conquering power of God and again teach the church to rely on him even though the world starts to become pitch dark. Through their words the church, shabby and on the run as she is, will garner new courage. Prayer life and a vibrant faith witness will greatly increase. Something of new life will invigorate the church of Christ and something of a holy joy of the Lord will blossom again, a wholesome willingness to surrender to God. There will come a time when, even to the farthest corners of the church, the joyful tidings of Christ's rising from the grave, will be heard again, the meaningful message that he lives and will come again to the eternal redemption of those who belong to him. Then the eyes will regain their sparkle, then again till late at night the songs of the Lord will resound. And again there will be real communion with one another, the communion of saints. The lonely and downhearted will again find a refuge in the church, will find joy among the people of God, and in that holy union all will find themselves enclosed as in a unbreakable bond.

At the same time these two witnesses will raise their voices in the world. The time for missionary work has past. Come and gone. The good news has done its job in the world. We now live in a time of apostasy, of chaos, and dissolution. Amidst this witless and disoriented generation these two persons, perhaps a man and a woman, will arise in the name of God. They are assured that the entire church of Christ will back them up and they will realize that they are carried by the prayers of the saints. Undeterred, they will call back to God all these embittered people, adrift in an ocean of intense insecurity. Their words will be seen and heard and read throughout the world. The electronic media will bring their words to the utmost ends of the world, be read throughout the most distant shores. These two witnesses will rise up in the midst of the utmost insanity of a world swiftly speeding to complete collapse. Millions will monitor their message. Are they the ones who can give new hope to a generation that is so tired and has lost its foothold? Do they have a new message for a world that is dying from uncertainty and insecurity? Again they will hold high the old-time religion that only Jesus Christ is Lord, and that only in returning to him there is salvation. And when they proclaim this, the word will sound as something new, as something fresh, as something that deals with all the problems of the then living generation. Nothing stale, nothing withered, nothing that sounds like platitudes or lacks fire, no, every word will sparkle with spirit and be expressed with extraordinary eloquence. Even the most unrepentant unbeliever will realize that this couple knows what they are talking about and what they say is not some old wives tale, but is the bruising reality.

Will that mean that a general conversion will come about? Will this couple really generate a following? There will be moments when it will look that this would actually happen, especially when, in their blind hate, some of them will try to kill them, and find out that this is impossible because they are authorized by God. That especially will force many to openly consider to follow these two witnesses and to accept their words.

In those days in the church too there will be those who expect the arrival of a new era. It is as if a few red stripes on the dark sky announce the dawning of a new day. These two witnesses firmly stand there amongst all that unsure and confused chatter of the people of those days. The do not bear crowns, but every single word they speak mirrors their majesty.

And still, their performance will not lead to universal conversion. The people of those days cannot really accept them as sent by God. Their message is too old-fashioned, too opposed to their deepest and most secret thoughts. After all, they say things that has been heard from time immemorial and already then rejected as useless. They bring something to the fore that has, for centuries, been repeated ad nauseam and already then seen as something impossible for the modernity to embrace. They come through as upright and strong, these two witnesses, but they are simply dated, and belong to earlier times. Their words convey strength but what they say they have so often heard before. No, even though they are well-spoken and their holy zeal is impressive, will the people become their disciples? No way. Countless hands, earlier eagerly extended to them, are slowly withdrawn. Countless ears first so eagerly hanging on every word are slowly turned off. Why listen to a story of a certain Jesus who had been killed on a wooden cross thousands of years ago while we live in a world with heaven-high skyscrapers and fast-flying airplanes and instant worldwide communication? Don't for a minute think that we will fall for that. It would be foolish to assume that this would mean anything for us. True, this couple looks quite up-to-date, quite forthright in their presentation, but, no, all things considered, they are dreamers, offer some fantasy, come proclaiming some Middle Age fairy tales. And the world hums and ferments and the ages roll on and on and the desacralizing escalates, and the despair increases. It is as if humanity for the last time goes directly past Calvary but cannot see the cross on which the only possibility for salvation hangs.

These two witnesses, the carriers of the very last exhortation on behalf of God, will perish in the end, as did so many other prophets and apostles before them. But that will not yet happen in the days of universal confusion and disintegration. No, that will only take place when, out of these chaotic conditions a new government has arisen, a regime of a strong dictatorship and firm measures, a new authority that was bound to come. These moods of despair and unbridled disruptions, the widespread forming of gangs and complete civil disorder could simply not continue. There was bound to eventually emerge a new sort of government that with an iron rod would force an end to this free-for-all lawlessness. A new authority was bound to emerge, a regime that wouldn't fool around and not be afraid to rule with an iron fist. The world was ripe for tyranny, was tired of the freedom because it had become estranged from the sort of freedom that meant real freedom, that is to say the strong inner ties to the divine norms they no longer knew. The word *freedom* had become a curse, synonymous with arbitrariness, chaotic conditions, unrestrained indulging in passionate living. That sort of world can only end one way: and that is in tyranny. This tyranny is first welcomed as beneficial, as a real blessing. At last there is an end to all that insanity, at last there is somebody who says what has to be done and can back it up. That is the new government that will be born from this period of total confusion.

And in the days of the new regime the two witnesses will ignominiously disappear. Perhaps *ignominiously* is not the right word. Even in their death they will be the bearers of divine majesty. They, in the very sight of their enemies, will rise from the dead and be taken up in heaven. I have no idea whether TV cameras will be there to record that miraculous event. No doubt it would have appeared on the front pages in fat print of all the papers in the world as the most sensational event of the week. But censure will quickly forbid to spread the news and the film, and the TV cameras will be destroyed. Forcefully the authorities will suppress all gossip related to it. These two witnesses are now old news. They were clever operators, but their time is up. We now must look ahead. Forget about the nonsense of these old-fashioned preachers. We now forge ahead to a new future!

We will come back to that new government later, because the book of Revelation also spends a great deal of attention to it. At this time we are only concerned how the world is slowly approaching that awesome moment that we call the end of time. In the approach to this final moment all these factors play a role. First the proceeding of the white horse. Then the wars and its consequences. After that the persecution and then the earthquake and what all this entails. The church too plays a role in all this, in her relationship with God, her witness to the world, her prayer for liberation. It is that particular prayer that will unlock the last things. New calamities will come and wreak havoc, catastrophes resulting in untold suffering, resulting in a fierce reaction of determined obstinacy and hate against God and against his authority. Demonic powers will be unleashed on humanity, desperation and despair will destroy the final vestiges of normativity, chaos and madness will gain the upper hand. It is at that time, in those days when it is everybody against everybody, in the days of total social upheaval that these two witnesses will arise as God's final appeal.

This is somewhat how we must interpret the depressing series of scenarios John outlines for us. There is progress, a certain push, but also stagnation. It is as if there constantly is a certain force at work that prevents the great day from coming, that inevitable and so deeply desired day. There certainly are restraining elements. The seals are broken, one after the other, but there are forces at work that stall the entire process. Some of these forces we have traced: the church has failed in her missionary calling, and also she has prayed far too little.

But apart from blaming the church there is another factor that acts as a delaying agent, something that now slowly is becoming visible. The very end can come only when the world has first degenerated into a condition where, in the most radical sense, the entire earth has become rebellious, godless, chaotic, and lawless. Sin must become public, sin must be revealed what it in the most explicit sense really is and always has been. Everything must become what it is. That is one of the dominating motifs of this remarkable book of the Bible, and motif that only at the very end of comes to us in its naked reality: "Let they who do wrong, let them continue to do wrong; let they who are vile, continue to be vile; let they who are right, continue to do right; let they who are holy, continue to be holy."

Right now his world is covered by a haze of untruthfulness: all things seem different than they are. The devil disguises himself as an angel of light, while the children of God often poorly reflect God's image in their daily walk of life. Everything is unclear, unreal, non-transparent. We still see far too many expressions coming from this sinful humanity, which in its deepest essence has always rebelled against its creator and king.

Under the force of constant hammer blows, still raining upon this pseudo world, humanity finally becomes the humanity it was meant to be in the most detestable sense of the word, the real human, that is the rebel, the prisoner, the doubting, the unconverted. World history, stripped bare from all pretenses, is not simply a record of events: it is nothing else than that through all these happenings, through prosperity and adversity, through wars and peace, through increase in knowledge and culture, that through all this and more, in the end everything becomes what it always has been. That's why the kingdom of the Son of Man, the reign of humanity personified, can only come when the kingdom of the beast has had the entire world in its grasping hands.

CHAPTER SIX

The Very Last Unmasking
(Revelation 13–19)

OVERVIEW

In our deliberations about the book of the Revelation of John we have started with chapter 12. The reason for this was that this chapter, in a few lines, gave a general overview of what was going on in the church. That church is a strange phenomenon in this mixed-up world. She carries a crown, is the mother of the great victor, Jesus Christ, and shares in his victory. Nevertheless she flees away as a victim, as one persecuted, and as one in deep distress. In the history of the world she always is what she is not, and she never is what she, by the grace of God, already in the deepest sense has been from of old. Her existence on earth is through and through puzzling, paradoxical, and mysterious. Even though she carries the diadem of eternal glory, she traverses through history under the disguise of poverty, loneliness, and impotence.

Paul at times can look at all this with silent amazement. Without any hesitation he writes: "In all this we are more than conquerors" (Rom 7:37), but in the next instance he also confesses: "Up to this moment we have become the scum of the earth, the refuse of the world" (1 Cor 4:13). "We have this treasure in jars of clay . . . We are hard pressed on every side, but not crushed, perplexed, but not in despair, persecuted, but not abandoned; struck down, but not destroyed. We always carry around in our body the death of Jesus, so that the life of Jesus may also be revealed in our body" (2 Cor 7:7–10). The secret of the church cannot be expressed in clearer and more direct terms. She's always the underdog, chased from her final hiding places, and yet there's always something that keeps her standing and saves her from a definite demise. But the victory crown is never totally visible, the disguise never totally disappears.

It is that picture of the church that in vivid colors is portrayed for us in the twelfth chapter of the Revelation of John. That too is the image that dominates the entire remainder of this last book of the Bible. The first eleven chapters are in all aspects simply an introduction. In stark but simple lines they show how this church conducted herself in the disguise. She can do this in the manner of Pergamum, courageously but yet too weak, she can do it as Smyrna did, upright and strong, or follow the example of Laodicea, dull and cold. But she never is totally the same, there's never a hint of monotony and always a rich variety, a rich variety of light and shadows. After this these chapters tell us how the last things gain their momentum. The proclamation of the gospel made inroads, wars ravaged the world, a broad stream of deep sorrow inundated the nations of the world. Disasters of cosmic proportions popped up, eclipses of the sun, earthquakes occurred. The tsunamis of terror tore into the earth's territories and generated general animosity and brought on boundless chaos, roaring rage and introduced the age of the king of madness. From all this incoherent confusion emerged in the end the vague forms of the new kingdom, the kingdom of men, dominated by cruel tyranny. All that is briefly the image that was further worked out in chapters five to eleven.

After the twelfth chapter it is the new kingdom that rules over all. That kingdom is now present and we receive a complete picture. In colorful ways we are also shown what is happening there and how it copes with it all. At the end of the book we witness the destruction of that kingdom in a way that shakes us to the very core. All this is the theme of the second part of this wonderful book.

THE ARCHITECTURE OF THE HUMAN KINGDOM

"And I saw a beast coming out of the sea." That's simply how this thirteenth chapter starts. These sober words appear without any further ado, no exclamations of astonishment, no extra emphasis.

What right away strikes us is the past tense: "I saw." These are events that are still to come in the faraway future. John himself would not have suspected that it would take a few thousand years before these matters would be realized. "I saw." In the heaven it is already past tense while on earth it still is in the far, far future. For a moment we sense that our earthly time concept is quite limited and unilateral. What for us is the future tense is in certain ways already a matter of the past, thus past and future are much more closely intertwined than we often suspect. When, at last, the true state of affairs of what John has seen, will become evident and there really appears a great anti-Christian realm under some sort of ruler or tyrant or dictator or president or under whatever name, then this world ruler will be convinced that he is doing something entirely original and that he has founded a new regime of an unlimited extent. He will dream that his actions are totally novel, something that never before has occurred in world history. And he will not have the faintest idea that already many centuries before, the seer of Patmos has seen him. He also will also not in the least suspect that his action has already been observed and described in detail. And he certainly will not be able to grasp that somehow he fits into God's great plan concerning the last things. It all is going to happen: he will arise out of the seething sea of the world's happenings, but in the final analysis it will be God who will appear there as the great doer. God will allow him to rise up, not a minute earlier and not a minute later than is indicated in that unfathomable book of the end times. In that way also the divine and the human acts are much more closely interwoven than we as a rule are able to understand.

The beast that John saw rising out of the sea poses all sorts of difficult questions. That it is a "beast" is a foregone conclusion. In any case this already means that when the human kingdom formerly reveals itself, it clearly is bestial in its total being. The bestiality is always dormant in us humans, clearly evident in the Holocaust during World War II and now in ISIS. It certainly is not an exception, not the last remnant of an as yet not conquered form of barbarity, no, bestiality is essentially a true feature of humanity. Yes, it is humanity to the core. As soon as the brakes are released, as soon as God pushes the bolts away, perversity pours out from all pores, because we humans, however cultivated we seem to be and however humane, in ourselves we are cruel, hard, indifferent, and bloodthirsty. That's why this kingdom of man can never be better described than by the image of a beast that suddenly rises up out of the sea, out of the chaos of the world's happenings.

When we examine the beast more closely, a few features stand out right away. In the first place it is striking that it closely resembles the dragon described for us in chapter 12. That dragon had seven heads and ten horns, the same as the beast that rises up out of the sea, except the order is reversed. That here the horns are mentioned first is because John sees first the horns breaking the surface of the sea and only then are his eyes fixed on the heads.

In the second place this entire passage clearly reminds us of Daniel 7, where successively four animals emerge from the turbulent ocean. The first animal there resembles a lion, the second that of a bear, the third a leopard, while the fourth animal appeared to be a great monster full of mind-boggling cruelty and godlessness. Here, in Revelation 13, only one animal is annotated, but that one animal evidently combines the several features of the four animals Daniel has observed. The build of that one animal is that of a leopard, but its paws are that of a bear, the mouth is that of a lion, while the horns are clearly associated with the fourth animal. In other words, that one animal seen by John is an amalgam, a composition of the four animals Daniel many centuries ago has observed in his dream. With both Daniel and John, these animals signify world empires. Throughout the history of the world we can notice a very remarkable push toward the formation of world empires: rulers love to establish superpowers. The Bible in many places shows us this phenomenon and opens our eyes for this desire, because the urge to form world empires indicates the human hubris that has destroyed the kingdom of God and now attempts to create its own kingdom. He has escaped from God's guidance and now wants to establish something new that reflects his own personality. This urge to form a world power is as ancient as humanity itself, and it also is, judging by history, a permanent feature. Here this prophecy reveals its raw rebellious energy.

The forming of super powers, however, differs in methods and motives. The variety of animals explains this. There are nations that show the features of a lion. They probably indicate that these nations are the products of unrestrained pride. There are populations that imagine themselves as superior, far above all other nations. The German National Socialism displayed this pride, and preached the superiority of the German race above all others. That was its motivation to found its empire. We can see this perhaps even more pronounced in Japanese nationalism as it was displayed before the war when it openly preached this. One of the religious movements in prewar Japan publicly confessed that "Japan must dominate the foreign nations. Japan is the root of the world and its people are the chosen of God, it is the tree while the other nations are mere branches. Someday in the future the day will come when all will confess one God. Until that time Japan and the other nations will have been separate, and after that only one will remain: Japan." These are striking hallmarks of a "lion-nation." A lion, after all, is a destructive animal, the same as lion-kingdoms. Ancient Israel has learned to see proud Babylon as a lion-kingdom and experienced its bloodthirsty nature. We also, in our days, know to some extent the nature of a lion-state.

There also are states resembling a bear. Daniel offers here a brief characterization: "It had three ribs in its mouth between his teeth, and it was told: rise and eat much meat." In all likelihood this means that these bear-like nations were exceedingly greedy. With them it is not so much the pride factor that stimulates it to become a super-power, but more the economic advantage. They want to control raw material, the rubber, oil, the iron ore, and the grain market. They want to dominate the world's mineral riches. They have no interest in color or creed nor do they suffer from a superiority complex, but they are keen on anything to do with money and strive to completely manage the world's entire production process. These "bear-like" empires with their economic expansion goals are a well-known item in world history and frequently appear in the history books even up to today. Ancient Israel saw the Persian Empire as a good example of this.

And then there are the leopard nations. What this indicates is not entirely clear. The leopard or panther was, in the time of the ancient Israel nation, feared for its unequalled speed of operation. In Habakkuk 1:8 there is mention of this speed. Apparently these panther-resembling nations were famous for their blitzkrieg action, their lightning quick striking force, their unexpected, surprisingly fast war machine. It seems that the sort of imperialism they displayed contained an element of sport, was some sort of game, almost some daredevil act. They don't have a hubris complex, are not primarily interested in some rich booty, but they invade just for the heck of it, they go on some quick plunder trip to grab whatever comes their way. Like a panther they leap up on the unsuspecting prey; their entire demeanor is one of stealth and speed. Israel especially saw the Greek state under Alexander the Great as such a panther-like nation. In a newer context Napoleon could be compared to such a regime.

There are three kinds of empires. Their motifs differ: the one displays hubris, the other economic expansion, a third is opportunistic. In their nature they resemble three animals: the lion, the bear, and the panther. But John sees these three animals in one body. The panther body dominates because the animal he sees is "like a panther," but it has the feet of a bear and the mouth like a lion. It is lightning-fast, surprising, amazingly quick in its attack, but at the same time eager for riches, and uncannily proud. In that one nation-kingdom culminate all previous super powers the world's history has ever experienced, from the first till the last, from Babylon, Persia, the Roman Empire, the ever-still expanding Islam, the Middle Age German Empire, that of Napoleon, Great Britain under Queen Victoria, Germany under Hitler, the USA after World War II, and all others: they all are reflected in that one kingdom that now is appearing on the horizon. But because it unites in it all these features, it is at the same time a misshapen phenomenon, a terrifying monster.

The chapter tells us something about the beast's heads and horns. These horns carry crowns while one of the heads is mortally wounded but, at the amazement of the nations, it completely heals itself. What all these symbols mean is not quite clear. These crowned horns, do they point to crowned kings who reign in succession, or dynasties, or does it have a different meaning, where they depict how that one particular empire will be construed from several different realms or provinces? It compels us only to do some guesswork here, and the same applies to the seven heads. What is recorded in verse 3 about that one head that was mortally wounded, but later healed itself, applies to Nero, according to some commentators, about whom the rumor made the rounds that he had not really died but suddenly reappeared fully alive. It is possible that this legend was accepted as truth also for a while in Christian circles, but it is very unlikely that this is the true explanation. In Daniel's vision a similar description appears.

Of the fourth animal it is said that three of its horns were pulled out to make place for a small horn that suddenly rose up instead. We will be pretty close to the truth when we assume that this in veiled terms indicates that right from the birth of the new world empire, events will take place that show that the sword of Damocles already hangs above the head of this world ruler. There will be a temporary revival but the germ of defeat is already visible.

In the meantime the book of Revelation tells us of some horrible features typifying this human realm and its supreme commander, matters that give us some insight into the principles upon which this kingdom is built.

The first item mentioned here is that the world ruler owes his power courtesy the "the dragon," and its occult, demonic powers. We can reasonably assume that this total world power is the last and most energetic of Satan's attempts to unite all of humanity into one formidable anti-god coalition. This demonic character will visibly become apparent, that is to say, humanity in general will become aware one way or another that here not merely human craftiness, but that this dictator also has some unusual, even some supernatural features. What is at work here is not just a matter of devising a grand plan but mysterious matters play a dominating role here such as prophetic visions, fortune-telling, and unfailing intuition. People will be impressed by the enchanting energy that emanates from this peculiar personality. People will be astounded how everything he does proves successful, even when this initially looks like a daredevil act. Time and again people will conclude that this is abnormal, that unfathomable and irresistible powers are at work here. When the mortal wound from which this ruler has suffered will be healed, people in general will not only start to praise him to high heavens but also attribute supernatural powers to him that keep him alive up and make him prosper.

The second peculiarity is that this dictator speaks proud words and blasphemies. That indicates that he is full of rancor, harbors thoughts of revenge and bitterness. In that sense he is not like the modern people who have ceased to be angry with God because they no longer sense God's presence in life. Somehow is an almost naïve human feature evident in that he is eager to unburden himself by uttering detestable curses against God by way of blatant blasphemy. His audience may not completely understand all this as it is composed of people who no longer understand the concept of God. They have become completely taken in by material possessions, have totally turned nihilists. They can talk about what appears on television and and other related matters, but they have no notion what in earlier times such concepts as morality, good and evil, sin and life after life stood for. The new world ruler is in that respect not a nihilist. For him God is definitely a reality and he certainly knows what is meant by that concept. When he is reminded of that "God" word then waves of bitterness gush through his veins, his eyes spark flames, and his temper flares up. For him God is the most despicable matter that can be imagined and he is proud that he dares to cast that great name of God away like a piece of filth, a name that millions upon millions have revered as holy. In that respect he is more childish than most of this modern generation, which is far beyond the stage of getting angry at God. This man is much more attached to God than they.

This man, I must admit, definitely has the gift of leadership. His armies have gained entrance into all earth's regions, and managed to conquer all existing rulers. The incomparable success in his military expeditions is based not so much on his modern warfare equipment but is mostly the result of the mysterious, frightening, goal-oriented direction that dominates everything he does. This ruler gives the impression that with every step he takes he knows that he will succeed, and so he does. No wonder that in a very short time the entire world fears him; he also in the space of a few months takes over all economic resources, with the result that he has become the undeniable ruler of the earth. All attempts to revolt have disappeared, all nationalistic movements aimed at his overthrow have gone. The world has become dead-quiet, the press no longer reports any armed conflicts: now their only theme is the song of praise to him who accomplished all this, which does not mean that this greatest ruler of all times is not mocked and vilified and cursed in some places. But all that mockery amounts to nothing because the secret police are quick to bloodily suppress even the tiniest attempt to disobedience. Indeed all is quiet on all fronts. The press has little else to report than some sport events and perhaps another technological breakthrough.

Yet something is brewing out there, even though no newspaper has an inkling of it. The now so famous ruler in his burning hate stretches out his hands to "the tent and to those who live in heaven." The literal text says "those who dwell in the heavenly tabernacles." There is a direct reference to those who live in tents, as the tabernacle was. Here we again have the impression (just as in Rev 12:12) that the tent-dwellers in heaven are not meant to be the angels and the saints there but rather the believers who, even though they are still on earth, have their citizenship already in heaven (Phil 3:20), and have received a place "in the heavenly realms in Jesus Christ" (Eph 2:6). It seems that this is the reason why the word *tabernacles* is mentioned and not dwellings in the real solid sense. Those believers who in these days of persecution are more than ever conscious of the circumstance that they already belong to the "heavenly realms" are bodily subjected to the cruel ire of this blasphemer. He goes beyond cursing and slander and starts a war against "the saints." He receives that opportunity, says John meaningfully. He is allowed to do so, God makes it possible. God, for a moment, withdraws his protection and leaves his people at the mercy of the wild animal that spares no wrath. That war is, of course, child's play for this redoubtable world ruler. The Bible does not record where these saints have hidden, to which desert or cave or catacomb they have fled. Of course they have no sophisticated weaponry, so it becomes a rather one-sided affair, a war against the defenseless. The result is a sad parade of chained Christians flanked by heavily armed soldiers. That is the somber end of this brief "war." The press, of course, praises the accomplishments of our "heroic military."

The result is that everybody is dead scared. Nobody dares to associate with the believers. The few of those still confessing the name of Christ wander about feeling totally abandoned, with no access anywhere. The entire world worships "the beast," worships not in the sense of altars and temples, but in mass meetings, with flags and banners with extravagant praise from the press, with hollow humbug and boastful bragging. But the throne of him who has assumed the direction of the world in his insecure hands still stands unshaken.

In those days there are still some who refuse to pray to the beast. These are the wandering Christ confessors, nowhere safe, driven from home and hearth. They refuse to budge. They remain steadfast in a world of brass bands and flattering tributes. It is not their good works that make them do this, it is only that their names have been written in the Book of Life. They are preserved by their Lord and savior, are in his firm grip; that's why they cannot join in the choir of the demonic powers. They are the followers of the "Lamb that has been slain since the foundation of the world."

These last words contain something astonishing. It is as if the happening on Calvary, the cross of Jesus Christ, is seen here as the synopsis of what always takes place: "since the foundation of the world." All ages are always active in crucifying him, all nations and all generations want to lay their hands on him. That was the cruel, historical reality under Pontius Pilate, is now also the expression of something supra-temporal, something that in every age takes place all the time. It reminds me of the well-known words of Pascal: "Jesus is in his death struggle till the end of the world." Of course this boastful world ruler of the kingdom of men will not succeed in chaining Jesus Christ and let him languish in a dirty prison camp. But when he eagerly stretches out his hands to Christ's followers, the ones who confess his name, then his aim is to get at Christ, then his utmost meaning is to drag Christ to the guillotine. In their tears are his tears, in their blood that freely flows, is his blood. According to the moving words of the Apostle Paul, they are engaged in their own bodies "to fill up what is still lacking in regard to Christ's afflictions" (Col 1:24). In this one sentence is the martyrdom of these last believers at once placed in a new light. For a moment we get a glimpse of him who stands behind these persecuted and deprived people, the one who has borne the crown of thorns and travels through history as an abandoned loner.

The Prophet of the Kingdom of Humanity

With an almost boring regularity John continues to describe one scenario after another. "Then I saw another beast coming out of the earth. He had two horns like a lamb but he spoke like a dragon" (Rev 13:11). Here we see a new creature looming up before our astonished eyes.

That this animal rises up from the earth can possibly be connected to the life-producing earth that the nations of antiquity always considered to be the keeper of the secret. Everything comes forth from the earth that carries us all, and maintains us all. We too originate from the earth and we all return to the earth. The earth is the keeper of life's most valuable secret. This prophet has its origin in this earth. That at the same time also indicates his un-heavenly origin because he does not come in the name of God but comes up out of nature itself, is a product of the earth. His total appearance has the character of duplicity. His horns evidently are lamb's horns, small, posing no danger, hardly visible, but his voice is the voice of a dragon, his language is demonic, but not in a way that is right away noticeable. There's something striking about him, something fascinating. At times he resembles the lamb itself, but when listening to his voice, we recognize his employer. The entire picture suggests that here we don't deal with a prince, but a prophet, a counselor and also a propaganda minister.

The theme of the relationship between king and prophet is a cherished topic in the Bible, especially in the Old Testament. The prophet seldom strays far from the palace. He often enters there, he reminds kings to keep the law and is not afraid to call them to account. At times there appear false prophets, who flatter the kings and offer the most favorable predictions, but as a rule we encounter the prophets as fearless witnesses of God's truth. This prophet here also frequents the court, and, apparently, is the confidant of the dictator. His main task is to go out and sing the praises of the dictator. He urges the people to worship the beast, that same beast that for a while was suffering from a mortal wound but later recovered.

The prophet has the ability to adorn his speeches with sensational examples of his miraculous powers. Before an enthusiastic crowd he commands fire to come from heaven. That miracle is totally senseless and serves no purpose, and is nothing else but a demonstration of the prophet's capability. Jesus and the Old Testament prophets always have resisted such sort of demonstrations, because they did not want to use their power to enhance their own image. Jesus only performed miracles when there was an explicit need when people required help, but he emphatically refused to leap from the top of the temple just for the sake of being admired. This prophet is different and is not afraid to do so. On the contrary, he delights in doing this sort of sensational showpieces. Whether he does this with the aid of cleverly constructed components or whether he indeed possesses supernatural talents remains a matter of speculation. The fact is that the assembled crowds are deeply impressed and respond with enthusiastic applause.

The prophet continues to do some remarkable feats. He has an image made of the dictator and as soon as this replica is ready he infuses it with a "spirit" so that, to the astonishment of the onlookers, it starts to speak and to pronounce that all those who refuse to worship the beast will be killed. For a moment we are tempted to see this as tomfoolery. It would not be the first time in world history that a human being is concealed in a statue, which at a certain moment can produce sounds. Today, of course, we have numerous examples of this sort of thing, but the way John talks about this he is quite convinced that we are not dealing here with some sort of deception. On the contrary, he quite solemnly says that the beast was "given" the power to infuse the image with a "spirit." It really looks that we must think here that something abnormal was taking place, something supra-natural. That elevates this miracle to the sphere of a mystery; here the

Satan manifests himself as the great imitator of God. What this made-alive image is proclaiming is nothing else but a fanatic call to kill all those who do not reverently honor the dictator.

And the crowds obey, these subdued, terrorized, propaganda-poisoned people swallow the party line. Measures are devised to determine who the people are that warrant the death penalty. They find the solution: the faithful followers of the prophet and consequently the true adherents of the dictator will receive a sign either on their right hand or on their forehead. Perhaps the laborers will carry the sign on their hand, while the thinkers, the intellectuals, will carry it on their foreheads. Is all this an indication that from now on everybody must see as their life calling to devote all their energy to the greater glorification of the beast? No doubt that is exactly the aim of this sign. Severe penalties are posted to prevent anyone who does not display the sign from buying or selling. That is a beautiful way to detect those who act illegally, those who do not worship the beast and do not acknowledge the prophet. Those who act illegally are simply boycotted, are not allowed to enter any store, and must somehow manage to survive. No longer will there be people willing to hide or feed them because those who do will be judged as having lost the sign. And with this resolution all loopholes are closed. The dictator now has eliminated all opposition, is the undisputed ruler. The prophet, using all available communication channels, day-in-day-out praises the success of the kingdom of man. All commerce and industry and agriculture are now serving the state. The press and all institutes of learning obediently fall in line, all broadcasting systems have become tools of the regime and totally devoted to the glorification of the new realm, the realm of men that finally, after many centuries of struggle, has established permanent peace on earth. The maintenance of armies is a matter of the past; abolished is the industrial complex that always was so feverishly busy with building a war machine. Now everything can be prepared for peaceful purposes and fear is forever banned. That's exactly what, for centuries, humanity has yearned for; now, finally, peace has been given a chance.

But is that really peace? Yes, if we regard peace as a situation where everybody says and thinks the same thing. Yes, if we understand by peace that whoever utters a different opinion is right away incarcerated somewhere or shipped to some inhospitable island. Yes, if we mean by peace that those are swiftly eliminated who, in spite of all threats, still feel and confess that the word "we" includes to be responsible for their conduct. Now humans lack all personal responsibility. Now humans simply are a small cog in the mighty machine of the state. Now nobody ever speaks their mind because he or she has been submerged in the collective of the state. When the state day after day suggests that all authority rests with men and that above all humanity rules the unfathomable, exalted, worshipful figure of some leader, emperor, president, or whatever his or her title may be, then they humbly hug the message presented to them as the ultimate truth. The result is that slowly there's nobody left who can allow themselves the luxury to voice a private opinion. The state is omniscient, the media incessantly spouts its confession of faith into a submissive world, the children swallow it whole, are constantly inundated with it in school. Families no longer count, parents have become meaningless, personal ideals, expectations, awareness of sin, all these have become superfluous and even dangerous. Everything needs to be wiped away because the only matter that firmly and resolutely may take root in the hearts of people is the certainty that the state is everything, that the leader is wise and powerful, and that only the minister of information, the prophet of all prophets, knows what is true and useful. It becomes a beautiful era for the mindless, for those who find it difficult to engage one's brain, who rather long to be dictated to and be led. For them life is golden, because the state only recognizes those who can easily be cajoled, who willingly go where the strong hand of the state puts them.

And peacefully life goes on. Peaceful, yes by all outward indications, but in the prisons where the asocial elements have been taken, those who do not believe in the legitimacy of that state, there matters are not peaceful. And in many an attic in the major cities, people quietly sigh and moan, thinking and whispering, "The state is grinding us so fine that every bone in our bodies is cracking and the last of our personality has vanished." Others lament, "We are reduced to things, not knowing anymore whether we exist or not." Those are the complaints murmured here and there. They are hardly audible, because even their spouses or children can no longer be trusted. To be on the safe side it's preferable to always wear that sign and honor the leaders when needed, and fully join in when the joyful words of the national anthem are heard. But in the bottom of their heart people start to curse this make-believe world and begin to despise it.

And somewhere far away, somewhere in nowhere, there lives a small band of Christians: the roaming remnant of religious refugees. So far they have managed to escape from the ever-searching hand of the authorities and avoid capture. They don't carry the required sign either on the hand or the forehead because they carry the sign of baptism, of their covenant with him who entered death and is risen. They exist on what they can find and never remain long in one place because everywhere danger lurks. The Laodicea-Christians have long ago given up, and have gone back to the cities, to their places of employment, and stand in line to receive their sign. The Nicolaitans have long gone because heresies are no longer in fashion. This is not the time to indulge in outlandish theological speculations. This is the time of all times. Now there is only one thing that counts: whether you really are one with Jesus Christ in a living faith relationship. You can only keep body and soul together when you know that this entire senseless game of the kingdom of man will come to an end and that only the kingdom of Jesus Christ will prove victorious. And if you do not have that irrevocable security then you better return to the city. There in the urban surroundings you may hear curses and blasphemy, there you will also find distraction in many forms and so lose yourself into wild entertainment. But here in the silent solitude, here you can only manage to survive when you can look through the total vacuity of that human authority apparatus.

Here you can only survive when you love Christ with all the passion of your total being.

In these short snapshots John pictures the end of history. There is peace in the world. There is universal prosperity. Productivity rises considerably now that the war industry hardly consumes anything. Now a four-day work week is standard, and commerce is flourishing more than ever. Gone are all money-exchange problems and all custom officials have been furloughed. There's plenty of opportunity for play and pleasure, for trips and for sports, exactly the way the tyrant and his propaganda machine had planned: fun is the key to happiness. In the merry-go-round of frolicking the men and women push away any thought of rebellion, while it paves the way for total submission. It is indeed a world to be proud of. If these people totally forget that little word "I," forget that they live, forget that they think, forget that they carry responsibility, and forget that they will die, when they keep on dancing on the music of the state, and spend their personality away in the pursuit of pleasure, then all the doors to complete happiness are wide open. Then all worries in the world disappear and all anxieties evaporate. Then there is food for all and you'll never have to worry where the next meal will come from. Then finally the people of the world, the fatigued and famine-stricken family of men, can relax in complete surrender. At last the triumphant slogan of the state, "peace on earth," resounds over their tired and bended heads. And the airplanes are loaded and the new cars are shown off and the rock festivals flourish and there are no bounds to spending. It's all fanciful and fine and the future never looked better. And in the heart of that empire, at the center of all these marvelous happenings, there the creator of all these wonderful blessings sits on his throne.

It is striking that today we can understand John so well. We all have experienced this, we all have become experts in this sort of living. We exactly know how the state will develop. We know what these signs mean; we know what the right connections entail; we know that with the proper education, with the proper political ties, the correct career is assured. We also know what it means that people lose their "I" and are wiped away as a zero. We know what it is that the cadence of current affairs becomes so penetrating and so all-consuming that those so exposed feel like becoming a dimwit. It makes one think of the wartime 1940 to 1945 when Germany occupied Europe. The Nazi regime under Hitler strongly resembled what John depicts here in such somber terms. The nucleus of the thinking then was that every person would sacrifice his or her personality for the greater good of the state. Nobody needs to think because the führer thinks. Nobody needs to decide because he decides. Nobody needs to require anything because he requires for everybody. And if they only would understand what this sort of gospel wants to attain and obediently would comply, then indeed the peaceable kingdom would have come. Today it is becoming more and more evident that the countries under the capitalistic system, with its infinite growth religion, could be subjected to this same sort of punishment. By and large we are slowly becoming aware that today too life is increasingly becoming emptied of what is meaningful, that today too millions are sinking into a state of nothingness. During working hours they are stuck on the treadmill of big business and in the free hours glued to the screen of whatever, often too tired to think, not enough energy left for a moment of reflection and self-examination. The droning of modern life with all its noise, its emptiness and insanity, cascades over the lives of billions and chokes off the last spark of life in humanity. Yet they all are people who, each personally, will someday stand before God's face. Youth today, with TV as its babysitter, are, from their first eye-opening glance, already saturated with all the superficiality and smallness of contemporary life, are thoroughly brainwashed by its utter vulgarity. The noise of the never-silent voices stuffing them with secularism, breeds total indifference for any spiritual influence, stifles forever an inclination for self-analysis and independence. They never learn how to think from a central point of faith commitment and are never taught to take everlasting ideas into account. The thirst for meaning is, in a way, the only factor that gives existence still a bit of sparkle and shine. There are untold many nowadays who no longer can spell the word *life*, who no longer know what it means to be "alive'" human beings.

Our entire modern society is in a breathtaking tempo forced to exist in a nihilistic mode of life in which everyone sinks away as in a morass. John saw all this quite clearly. And above this entire new world scene he saw the figure of the tyrant who in bitter hate carried all this in his almighty hands. He took extreme care to provide a veneer of romanticism and sentimentality so that everything had the appearance of beauty and magnificence. But in the meantime these masses, these characterless and shapeless masses, these malleable and submissive masses, were incapable of change.

All this is now also affecting us when we see the world around us. We are definitely at its initial stage: it lurks in the shadows from all sides.

The Great Catastrophe

Something is going to happen. We sensed right from the start that somehow the portrayal John offered could not last for long. Everything is simply too artificial, too downright crazy, too terrifying for it to endure. Something is bound to happen, something that will cause this so elaborately structured set-up to collapse. The description of that regime makes that quite clear. The main plank of this governing body is its hate against God. Its confession of faith is based on unlimited trust in human power. Its only hope in life on earth is to fully immerse oneself in the pursuit of pleasure. The basis of its morality is that nobody can be a somebody, that nobody can believe in their own responsibility, and is ultimately answerable to God. The regime of the beast has as sole purpose the extinguishing of even the tiniest part of personal life, personal joy, and a personal connection to God. It all is built on one colossal lie, on the total denial of the most fundamental and decisive reality. The culture of the new regime constitutes a tremendous push to suppress, to close off peoples' minds so that it deprives humanity of the very essence to be human. It is a culture that promotes escaping what is truly human. Its most primary goal is to live totally without God.

And this can simply not continue. Eventually the powerful presence of God will penetrate all pores. It is simply impossible to suppress it forever. All this nonsense will have to be exposed someday when, finally, that what was so perseveringly suppressed will break through after all. On every page of the book of Revelation of John it is clearly shown that someday this house of cards will collapse. The only question remains how and when this will happen.

But, exactly at what point this will take place, John's book is not quite clear. When we observe how that kingdom is experiencing its highest expression then a new series of visions appear, visions all directly related to the last things, but which also leave us with a barrage of other questions.

It starts with a vision of the infinite majesty of the lamb. After all these deplorable depictions of the kingdom of man we urgently need some more information of the world behind the world. "And I looked, and there before me was the Lamb, standing on Mount Zion." Just a short snapshot of indescribable grandeur: the lamb amidst the thousands who belong to him. That short vision for a brief moment interrupts that insanely dark and somber picture of that human busyness.

And right after this we see the first signs of the coming deterioration. The walls start to crumble, and the initial symptoms of decay and fall are visible. But it now looks as if John starts to hesitate. He already hears the rumbling of the approaching storm but it looks as if he isn't yet ready for it. It all is so terribly unsettling, so intensely horrible that he can hardly absorb it. Here, finally, the age-long suppressed truth knocks at the portals of the human heart with loud and ineradicable force. Here, finally, the forever scorned, the nailed-to-the-cross Christ, stands, in his full majesty, before the door of the kingdom of man. This time he cannot be refused entrance, he cannot again be dragged outside Jerusalem's city limits, he cannot again be pushed away as an unwelcome stranger. His knocking at the door becomes louder and more insistent. And that human structure that was built with so much artifice and cunning, that entire building starts to shake.

John sees it all happening. He first starts to outline how he heard the announcement of the approaching judgment. He observes an angel who flies in the center of heaven while carrying the eternal gospel upon him. The content of that eternal gospel is right away described: "Fear God and give him glory, because the hour of his judgment has come." It is not a new message; it is nothing other than what throughout the ages God's prophets have already said. What is new is that now it is not spoken by a human voice, but by an angel who loudly proclaims it over the entire earth. Will he be seen by all the people? Will that man who still holds the reins of the entire world in his hands, will he notice his sparkling appearance? That is difficult to say. What definitely is the aim here is that all these billions of people, then alive, will receive something like an electric shock. For a moment they'll be confronted with the clarion call to wake up from their intoxication and their insanity, gripped as they suddenly are by a growing panic. For a brief moment this jolt will sufficiently electrify them to see that this entire exceptional enterprise of human hubris is doomed to failure. There, suddenly they are forcefully confronted with the knowledge that God is still there, this always-scorned God, this ever-banned-from-view God, this constantly-run-away-from God. "Fear God, and give him glory." Not the senselessness of human idolatry, not a reverently prostrating before human greatness and pride. Only God is great. Only God is worthy to receive our praise and our humble service.

Where does this uneasy-making truth come from, this uncomfortable foreign voice that suddenly soars through these masses? Does it bounce back and forth in the hollow chambers of their own heart? Or does it descend from above, and bury them as under a quickly advancing avalanche? And why is it that they just can't get rid of that voice, that somehow clings to them, that makes them bow their heads now that they hear that word *God*?

Now for the last time, now for the very last time God tells the world, on the point of disintegrating, to stop.

And God's last appeal here is called the gospel. In reality it is nothing else but a warning, a call to action. It is a command to once and for all abandon the notion that humanity is able to erect a society of security and peace. It is a powerful cry to wake up and to turn to God who rules the entire world. It can hardly be called a gospel, it is more an exhortation, and it also is a favor, God's very last sign of leniency. In that age-long dialogue between God and the proud, arrogant humanity, God has the last word. Once more he stands before us, and once more he calls us back from the fateful road we have chosen. That is what John sees first.

Quite concretely this last admonition pointedly becomes a direct call to wrestle oneself free from the tyranny of that despot and the paralyzing influence of the false prophet. God perfectly knows that those who heed the divine call will quickly be dragged to filthy prisons and incarcerated in cruel camps. It would require a very valiant act to now, at the very last moment withdraw from the enchantment of this rudderless world and go and serve Christ. But it is possible. And happy are those who do. "Here is apparent that perseverance of the saints who keep the commands of God and the faith in Jesus Christ." And a sweet melody permeates this saying: "Write: blessed are they who die in the Lord from now on. Yes, says the Spirit, they will rest from their labor, for their deeds will follow them." Yes, there are those who take this step, who display the unbelievable courage to defy the threat of violence and declare themselves for God. The world will totally deprive them of all ease because the defiant authorities will not spare them and will try to physically and painfully punish them.

A new tableau unfolds (Rev 14:14–20). Now all bets are off. John sees how in the heavenly realms everything is made ready for the last battle. On earth for the time being nobody notices this because there the danse macabre of that vain existence continues unabated. But in the heavenly temple the last preparations are being made, hanging as a dark cloud over the world, appearing as a frightening tornado spout that comes perilously close.

Suddenly John's attention is focused on something he has not noticed before (Rev 15:1–4). He sees a sea of glass, mixed with fire and beside the sea are standing those who had been victorious over the beast and his image. For a minute we wonder: victors? The beast certainly has not yet vanquished as on earth his tyranny continues unabated. Only in chapter 19, thus much later, is it described how indeed the beast has been defeated. How then is it possible that we read here about those who have been victorious? Again we should remember that heaven maintains a different timetable than we do. What for us is the future tense has already happened there. What we are still expecting is already a done fact there, because the beast has indeed been conquered. In the heavenly realms his fate has already been sealed, and his fall is history. What later on will happen on earth is nothing else but the aftereffect of what in its deepest sense is already a truth. That's why it is not at all unusual that before the last battle has started the victors are already ready to celebrate at the sea of glass. This time also this sea of glass is a reflection of God's majesty, fully showing his holy being. That this sea is described here as glass mixed with fire is simply to indicate that God's wrath has been kindled and that the end is now near. As yet life on earth continues its relaxed pace, as yet the persecuted, counting in the millions, daily suffer pain and humiliation. As yet the industrial complex keeps on functioning. As yet the flowers bloom, the harvests ripen, and the heavens above the earth seem peaceful, revealing nothing of the bitter battles fought there between the powers of heaven and the powers of hell. But all this is soon to end. There is a spirit of despair in the air, there is something of skittishness affecting all of nature. All human certainties are now under threat and all fundamental facts now appear as founded on fiction. That's what John observes with growing amazement.

In the next scenario (Rev 15:5 through 16:21) the last things are set into motion. The picture John provides us with is again a sad succession of disasters. In several aspects they remind us of what happened in Egypt during the ancient pharaoh's regime, but here they are much more intense and dangerous. They are of cosmic implications as even the sun and the earth are part of all this. Pandemics produce panic in the planet's population, deadly droughts, hellish heat devastates the crops. The culmination of the natural disasters and the pinnacle of pain are caused by an earthquake (16:18). "No earthquake like it has ever occurred since man has been on earth." The seismographs in the capitals shake wildly and record numbers beyond any ever registered. And the houses tumble, the palaces are ruined. No human technological expertise is any help. Nothing can withstand this force of nature: no nuclear bomb has this devastating power. Now an endless series of ever more frightening events roll over the world.

The catastrophes mentioned here extend to the entire cosmos. They affect people everywhere. Earlier we have seen how in the disastrous happenings preceding the last things, two types of distress can be detected. There are calamities that originate from above, that find their source in nature, and there are those that are the result of human action. Here only the first type is mentioned. It is as if the tamed earth, given by God as a gift to humanity as his own domain, is now rebelling, is now rising up against her tormentor. It is as if nature that, for so long, for so many centuries, has faithfully furnished humanity with all its needs, has now become recalcitrant, and full of revenge has thrown itself upon humanity. And this humanity, this so superior human race, with her atomic energy, her mighty medical system, her military prowess, and her entertainment establishment, all of which made her feel so immensely mighty and strong, these same men and women are now in a totally humiliating fashion confronted with the fact that in the final analysis they amount to nothing, that they are a mere rag that is thrown out as useless.

It is apparent that this catastrophe is especially aimed at the heart of the state, the capital, at the government offices. There the epidemic hits the hardest; there the earthquake is experienced as the most extreme. "The great city split into three parts" (verse 19). We can only guess what the meaning is of this great city.

In antiquity an empire was always portrayed around a big city, such as Babylon, Nineveh or Rome. It also seems probable that we must see this great city as the heart of the new kingdom, the center from where this worldwide empire is being governed. So, it is this great city that is hit the most, its office towers and high condo buildings collapse, and its squares become places where the rubble piles up, while the entire governmental structure is ground to dust.

What is again so very interesting here is how the population reacts to all this. Do they become mired in dull despair? Do they flee from the big cities to the wilderness and seek refuge somewhere in the quietness of the countryside? Do they abandon all norms of decency and start fighting each other as wild animals? Does this society, so cleverly constructed, in a few days degenerate in a desperate mass of people, a wildly possessed crowd? Or does the central authority manage to keep order in a time of universal disintegration? Those are the questions that particularly concern us especially when at an earlier series of disasters (when the trumpets sounded) confusion reigned almost beyond control.

But not now. There's not a trace of confusion to be noticed. Of course people are unsure. Of course there also is a good amount of despair. But conversion? No, they cursed God the God of the heavens! Strange, these modern men and women, who had become convinced that the concept *God* did not exist anymore, all these people started to curse. They always had told themselves that they no longer believed in God, that this fairy tale was something they had ridiculed all their lives. They had left the church in droves already long ago and had assured their neighbors that God was dead and that they, in line with the spirit of the age, had nothing to do with him anymore. On the census they had written "no church affiliation," so how was it now possible that suddenly God was back, risen from the dead? How come that these educated people, so up-to-date with everything, with the latest gadgets, who never did need God, now suddenly seem to remember that he exists after all? Was there in the deepest crevices of their mind a secret notion that the meaning of life is that we always are in a conversation with him who made our lives and even guides us? Have they understood this more profoundly than they would admit to themselves and to others? In any case, at this so-critical juncture, now that the flames of defeat leap up high and start to scorch their fragile body frames, now irrepressibly the certainty arises that God is there after all. And these nervous, these out-of-balance persons clench their small fists threatening the Lord of the heavens. They wished they could aim a guided missile and so shoot God from his throne. They would crucify him again if they could, would cast him into the deepest black hole, dead, forever defeated. But all they can do is belch out their powerless rage against him who now so mightily intervenes in this minor league game of human creation and construction.

In the meantime the world of humanity is astir. Humanity gets ready for battle. John relates it in a few tiny flashes. The river Euphrates dries up, opening the way for the kings of the east. The Euphrates is the borderline that separates the Asia Minor culture from the barbarians in the East, the Scythes and the Parthians, whose masses have overrun the old (Western) world. The Euphrates is the last frontier, the last protection against chaos. Now that same Euphrates River has dried up. I imagine that this indicates that the kingdom suddenly has become vulnerable. Apparently there still are nations who have refused to submit to the authority of the tyrant. They never bothered this strongman because they were powerless anyway. But now that the capital has been reduced to rubble, now that universal lawlessness is threatening to overwhelm the realm, now there is a real danger that they will invade the kingdom and destroy it. Again there is a real threat of war and the nation prepares for the worst.

Out of the mouth of the dragon and out of the mouth of the beast and of the false prophet came demons in the form of frogs. This must indicate that now the demonic powers are at full strength. Humanity now removes all holds and goes all out. Nothing can keep them; human cruelty and insanity have no more limits. Now this wounded nation, this tortured tyrant, this world emperor once more unveils his full magnitude and more powerful than ever he unfolds his majesty.

He assembles an army, an innumerably great fighting force. Why? Against whom? Against those hordes who come from afar and came to plunder his territory? Against the recalcitrant heads of the provinces who no longer want to be subjected to the central seat of power? Has the revolution now become a popular uprising? Or is the army assembled against the church, against that poor roaming remainder of religious refugees that has found a hiding place somewhere in the desert? Or is that saber-rattling all for show, nothing but a publicity stunt, only a childish demonstration that the kingdom, in spite of everything, still packs a lot of punch? John here means that in fact this army has been assembled to fight against God. Of course you can't fight against God as you battle a human enemy. But this wild species of humanity who is seeing his ideals go up in smoke, this human being wants to defend himself and he wants to put up a front which is all he still can do. Without him realizing it, this entire display of senseless mobilization expresses an inextinguishable hatred against God. And while the earth quakes, while the cities crumble, here the soldiers assemble, place the pieces of artillery in position, the tank engines roar, the planes are fueled up, the war can start. War it is. War, against whom?

THE FALL OF BABYLON

In veiled, secretive language John continues to tell us how all this is unfolding. The entire eighteenth chapter is devoted to the fall of Babylon.

Babylon! How deeply has been the impression Babylon has made on the ancient people of Israel, that after many centuries the name of this city appears in this prophecy. That ancient Babylon, the city of Nebuchadnezzar, the city where Belshazzar spoke his haughty words, where he received a rude awakening when the Persian armies secretly invaded it during the night. That city is long gone, completely destroyed. Desert sand has covered it all, has crawled into its deserted defenses, and has blanketed the old ruins with a carpet of oblivion. No, the prophecy has nothing to do with that ancient world city. It is clear that John has Rome in mind here, that city vested on the seven hills, the queen of the earth. It is from there, out from the heart of Rome that the military roads branched out to the far corners of the mighty empire. Roman legions penetrated to the very edges of the then known world. From Britain to India's borders, the scepter of the Roman emperors held sway. When John wrote this all, the image of Rome was constantly in his mind. Rome is the city around which the entire empire is arranged as an immensely wide steppe surrounds a high mountain top. And, yes, in the days of John, the emperors in all aspects resembled the signs of the beast. It is undeniable that John thought of Rome. Of course that does not mean that all this ultimately has to do with that city because the word *Rome* here is only a vague indication of the city of the last days that then— that is now!—will function as the core of the world that is to disappear. It serves no purpose to speculate which city is indicated here. (Now with the entire world "urbanized" it simply indicates our contemporary world.)

In the scenario John tells us about, four important entities appear. In the first place there is the beast, the emperor or tyrant or by whatever name he or she goes. This personality is the undisputed ruler of the entire world. This tyrant apparently has a place of residence, that mysterious Babylon, where everything converges. There are the government offices, there is the head office of the CIA or CSIS or whatever name this secret police apparatus possesses: it is the place where money and power rules. Next to the tyrant we see the beast that rises out of the earth, the false prophet or the minister of information or propaganda, the advertising world, perhaps. And in the third place there is the state, the realm, that all-powerful empire spanning the world. Foreign wars are no longer an issue, because outside the boundaries of the empire there are no more forces that can match the power Babylon has. The only threat of fear must come either from God, from above, or from inside.

And that, indeed, is the case. Trouble threatens from within, and that same threat also comes from above. God infects this empire with itself, curses it with insanity. That, in short, is the theme of this amazing chapter. The city of Babylon, situated on seven hills, is pictured here as a woman, a prostitute. It seems that the prophet wants to indicate that this entire world, with all its culture, its science, its perpetual search for progress, and its never-ending dream for future growth and happiness, portrays something typically feminine. Men may dominate world history, men may declare war and govern nations, but the overall image of humanity is foremost feminine. And this world-city, this Babylon, with its constant clamor of human voices, her illuminated squares, her theaters and concert halls, her display of beauty, the world is typically feminine in character.

But John has a deeper meaning here. He has in mind here that this woman belongs to God. She can only find her full peace and safety in God. Humanity as such is not complete, is only an unfinished product. There remains a profound dissatisfaction in it as long as God is left out. We humans have been fashioned for an eternal marriage with God. That's the reason John calls this woman a prostitute, because she has associated herself with other men instead of with God. She has abstained herself from God who was hers and has instead offered herself to an endless playing around, seeking sensual amusement, and showing off her attributes. She has the most noble in her, that being of service to others, radically discarded and scorned. Instead she has prostituted herself for the sake of wealth and for the exterior glory of the world, and also willingly offered herself to everyone who sought her out for carnal pleasures. Cast a last look at that mighty city, surrounded by fortifications and vast airports. That city with her all-seeing radar, spotting whatever is up there in the air, that city with her ever taller buildings, her ever larger warehouses, her ever greater glaring signs. That city belongs to God. She is situated there as an unscrupulous seductress, as a woman who sells herself for a moment of sensual pleasure, who forgets who is her rightful Lord and king. That woman sits somewhere in the desert. Again there is the similarity with that other woman, the one of Revelation 12, the church of Jesus Christ, that woman with the crown of stars, who also flees to the desert, persecuted by the dragon. This woman here, the one who has given herself to every pursuer who approached her, also finds herself in the desert. Apparently the aim here is that this world-city with all her noise and glittering, in essence is just something totally pitiable, is a thoroughly unhappy and dissatisfied creature. The desert will soon bury the city in its finely grained sand, when chaos will cause it to sink away in nothingness.

In vivid colors the vision sees the woman seated upon a scarlet beast. That beast is apparently the same as described in 13:1. It is the beast that emerges from the world's stormy sea, the image of the Antichrist, the great tyrant of the empire. In 13:1 it says that on his heads he carries blasphemous names, but here his entire body is covered with blasphemous names. This means that there is a growing process of dissolution and disintegration. This beast is completely filled with bitter hate against God. On top of that beast the world's capital is mounted. That means that this so mighty world-city owes her glory and power to the tyrant who makes his domicile inside her safe surroundings. Just imagine all the innocent blood shed in that city, in that horrible Babylon! How many of God's true children gave their lives there for their faith in their savior? It is a city of luxury and glamor but also a place of tears and want.

There is something rather different about this city: John mentions it with growing apprehension. Its tyrant, its master, "was and is not and yet shall be." Apparently this is aimed at the same phenomenon that also was mentioned in Revelation 13:3, which indicates that the supreme leader will become mortally wounded and yet will recover. People will one moment think that he has died and then right away he will rise up full alive. First to exist, then not so, and then yet being alive again lends to this beast an aura of romanticism, something striking and fascinating that produces popular appeal. John's aim here is to show that this "wonderful" beast, this world ruler, indeed this Antichrist did do what Jesus so emphatically refused to do, that is bow down for Satan in order to obtain dominion over the earth, that this world ruler, also shows a very remarkable resemblance with Christ himself. To Christ too applies this glorious description: "I am the living one, I have died, and behold, I am alive into all eternity." In the same way, of this tyrant too, it can be said that he was, and is not, and yet shall be. But for him there is only one ending: he is on his way to total ruin. For awhile he may show a remarkable resemblance with him who carried a crown of thorns, who was crucified and who, fully alive, rose on the third day, but he will in one aspect be totally different, and that is that, after rising from the abyss, he, the tyrant, is destined to perish once and for all. It takes precise insight to really detect this and to see the actual issue here, but for those whose name is written in the Book of Life they will not be deceived by this exterior similarity.

There are four major indicators: the world empire, and in the center of that realm the capital, that mighty Babylon with its luxuries and security. In Babylon lives the tyrant, the world ruler, the beast with on his side his prophet. For all practical purposes these four form an integral unity, they are inseparably connected to each other, so much that when one falls the others do too.

Revelation 17:14 has a brief statement: "They will make war against the Lamb, but the Lamb will overcome, because he is the Lord of Lords and the King of Kings, and with him will be his called, chosen and faithful followers." But that is yet something in the future, just a short indication of what is to take place but now is still hidden behind fog and darkness.

The first indication of the coming judgment is described as: "The beast and the ten horns you saw will hate the prostitute. They will bring her to ruin and leave her naked; they will eat her flesh and burn her with fire. For God has put it into their hearts to accomplish his purpose by agreeing to give the beast their power to rule, until God's words are fulfilled." From this quite condensed summary we gain the impression that the situation of the world empire is quite shaky, that it is much more vulnerable than we first suspected. It still looks strong and invincible but apparently there are within the realm unbridgeable contrasts, evident in distrust, deeply ingrained jealousy, anguish, envy, and hate. The beast, the tyrant and his ten horns, his underlings and his governors, they all fear that a revolution is brewing in the capital. They very much suspect that an insurrection is in the offing, that they no longer can rely on the world-city's power. Here and there are signs of resistance. The secret police is actively busy to subdue any signs of rebellion. There are strikes in spite of violent suppression. There are riots. The core of the realm is becoming unsafe. When the tyrant travels through the city in his specially reinforced vehicle, he is surrounded by a small army of policemen because danger lurks everywhere. Before he arrives in his helicopter on his private airport next to the palace, the field is first completely cleared. No longer is it a matter of some easily subdued dissatisfied citizens. No longer is it a few rebels who are quickly apprehended. No, this is becoming serious: there is in Babylon a simmering spark of resistance that in an instant can burst into roaring flames and a full-fledged revolution. There is only one solution, one radical and total cure: a nuclear bomb. For the sake of preserving the realm, the capital must be sacrificed. All these grand buildings and its beautiful squares, all its magnificence has to go. It takes a while before they dare to make that decision, but in the end the world ruler, in consultation with his ten governors, is not afraid to execute this extreme edict. During the night one single plane from a remote airport flies high in the sky over the sleeping city, never to wake again. A bomb is released, slowly a mushroom cloud ensues, and . . . a rebellious Babylon is abolished forever.

When this decision was made in the assembly upon a motion that carried unanimously nobody present there was aware that they just had realized God's intention. None of these governors had even the slightest notion that God had given them this plan. People today too regard themselves as autonomous, acting on their own, and never acknowledge that they are being led. And yet that was the case then and is now. That fatal decision contains something of God's sense of humor over against this proud world, the chuckle that the poet of Psalm 2 already had heard: "The One in heaven laughs, the Lord scoffs at them." Yes, indeed, that happens here. The final judgment is upon the world in the form of natural disasters, earthquakes, pandemics, and so on, all happenings neither human technology nor medical science can prevent. But that is only the start. Matters will become a lot worse. The final judgment over this terrified world will reveal itself in its inevitable self-destruction of the culture. Emperor Nero set his own capital, Rome, on fire. He had no clue what he was doing. He had not the faintest idea that his act foreshadowed the horrible fate that as a sword hangs above all human might and civilization. Humanity, totally estranged from God, that capricious and fickle woman that has her one-night stands with whomever, that has become drunk on her own delusion and impressed by her own grandeur, this same humanity ends herself by means of her own radical self-destruction. She bombs herself into oblivion, destroys what she has built, commits suicide. World history is, indeed, suicide, world history is a leap into the abyss. That is what humanity does without prompting: God does not have a hand in all this.

Or is that the case anyway? Is perhaps that unanimity, is that dire decision a result of divine intervention? Was God present in that chamber and did he chair that meeting? Was there, unrecognized and unwittingly, behind that unbelievable decision, the hidden power of his avenging justice? Is that really God at work? Does this God, who so carefully, throughout the ages preserves his incognito, does this God cause humanity to destroy itself? Or does he allow it to perish through its own insanity? Yes, John sees this quite clearly before him. This judgment erupts from the bottom up. It is pure self-decomposition, pure self-destruction. Humanity causes its own downfall. And still it has no idea that behind all this, behind this foolish thinking, stands God. That same God whom it has scorned, has forgotten, whom it has deserted, fled away from in its desperate anguish, whom it has nailed to the cross in its unrivaled bitterness.

The fall of Babylon appears to be more than a small incident in that grand picture we call world history. Not counting the fact that its fall entails tremendous consequences on the political scene and especially for its economy, the entire world sees it as a sign of what is in store for it in the future. That's the reason why there are enormous reactions everywhere, all over the world. An angel calls out with a mighty voice audible throughout the world while another angel appeals to the church to right away take distance from her fate and leave Babylon and free itself from her embrace.

Then there are the kings of the earth, those who held positions of power, political as well as economic and commercial, and those engaged in the transport of merchandise. They all have done well during the times of extreme prosperity, they have benefited from the luxuries and grown rich and have enjoyed the perks that came with their positions of influence. They observe the carnage and sing a dirge for the bygone benefits.

The Bible itself is not a tragic book. The word *tragedy* always connotes being overtaken by a sort of fate, by something we cannot fight. In that sense the Bible is not tragic because it far too really sees the disturbing matter it calls sin. The world history is not tragic either because fate does not suddenly overwhelm our innocent selves. So what is world history? It certainly is unspeakably sad because it leads inescapably to a disastrous finale. The fall of Babel is not tragic either, because it is the inevitable result of what Babylon represents. That fall had to come because of what constitutes God's holy justice. But these merchants and these politicians and these bankers and the money manipulators, they thought it was tragic. In their monotonous mourning melodies they did not mention the question of responsibility. They did no wonder why this awesome city had to come to such an ignominious end. That question they do not ask. They only sing their litanies on the tragic destruction of so much beauty and so much value.

John gives full play to this tragic song. He gives full coverage to all these lamentations without any comment or interruptions. In a few meaningful words he displays how people experience their fate. They consider this as "fate," perplexed by all these setbacks, they are witless, because this entire event is so very foreign, so utterly flabbergasting. They sing their somber litanies, while standing at these ruins, even though these are products of their own making. They stand there, totally stunned by what they themselves have wrought, muttering dark mourning dirges that sound like rumbling thunder. Standing some distance away they really want to say "these poor people, that miserable Babylon. Woe, woe, o great city, in one instant your doom has come!" Being part of history is being involved in a drama of such great magnitude and so serious, that it makes one dizzy. We people, we experience the actions that are the result of our own decisions as if an avalanche has buried us.

No, John does not interrupt these lamentations. It is tragic, this fall of Babylon. But then, suddenly, rising above all these mourning voices, there is the sound of a song of praise, so overwhelming, that it pierces through the deepest core of all. But who can be so cheerful when seeing the ruins of such greatness, and exclaim such joy? "Rejoice over her, O heaven! Rejoice, saints and apostles and prophets! God has judged her for the way she treated you." That is breathtaking. That is unbelievable. Does John not feel anything of the deep disturbance that has taken place here? Is it not possible for him to stand beside those rulers and those merchants and join them in their songs of sorrow? No, that is not possible for him. No, he is not insensitive, because an insensitive heart could never have described these events in such a touching way. But he is simply not capable of seeing all this as tragic. He understands far too well that what has taken place here is the ultimate outcome of a process that has gone on for centuries, a process of stubborn refusal to follow the divine directions, a process of unstrained surrender to superficiality and senselessness, a process of a never-ending escape from God and aversion to him. In Babylon so much blood has been shed, starting with Abel and ending with the blood of the last witnesses. That this blood was shed, is in itself not the worst, but that these hands of these executioners, these prisons, the horrible torture, that all this is the result of the determined refusal to listen to God's voice, that most certainly is the worst thing imaginable. By harming these holy men and prophets Babylon has repeatedly, in Nineveh, and in Babylon itself, but also in Rome and Jerusalem, in Baghdad and Damascus, stretched out her throttling hands to God himself, in a willful effort to silence God's voice. No, that is no longer a tragedy, this fall of Babylon. It is shocking, it is terrible and overwhelming, it calls for tears, both tears of dismay and tears of jubilation. Thank God that happens! Thank God that God exists and that, at last, he will triumph.

That's why this episode involving the bitter fall of Babylon ends in a hymn, so exceedingly beautiful, so marvelously moving, so clearly comforting that every trace of anguish is silenced: "Hallelujah! Salvation and glory and power belong to our God, for true and just are his judgments. He has condemned the great prostitute who corrupted the earth by her adulteries. He has avenged on her the blood of his servants." (Rev 19:1–2) There is no cruelty in there, no raw delight in the pain of others. It does contain cutting irony however. Babylon, Rome, Washington, or whatever the name of the city, they all have pretended that they have decided the world's well-being. But the large multitude in heaven says: Salvation is from God. Babylon always has claimed that its beauty, its science, the latest technical devices, its wealth belonged to her forever and ever, a luxury never to cease. But the multitude in the background says: the glory belongs to God. Babylon always has been convinced that it ruled the world, that it was the leading force in the world. The multitude on the stage exclaims triumphantly: all power belongs to God! All pretense is gone; Babylon's flush of victory has vanished.

That's why beyond this song of praise the hymn of the wedding of the Lamb resounds. "Hallelujah! For our Lord God Almighty reigns. Let us rejoice and be glad and give him glory! For the wedding of the Lamb has come and his bride has made herself ready." (Rev 19:6–8) God has accepted the kingship! Was there a time when this was not the case? No, but he has for many centuries kept this secret as something humanity was not able to see. It looked as if humanity was all powerful while God always the weakest. Everyone and his uncle could use the pages of the Bible as filler and be none the worse for it. God always was the lesser, you could push him and he would tip over. That's how it looked in this world. It certainly seems that the devil, this prince of the world, was the mightiest. He would roar and nobody dared to oppose him. He could incite the rulers of the world to persecute the church and to push them from the political forum and make then find refuge in the catacombs. All this was possible in this besotted world. It seems that God—if he existed at all—as a frightened old man somewhere far away looked on, to watch how the world pushed his people around. But all that was pure fabrication and total hallucination. Reality was totally different. God's voice was quite noticeable in the fall of world powers, in the total absence of adequate response and the ensuing chaos, in the misery and anxiety that in dense formations flew over this world as fearsome phantoms. God was present there in the earthquakes and natural disasters, laughing out loud at all technological tricks. God was present when those hubristic humans dug their own graves, but never anybody saw his face. Till the very end he was the grand mystery, the great incognito, the traveler disguised as the poor. And when he entered the world in Jesus Christ, he first emptied himself and took on the form of a servant, and was bedded in a manger, because that's exactly how he wanted it to be. Only on Easter morning the victory cry came, heard only in a small circle: it was not yet broadcast over the world. It remained a secret that yet has to be preached even though there was not an iota of evidence that God was king after all. That phrase *after all* only added to the confusion and enhanced its enigmatic character.

But now matters change, because God has accepted his royal status, no ifs, ands, and buts anymore. Now it is about to happen, what the prophets of the Old Testament have so greatly longed for. Now the heavens will open up and God will appear because the wedding of the lamb has come and his bride—his woman—has readied herself. There is that woman again. Not the prostitute who has her throne on the waters, but that other woman, the woman adorned with a crown of stars. That woman, the church of God, will at last experience the great encounter with the bridegroom, with him who rescued her.

THE EDGE OF THE HISTORY OF THE WORLD

That means the wedding is on. God is coming. Of course he was already there in the scenarios that have played out earlier, but there he was incognito, in disguise. There were angels who blew trumpets or who threw scales down to earth, and there were the eclipses of the sun, the epidemic disasters, and those earthquakes. People experienced all this but they never spotted the angel, never knew what was really behind all this. Then there is that world-dominating urban complex, now totally leveled in an instant. That was perhaps the worst event of all, but the people had not the faintest notion that all this had something to do with God. They did boast of what all they had done, of what their technical prowess could produce. But God never entered the picture. His footsteps throughout the history of the world went unmarked.

But now, at last, the fog retreats. Now appears the rider on a white horse, the victorious Christ. No longer does he carry a bow and arrow to gather his people to his church from all parts of the earth. He no longer comes under the guise of apostles or missionaries or under whatever name. No, he comes in person, visible, himself, in the form of terrifying majesty. His eyes flame flashes of fire and on his head are numerous crowns. And endless heavenly armies follow him. This is no longer history: here we are at the very edge of world history. Here we are at the finish line of human thought and action. Here the great victor steps up to the front. "Then I saw the beast and the kings of the earth and their armies gathered together to make war against the rider on the horse and his armies. But the beast was captured and with him the false prophets who had performed the miraculous signs on his behalf. They were thrown alive into the fiery lake of burning sulfur."

It does not behoove to add to this. Here all human imagination ceases. Here we are confronted with matters that go far beyond our thoughts and imagination. The history of the world ends in a collision with God, and is totally toppled by him who has been crucified. That fall of Babylon is much more than an accidental incident, a tragic moment from the capricious playing field of history. That fall is a symptom of something far bigger: it is the trumpet call that heralds the last event. Because we humans have started this, because we humans have turned our cruel hands on ourselves, and on all that we have wrought, we have brought this final verdict on our own heads. No longer can we surrender to the game of building our air castles, our own fantasies, and give full play to the demons of our own hubris, no, now we stand face to face before God. Now all our subterfuges and smart-alecky stuff have evaporated as useless fumes, and now only confronts us the flame of the wrath of him against we have fought throughout all ages.

That's all we dare to say about this final happening. Here the great unknown that has made the world history such a bitter and cruel game disappears, here the enchantment gives way, the blindfolds disappear, the fog dissipates. The last word of the world history is not *humanity* but it is that terrible, dreadful word *God*. Here time melts away in the embrace of eternity.

CHAPTER SEVEN

What Is Behind the End
(Revelation 20 and 21)

THE QUESTION OF THE 1000-YEAR KINGDOM

At the conclusion of the nineteenth chapter of the Revelation of John we gather the impression that the great happening we call world history is a thing of the past. The cruel world ruler and his prophet have been destroyed by Christ himself and his armies. All that is now past tense. We found ourselves at the edge of world history with our faces turned to the ocean of eternity.

And yet we are still faced with a short account of a few verses that deal with the binding of Satan during a period of a thousand years and how those who in their persecution have remained loyal to the savior will rule as kings together with Christ. Suddenly the scene changes again and, in a few sober words, it is said that after a thousand years Satan will be freed and again be allowed to deceive the nations. A fierce war will ensue between the Satan and the saints, a struggle that will end with a glorious victory by Christ. And that victory heralds the great judgment.

For many centuries people have pondered over these verses of this twentieth chapter and many have tried to solve the mysteries that they pose. Does the seer of Patmos want to reassure us that after the fall of Babylon and after the victory of the rider on the white horse a new period would commence, a sort of peaceable kingdom on earth where the saints will rule?

And must we expect that after this millennium of peace once more a re-awakening of satanic power will emerge? In other words: do these verses of this twentieth chapter really mean that the great triumph, so gloriously depicted in the nineteenth chapter, was only a preliminary one, only an interlude, while the final victory still had to come? Those are the questions we all wonder about when we carefully read this passage.

There are several factors that indicate that what is presented us in this chapter can hardly constitute signs that follow the fall of the rule of the Antichrist. In the first place the events so vividly shown in the nineteenth chapter are of such a definite nature that it is difficult to imagine that as yet an entirely new phase of world history is to follow. In the second place the first verses of this chapter give the impression that what is related there is of a total different order. There is talk about the souls of martyrs who are resurrected and, together with Christ, are allowed to rule. The thrones on which they are seated together with others who are saved are not earthly thrones but are far more described as thrones which have been made ready in heaven. That resurrection appears to me not to be aimed at a return to the earth but seems to refer to being crowned with honor and glory in the company of Christ in heaven. My reading of this passage gives me the impression that what is illustrated here in the first part of this twentieth chapter does not mean to be a happening that will take place after the return of Christ but that it rather contains in a new and grand vision of the entire struggle that has been described in the previous chapters. That means that once more everything that has taken place in the past is, in a very condensed way, repeated for us. For the last time we can go back to review that grand panorama involving that bitter fight against Satan who, throughout the ages has undermined the work of Jesus Christ and has been a constant threat for the church. So, this 1000-year period is not something new, but simply a repeat of the same happening that has been shown us before, but now in a new form and interpreted in a different manner.

Even though there is much in this chapter that remains obscure for us, this interpretation offers the most scriptural explanation. Nowhere does the Bible speak of two returns of Christ, and nowhere else has the Bible ever referred to a 1000 years of peace that is supposed to occur between these two returns, and this chapter, even though it has definite mysterious passages, does not point into that direction.

That's all we dare to comment here. It seems to me that we do well when referring to this passage to do so only in very provisional and moderate terms. It is simply impossible to pinpoint a period when such a 1000-year kingdom would have taken place in the church of Christ, when it would have started and when it would have ended. There are here numerous mysteries for which we at this time have no clear answers. An acceptable answer for all these questions welling up in us is not yet available and it seems to me that the best we can do is acknowledge that in all reverence. The main thing is that also in this so mysterious part, we must clearly remember that the path of the Christian church is one full of dark passages but that the great victory has, from its very start, been totally assured. At some time the Satan, against we often so struggle without clear results, will be crushed under our feet through the God of peace in Jesus Christ (Rom 16:20). That is the tiding of great joy that for us here too is such an outspoken assurance.

THE FINAL FINISH

When all this has taken place then high above this earth rises the throne of him for whose face earth and heaven flee. Then the books are opened, the volumes that contain the biographies of each person, depicting in minute details their deepest motives and penetrating into the heart's furthest secrets. No coercion will be needed to keep everybody in check. In complete submission every person who ever lived will stride along the ultimate line of separation, knowing exactly on which side to stand, sensing immediately what they have been and what they are. With a raw cry of realization there will be more than a few who have always seen themselves as pious and good and well-behaved and decent and honest and pure, who suddenly discover their true nature as godforsaken rebels, who basically have always pursued their own self interests. And also in wonderful delight many who ashamed and with a humble heart approach the throne hear the glad news: "I have been hungry and you have fed me." Many who have never seen themselves in their true state will be exposed. Also the life's secret of the many who have never understood their own nature will be revealed. Now at last everything will be what they are; now at last all false show is dissolved in the crystal-bright light of the face of God.

"And they were judged according to what they had done." Yes, according to what they had done, according to their works. Also according to that one work that is not our work, but that has been given to us in the faith of Christ and so has become our work, that incomparable and imperishable work of him who has died for our sins. Because in his death we too have died and in his resurrection the door of life is opened for us too. We won't have to say much on that day: it won't be necessary to present our résumé; we need not show in our curriculum vitae what we have done for (good) work. The only work that will count as our works, the only work that is valid, is our holding tight to the cross of him who has born our guilt before God.

From there the way is open to life eternal, to the immeasurable secret that God will be all and in all.

In the end the book of the Revelation of John runs resonantly into a restful rhythm. It ripples leisurely into an oasis of unfathomable peace. It is as if John, the great seer, for a moment looks back to that long, long road the people of God traversed as of times immemorial. Before his eyes flash all these scenes, but now in the light of what is to come.

His thoughts go to Jerusalem, that ancient holy city. How the children of Israel so enthusiastically ascended its hills and how they shouted out, "Our feet are within your gates, O Jerusalem!" But what is at hand now is different: this is going up to the true, the eternal Jerusalem that has descended from heaven. Here everything is different, here is shalom, here all thirst is quenched, all hunger stilled. Here everything imaginable is a combination of beauty and majesty. The walls no longer hem in, they no longer oppress, they now only exude quietness and security. The gates no longer signal danger, are no longer a sign of outside threat, because now they are guarded by angels. They no longer offer an invitation, a means to break out, and a way to escape from the face of God, no, now to be within the shelter of this eternal Jerusalem means that nobody will ever desire to leave this place of refuge. For a moment John's thoughts go back to the temple. He sees it clearly before him as it had been situated, high, glittering on Mount Zion. How elated were the pious pilgrims throughout the ages to go up there, how they longingly in song expressed their desire for the courts of the Lord. "As a deer pants for the streams of water, so my soul pants for you, O Lord! When can I go and meet with God?" That's how they sang, these poets of long, long ago. When they saw the temple then they had a burning desire to enter the courts of the Lord. All that is now history. At the time the temple was needed, but it now has accomplished its task as the foreshadowing of what was to come. Now all of that is no longer needed. The great, true temple was demolished and was rebuilt in three days. Christ is risen. And in him and on him as the utmost cornerstone God has built a new temple, a temple that mysteriously throughout the ages has been molded, is now the holy and chosen nation of God, assembled here in this Jerusalem. No, no more temple is needed here, because this complete city, this entire earth, is one mighty temple, a mighty holy of holies. Or rather, the Lord God here is the temple and the lamb.

Then again John's thoughts wander to something else again. He remembers how many years ago he together with Jesus, James, Peter, and Andrew were sitting on the Mount of Olives and had looked over the city of Jerusalem, above which the rays of the dying day were just visible. Jesus then had told them some frightening facts regarding the approaching fall of Jerusalem, matters which for the most part had taken place. While Jesus spoke the sky above the city has become quite dark so that only the contours of the big buildings were still visible. That prophecy has made a deep impression on John: Jerusalem that slowly disappeared into the night whose demise was approaching fast. And then suddenly it dawns on him that this can never happen in this new, true Jerusalem. "The city does not need the sun or the moon to shine on it, for the glory of the Lord gives it light and the Lamb is it light." From that city a bright light radiates that far, infinitely far flashes out brilliantly so that the entire world is full of its splendor.

Suddenly John hears the trampling of horses, approaching armies, soldiers coming from other countries and lay siege to Jerusalem. In this same way in times of old the Assyrians came under Zerubbabel and later the Babylonians. They smashed down the gates and plundered the city and destroyed all these holy buildings. And now, only a little while ago the Romans destroyed Jerusalem. They burned down its palaces, they demolished all these temple buildings and carried away all these precious temple treasures as their booty, the golden plates and goblins and lampstands. These soldiers carried all these valuable treasures away as their rightful possessions to barter them or adorn their own houses and cities. Jerusalem: how often have you been ransacked! You've repeatedly been the prey when foreign forces cast their greedy eyes on you. But now John knows that all this will never be repeated again. No more stamping horse hooves will approach the city walls, never again will eager riders come from afar to plunder her treasures. The exact opposite will happen: "The kings of the earth will bring their glory and honor to her." They will come on their own accord, the princes of the people, with the most precious they have wrought or the most imaginative that have entered their brains to offer it to him who is the light of all light, and from whom and through whom and with whom all things are.

Again another image flashes through John's thoughts. In earlier times kings and artists brought their treasures from afar to Jerusalem, but these often were also sources of terrible temptation. Idols they brought into the city, they carried foreign altars from far away, honoring different gods. They imported their alluring god-deviating customs, carried to them God-dishonoring practices, and the inhabitants of the old Jerusalem so often openly embraced them.

But here and now, in this new Jerusalem, none of these dangers are a cause for fear. The nations of the earth would still bring their honor and glory but "in her nothing impure will enter and nobody who does what is shameful or deceitful." Yes, all that is gone forever. Gone is the ever-present temptation, the extorting enchantment of paganism, the enticement of foreign gods. That nightmare is now gone, forever. In this New Jerusalem this is no longer possible. Here the eye is fixed no longer on what detracts from God, here the ear no longer hears the sounds that cause sinful thoughts. Here only are present those whose names are written in the Book of Life, in the book of the Lamb.

Strange, John's thoughts go back, far back, to where the cradle of humanity had stood, there where once a garden had been, full of all sorts of trees, a garden surrounded on all sides by the river of life. And somewhere in its center stood the tree of life, full of promise and full of holy certainty. The humans, formed from the earth, had sinned, had trespassed the law of their creator. Into that garden penetrated evil and lie, and the poison of that lie most certainly had its devastating effect. This caused the human to be driven out; those who wanted to be like God were chased away from the tree of life, and the cherubim with the flaming swords had closed off the entrance there. And from that moment humanity had become an exile, a lonely wanderer, who nowhere and never could really find perfect tranquility because, in spite of all riches and accomplishments, he would always carry a feeling of dissatisfaction and dispossession. They were and remained the harassed, the restless, the pilgrims who never knew where their pilgrimage would bring them. All that is like a permanent secret hidden behind this frightening world history, and every event in this world history must be viewed in that light and from that perspective.

But, again, all this is now past, never to happen again. That one human being, Christ, had broken that curse. He took upon himself the death that afflicted humanity. He had been mortally wounded by that flaming sword, but he is risen from the dead and has taken along in his triumphant act all those who belong to him. And when John's thoughts turn to that event then it seems that the centuries contract and he again is there on the place where the pilgrimage had its starting point. But now the cherubim, these angels with their flaming swords are gone. He hears the murmuring of the water of life that feeds the garden. That life-bringing water streams forth from the throne of God and of the Lamb. Just as the brook Siloam streamed from the temple mount, just as Ezekiel in his mighty vision saw the river originating in the temple itself, so John sees here the river of the water of life spring forth from the throne of God and the Lamb. Yes, the Lamb also. World history has not been a dream, yes, Calvary has been a reality, yes, Christ has gone through death, yes, all these horrible matters have taken place, and even here, in this new paradise, these events are visible. But their terrifying effects are gone, the anguish is vanished, the threat has disappeared. Here the Lamb is no longer the ridiculed target, the butt of all teasers, but he is the Lamb, the Lord of lords and the king of kings. And from the thrones of

God and the Lamb streams the never-ending stream of the highest good worthy of only to be called the essence of life for "this is eternal life: that they may know you, the only true God and Jesus Christ, whom you have sent" (John 17:3).

Here's where the tree of life grows. No, not just a single tree, but on both sides of the river, everywhere grows that foliage of life, the "arbor vitae" that bears fruit twelve times for year, and the leaves of the trees are for the healing of the nations.

The more John meditates on all this, the more he understands that only here all factors in life are fully coming into their own. That tree of life in the old paradise was only a foreshadowing of what is being found here. Here all those realities of former ages are finally fully flourishing; here they become what they essentially are. This is the true paradise and here is the true water of life. This is the eternal Canaan, the land of God's promise, of which the old Canaan was only a faint reflection. This is the true Jerusalem, the city with the true foundations, and of this Jerusalem the old Jerusalem was merely a very imperfect replica. This is the true temple and the entire world now becomes one tremendous temple of God. This also is the true holy of holies, the holiness of the saints that absorbs everything, that encompasses everything, that comprises everything. Here there is nothing that is not holy, nothing that is profane, nothing that is common, nothing that is ordinary, nothing that is secular. Here every gesture, every word, every deed, here all music, all science, here all of life and thought is part of the harmony of the kingdom of God, because here God is all and in all. All these innumerably many encounters the church has experienced in her long and arduous road through all of history that were signs of encouragement, something to hold on to, they are now, seen from here, mere shadows, mere symbols, more passing indications of what at one time will become reality. Every word gets only here its deepest meaning. The words *rest* and *peace*, the word *salvation*, in ages past only faint indications, only conjectures, here they become deep and unshakeable realities. This is the first true Sabbath, the crown of all days, the day of all days. Here all differentiations, all nuances, flow naturally into the eternal, unfathomable kingdom of God. Here everything that is and that happens and that will happen is included into the hymn of praise of ecstasy before the face of God. The first things have passed, our feet are standing in your gates, o eternal holy Jerusalem!

CHAPTER EIGHT

On and On the Ages Roll

IMAGE AND COUNTERIMAGE

We now have come to the end of our journey through the book of Revelation. We've not dealt with every detail, haven't solved every puzzle. But perhaps we provided enough of a survey to now at the finish line draw a few conclusions. And, based on that, we can better understand the message this wonderful book gives us for our day and age.

The first thing that strikes us, now that we can look back to what we have developed, is that this book is strongly dominated by the contrast of image and counterimage. Apparently John all the time sees images appear, and opposite them, counterimages. The latter closely resemble the former, but they are in essence in every respect totally different. We have, in our examination, already dealt with some of these images and counterimages, and, now that we are at the finish line, they are important enough to mention them again separately.

They are the following:

The woman	-	The prostitute
The Lamb	-	The beast arising from the sea
The two witnesses	-	The false prophet
Jerusalem	-	Babylon

As soon as we visualize these images, we right away feel their importance and sense the ideas connected to them.

First we see the contrast between the woman and that other woman who, as a prostitute, sits on a throne and rules the waters. We started our investigation with that first woman, the woman who is clothed with the sun, has the moon under her feet, and a crown of twelve stars on her head. It soon became clear that this woman is none other than the church of all ages, both of the old and new covenant. It is apparent that she stands in the heart of the universe and everything in the universe is concerned with her fate. All powers that dominate human life on earth, the sun coming up and going down, the moon with its changing phases, the stars in their courses, they all are subject to that woman. She derives this magnitude and power not from herself, but from the child that she bore and that has been fetched away to God and his throne. Actually it is not the woman that is important—it's all about the child. Indeed, honoring the woman means honoring the child. So, of this woman we saw that, in spite of her magnificence and majesty, she as one being driven, has to flee to the desert, persecuted by the dragon who tries his utmost to destroy her "knowing that his time is short." There's something mysterious about the woman, because she is not what she is. She comes through as insignificant in the earthly sphere, threatened, in great danger, weak, defenseless, and that's also mostly the way she feels. She's often dead-scared for the world around her, seeks compromises with the pagan world, acts like the Nicolaitans, becomes discouraged, worships as a mere habit, slinks away in lukewarmness, and loses all color in her religious life. Sardis and Laodicea are outspoken examples of the dangers which daily surround this woman. And yet this woman is at the center of it all, but, perhaps, she does not realize this. As a helpless child she grabs hold of every straw that might offer her some support. And there she is, hidden somewhere in the desert: even though she is the source to which all other things are subject.

And next to her, or rather opposite her, there is that other woman, the prostitute. She is so totally different! She has a golden vessel in her hand and is clothed in scarlet and purple, richly adorned with gold, precious stones and pearls. That woman is Babylon, and she is only now mentioned for the first time. But this woman is the symbol of all of humanity, now totally estranged from God, from days of old till now, and that's why she merits mention here. This woman indeed possesses authority and, what is remarkable, she also enjoys the goodwill, the appreciation of the rulers, of the captains of industry and commerce. She has political influence and also has a great impact on economic life. And, on top of that, on the cultural scene also she is of the highest importance. Through her the arts flourish, through her architecture is inspired to reach the pinnacle of prestige, and she also influences science so that it too reaches heights never before imagined. So what has been said about her is definitely not all negative. Yet almost everything about her is despicable and abhorrent. The reason for this is because she has frittered away the secret of her being, her femininity, her intimate connection to another, in this case to God, because she surrendered herself to outer glory, succumbed to the greed for power, to the accumulation of treasures, and to sensual passions. She was woman, exactly like the first woman, but she failed to find her destination, she has not remained loyal to her Lord and has forsaken her femininity, her "being a woman."

It is striking that she too goes through a desert period. In spite of all her glory and power, she is in the deepest sense a poor beggar, a thoroughly unhappy and dissatisfied human specimen, who is always in need of something and never finds satisfaction; she always has high aims and never reaches them. In her greedy eyes there always is a remnant of residual sorrow, and in her lascivious looks there always is a trace of difficult-to-disguise doubt.

So there are these two women, both in the desert. The one with her golden vessel and royal attire, and the other pushed away, hunted, unsure of herself, with an unquenchable longing for that day on which finally the glory of the Lord will surround her from everywhere.

The second contrast which dominates this total image is that of the Lamb on the one side and the beast that arises from the sea on the other. Actually this contrast is not entirely correct because the Lamb does not appear as such on the earthly plane. He was there in times long ago when he voiceless was led to slaughter. But now, after the Easter morning, the Lamb is no longer visible in this secular sphere. When it does appear then it is in a different form, as a rider on a white horse who, with a bow and arrow, traverses the globe, or as a different rider on a white horse, ready for battle. But as a Lamb it does not appear anymore in this world. And yet everything is ruled by the Lamb. It is the Lamb who breaks the seals of the Book that brings the world to its end. And that Lamb is also present at the end, in that new world where the never-ending stream of life flows from the throne of that Lamb.

The great opponent of the Lamb is also not the beast but the dragon, disguised as the beast. But that dragon also as a rule does not appear on the earth in visible form. He did do that when he brought the Son of Man to a high mountain and showed him all the earth's kingdoms. But ever since his infamous defeat in the heavenly realms he disguises himself as the creepy beast that emerges from the inhabited world.

That beast has some very remarkable features. We already saw that its most outstanding trait is its similarity with the Lamb. It too has suffered a deadly wound; it too has seemingly been destroyed and also has been resurrected as it were, from the dead. In that sense it too has known its Easter morning. In all these matters it has a remarkable similarity with the Lamb. The difference is that by the Lamb it is a threefold event: who lives, who has been dead, and behold, who lives into all eternity. With the beast it is a fourfold matter: it was, and is not, and will rise from the depth, and then perishes. After his Easter morning his ruination is assured. The beast does carry the signs of the Lamb but in essence they are totally different.

That beast appears to be a human, a very superior human. He manages for the very first time in human history to unite all nations under his scepter. He is more powerful than any king or emperor ever has been. He knows no bounds and does the most marvelous things. He is not just an ordinary human being, no, he is far more than that. There is something mysterious about that beast, because he has an aura of being supernatural. He is fortunate in all his undertakings, so much so that it is simply astounding. What he undertakes always seems to succeed. He apparently has gifts that go far beyond those of an average human being. No wonder he is feared beyond anybody who has ever existed, and also highly regarded and honored more than anybody ever. A mighty war strategist he is, a great politician, a clever organizer, a famous economist. He knows how to unite all the dispersed parts of the world into one effective whole, he rearranges a totally disorganized societal life so that it becomes a viable and effective unity. He is implacably severe when his will is thwarted, when his intentions are sabotaged. He knows how to hurt his opponents through economic boycott, by banning them from societal life, and not allowing them to buy or sell. And, when they persist in their opposition, they are "taken out of circulation" as the euphemistic term has it, which means that they are dispatched to a terrible labor camp where they will undergo a reeducation. That's how the beast works. He is both the great enemy and also the imitator of the Lamb. In the city of the Lamb nothing may enter that does not fit, nothing unclean, nobody who lies or cheats. In the city of the beast nobody may enter who is unwilling to totally be committed to way of the beast to the very end.

In the third contrast we see the two witnesses and the false prophet facing each other. The two witnesses are powerful personalities, who fearlessly proclaim their important and prophetic words in the midst of a degenerated environment. These are two persons who are able do marvelous deeds, who can rule over nature as none before them were able to do, who combined their inflammatory words with mighty acts. When their time has come God will allow them to be killed by the beast. Yes, they too will be brought low and their blood will be shed. But after three and a half days God will call them back from the land of the dead and God will pull them out from this world that is destined to perish and bring them before his throne.

And then there is the false prophet. This prophet has a much easier time than the two witnesses have had. He can point to the beast, the tyrant, the conqueror of the world and its ruler. He can point to concrete events, while these two witnesses must speak about an invisible Christ whose throne is in the heavens. This prophet can point people to a living and visible world ruler, who day in day out performs astonishing acts. The two witnesses must appeal to faith, to trust, while this prophet can appeal to submission to the man who exercises power here and now. That false prophet is also an exceedingly powerful person. He orders an image to be made, and manages to install in the image a spirit with the power to speak. His intention is to score one over the miracle of the two witnesses, who had risen from the dead, by doing something even more unbelievable in making a dumb, factory-made image come to life as a human being. Just as the magicians at Pharaoh's court overtrumped all the miracles Moses performed by doing their own displays of power, so this prophet too can best that miracle of miracles, the resurrection of the dead. In addition he also is quite cunning, a sly and a powerful speaker, and a clever debater. He knows exactly how to choose the right methods to shut up every voice of resistance. So there he is, standing before us as the indispensable right-hand man of the world-tyrant, his manager, his minister of propaganda, and the one to implement his ideology. Whatever the beast ordains he knows how to translate into the official policy of this mighty system in the form of a world vision and philosophy. He makes sense of and provides background for the ordinances of the ruler, and through his mesmerizing words he neatly fits everything into the framework of a salvation theology of universal extent.

Then there is the fourth contrast: Jerusalem and Babylon. That's the culmination of the book of the Revelation of John. Babylon, the city, the center of world culture. In her all threads converge, from there all modern life is pushed to the farthest nook and cradle of the world. There are the major media, all the news sources, from there the voice and image of the false prophet is broadcast all over the world. There are the stock markets, the central banks, there the economic policies of the world are formulated and implemented, there the world-class universities are located and the think tanks. From that Babylon humanity is fed a daily stream of new ideas and new slogans. That Babylon personifies the entire secular and disoriented human culture. There can be found urban paganism, people who only live by sensational stimuli and sensual self-gratifications. There are found the spiritually dead masses with blunted brains killed by oversaturation of incessant advertising and mind-killing entertainment, become unable to form an opinion because every hour of every day they are overwhelmed by contrary opinions. There are found the cunning trickster, the fast-talking salesman, the coquette young woman, the vote-buying politician, the Bible-clenching cleric, and whoever. There, in Babylon, foams and sings and complains and jubilates modern life in all its sharp contrasts. There the drunkard's grim laugh reverberates, there the tens of thousands rock and roll as maniacs, there the hundreds of thousands seek refuge from hunger and war and drought and civil strife, there are gunshots and mass murders. In Babylon there is anguish, unspeakable pain, there is terrible loneliness, there is bitterness, hate, doubt, passionate desire, burning ambition, despicable degeneration, and an indomitable deathly desire that craves for the ultimate depravity. That is a picture of Babylon, wonderfully beautiful, engaging, romantic, full of breathtaking entertainment, but also utterly miserable and disoriented.

In the book of Revelation, Jerusalem rises up far above Babylon. It is impossible to picture; no image is adequate. All that John writes is symbolic, is a faint attempt to verbalize the unspeakable. Jerusalem stands for inclusivity, safety, purity, peace, light. As soon as we ponder these matters, the images become blurred. We simply cannot imagine life in Jerusalem. We simply cannot say anything worthwhile about life there. For this Jerusalem there is only one word, one thought, one phrase: God will be all and in all, God will be the temple and the light, the joy and the power, the rest and the meaning of all existence. There will be nuances, but no tensions, there will be differences, but no hostility. The word *I* will not disappear but it will be spelled differently because God shall my small, human "I" illuminate and fill with his holy presence. And everything, creation with all its possibilities, the human race with all its gifts and talents, everything will be included in that indescribable and soul-jubilating harmony of the eternal kingdom of God.

EVERYTHING BECOMES WHAT IT IS

Now that we have seen a brief flash of the images and counterimages which play such an important role in the book of Revelation, now we can approach what can be seen as the heart of this book, its dominating theme. This can be captured in one phrase: everything becomes what it is. That's what it is all about, that is the meaning of all happenings and in particular of this final phase.

That simply means that we now live in a masked world, a world in disguise. Matters are not what they are, are different from what they are in fact. That is the secret that this world so carefully wants to conceal.

The Satan, that immense moving power behind the world's happenings, holds humanity in the clutches of the fateful illusion that God is dead matter, something stale situated in the past, a self-satisfied sugar uncle, far beyond being relevant. He has sold humanity on the notion that men and women everywhere are now fully in charge. That same Satan, that invincible enemy, the creator of the grand world illusion, this contemptible conjurer and mass murderer, has, in fact, been defeated a long time ago. He has been thrown out of heaven as one totally crushed, he is moribund, flung down into defeat. And yet he continues to sound like a victor, and continues to daily gain immense victories. He acts totally different from what he in reality is: this is a creature, exiled from heaven, the banned one, who carries his death sentence written on his forehead.

The woman, the church, she, in reality, is the queen of heaven. She carries the crown of stars on her head and the universe is reverently arranged around her, anxiously awaiting her glorification. But in the rough and tumble semblance of world history, she is the persecuted, time and again hoodwinked by evil promptings, the slow-moving, spineless, weak, threatened, tempted, stumbling one. She too is not what she is, her appearance is totally different than the way God sees her. That's why she goes her pilgrim way through the ages, sighing and stumbling. And often she no longer has a true recollection of what she really is. She imagines she is a beggar, while, in fact, she is immensely rich. She dreams she has been chased into the desert, while actually she stands at the entrance to God's eternal palace. She feels forlorn and ill, while angels are ready anytime to serve her. She thinks that she always is in the lesser, the weaker over against the booming powers of this world, while in reality she is even more than a conqueror through him who has loved her. She walks with head bowed down, while in reality the crown of life eternal already adorns her head. She is different, totally different than she herself thinks she is. She is different, totally different than what the world around her thinks she is. She stands in the heart of the universe and in the center of history, but she feels that she is poverty-stricken, discarded as useless, without value, adrift on the waves of history.

The beast, that horrible creature that will dominate the last phase of human history, that world-tyrant or world-ruler, in reality he is nothing. He is completely hollow and powerless. All his power is nothing more than a soap bubble, a piece of pumped-up psychosis. One little needle stab and it collapses. His authority is based on what may seem gigantic pillars of cruelty, devilish dexterity, bewitchment, relentless execution of a cleverly devised system, but each of these pillars hangs in a vacuum. There is no solid rocky ground on which this palace can rest. Solid ground is only the eternal strength and infallible word of God, and his authority. But that cleverly devised system of the Antichrist is in its deepest essence a pseudo-picture that has no real viability. But in the meantime we have to deal with it, and people by the millions are seduced by it to the point of ecstasy. In the meantime these prisons are gruesome realities where the rattling last breath of the martyrs is drowned out by the cruel curses and joyless jokes of cowardly brutes.

And Babylon, the glorious Babylon, with its infinite charm, it basically presents a pathetic picture. With it insistent advertising, with its tinkering and peddling, with its visual effects, it may entice the naïve, the easily fooled, who fail to see that Babylon is an empty shell, "who was and is not," the way John described this world-tyrant. It simply cannot endure because it is not vested in God. Outside God nothing is safe, outside God everything, however beautiful it may seem and however great it may appear, in essence is nothing other than vanity.

No, matters are not what they are. The one crowned with thorns is not the panting, powerless loser in the pantomime of the planetary history, and the "prince of the world," and "the ruler of the kingdom of the air," as Paul calls him (Eph 2:2), the one who "blinds the senses," he is not the potentate of all potentates, who is seated on the throne of the universe. In the final analysis he is nothing more than the doomed, the defeated, and, at this point, the almost demolished one under the feet of those who believe in Jesus Christ. What we call world history is one tremendous masquerade where each single item carries a disguise, where everything is different than it seems. But in time this entire masquerade will end and every mask will be removed. That is the meaning of everything that has happened and will happen, and that is what the last things are all about. That too is the deep thought of this astonishing book that John has seen and has described. Eventually the most profound reality must penetrate through all the pores of the ultimate illusion and the truth will triumph. In the last chapter this thought is poignantly expressed as: "Let those who do wrong, let them do wrong even more, let them who do vile, let them continue to do more so; let those who do right continue to do right; and let those who are holy continue to be holy" (Rev 22:11). That hits the nail on the head. The mask has to go, the secret must be unveiled, everything must in the end become what it always has been already.

Several factors are involved in this de-masking process. John gives insight into these from the point of view of divine judgment. That so carefully constructed and properly propped-up house of cards of human pride begins to crumble under the hammer blows of the divine judgments. These judgments are cosmic in character as the totality of the universe is connected to this. They are sketched in flowery images that speak to the imagination of the first readers of this book: creepy animals with strange tails and weird weapons, showers of stars, a burning mountain that is thrown into the sea. Some of these signs we cannot fathom in their entirety, because they in shrouded form relay what God will do in these great and awesome days. But what is sure beyond doubt is that humanity will be hit exactly where it imagines itself to be the strongest, in its technical know-how and in its mastery over nature. Nature will fall upon the human race as a provoked lion: nature will breach all the constrains humanity has laid upon it, and will explode into extraordinary catastrophes, earthquakes, floods, failed harvests, pandemics. All these will be more severe than ever. And as part of all this comes the dissolution of human society. Wars will come of an intensity and severity never before experienced, causing incalculable confusion. And all this will result in the coming of the kingdom of the one world-tyrant, the beast with his abhorrent body, arising out of the ocean of the community of nations. Again for a short spell the human throne will be established. Humanity has not turned to God, has only become more outspoken in his resistance, more spiteful in its hatred, more determined in its powerless hate, more relentless in its rage against God's children. Indeed, who is unjust, more injustice will ensue, who is vile, more vileness will follow. The mask falls off.

Apparently that is the total purpose of this picture. In the last empire, all motives, which have dominated the world's history from times immemorial, all these come to their unrestrained revelation. Sin is shown there in the full sense of the word, in its breathtaking hubris, in its self-elevation to God's throne, in its all-out discarding of everything that stands in the way of this brazen effort. Here human vilest intentions rise to the surface. All veneer is vanished, melted away in the heat of the last days. Humanity, not as single persons but in its totality, as a collective species, rises up in its dream of the totalitarian world empire, lauding its greatness, its power. It now only has the one idol, but the idol carries the same bizarre and distorted feature that it itself has. This idol is its own image, magnified into infinity. That is the Antichrist, the culmination of the world's history.

In these last chapters we hear little of the church. We often do hear heavenly songs of praise but the hidden ways of the church on earth are no longer shown. After the two witnesses are taken up in heaven, the church remains only in the background. History no longer concerns her. She lives closer than ever before by the eternal matters that come from heaven. Perhaps she, at last, becomes one, one communion of true believers, one church from which in panic all fear flees away, all that is unclean and smells of lies no longer is at home. In the melting pot of the final time the church too becomes more and more what she is; she too, in spite of all pressure and persecution, slowly assumes the features of her true character.

All this first has to reach a certain level of maturity, must first take on a definite final shape before all that for which the believers of all ages have hoped so fervently can come about. Then, in the end, the new kingdom, the kingdom of Jesus Christ, the New Jerusalem will dawn.

Actually, expressed in the language of John, this is not strange at all. At last everything in the world becomes what it should have been all along. When a person stands on top of a mountain it sometimes looks as if the world below is veiled in a haze of mists. The wind then suddenly can cause the last shreds of mist to disappear and reveal the world as it really is. In that same way, in the final events the world too will become what she has been all the time. The one with the crown of thorns is the ruler of the kings of the earth. He does not become that: he is that. The Satan is the one who is defeated, the opponent who has been thrown out of heaven. He does not become that: he is that. Nature has no independent existence but is an instrument in God's hand and is part of God's plan and does what God wants. She does not become that: she is that. And we humans, we who revolted against God, we who in the depth of our striving are the great fugitive from God, and always rebel against him, we grimly keep on embracing this world because this is our last and only refuge. That we do not become: that's what we are. And the church, that divided and ripped apart community of believers always tempted, always threatened, always walking on the edge of the abyss, she is the woman, clothed with the sun and wearing a crown of stars on her head. She does not become that, no, she is that already for a long time, in Christ Jesus, her Lord and her king. What happens in the end is not something new, is not something miraculous. No, all this amounts to is that when humanity has spoken its last and most important word, then God starts to speak his mighty word. That is the most radical revolution of all times, but in essence it is nothing else than that everything becomes what it is. The secret is dug up from every reality and exposed for everybody to see. The ultimate meaning of every creature becomes exposed and held up to public view in the hands of the true God. That is the judgment day, that is the most horrible that can be imagined and at the same time it is redemption, the eternal liberation of all who have loved Jesus' appearance on earth. At one time he exclaimed on Calvary the triumphal call: It is accomplished. Already then the great plea was settled, and already then everything was changed. On the last day it again will be exclaimed: "It is done!" (Rev 21:6). That second exclamation is exactly the same as the first. It is the same word, but now it is in the acute, present tense, is now the full reality. Now, indeed, it is for ever and ever "done."

AND WHAT ABOUT US?

There is now one question remaining: what about us? We are still here, part of the great masquerade, still in this world that hides its true nature. What is John's message to us? How then can we find our place in this ultimate hour? With what sort of expectation must we enter this future? It is not difficult to find the answer when reading this book. The first indication John gives is a word of beautiful encouragement. We are still far too much clued in to the false image of the seeming reality, that's why we are still far too afraid and far too alarmed. When we know Jesus and confess him and love him, then only one thing counts, and that is to start to understand who we are. You are "more than conquerors," "everything is yours," we are the woman clothed with the sun. Our citizenship, says Paul, is in the heavens. Be what we are! Be aware what our feelings ought to be and act accordingly. Don't stand shaking in your boots in the midst of the last gasp of the history of the world, and don't just stand there with eyes full of fear, sorely afraid of what is to come. What lies ahead can only be what already is, what has been there since Calvary, and what is there is nothing but light, radiating light. That's why this book, in spite of all its anxiety-provoking pictures, is, in its deepest sense, a book of rich encouragement. This is a case where we have nothing to lose and everything to gain. There is only one thing to worry about, and this is that we lose sight of what God in his grace in Jesus Christ has done for us, so that we, in our insecurity, will be tempted to compromise with the world, become a Nicolaitan and find security in an attitude of half-baked lukewarmness. That is the only matter that may give reason for anxiety. And if we really worry about that, then we need not be worried at all because then we are assured that this great Christ, the Lord of lords and the king of kings, in the midst of all temptation and danger, will embrace us with his strong arms. But there always remains that ever-present warning to persist till the end. "They who overcome, I will make pillars in the temple of my God and the name of the city of my God, the new Jerusalem and also write on them their new name" (Rev 3:12).

But the final chord that John sounds in his book is yet somewhat different from a word of encouragement and warning. It is a word of an infinite deep longing, a longing for God. "And the Spirit and the Bride say: Come!" The church can at times feel so at home in this fantastic world that she forgets her ultimate destination. She can become so fascinated by all the daily affairs that she forgets where she is headed. Then it really is necessary, amidst the earsplitting tumult of the cascading accumulation of the incessant catastrophes and the cessation of all certainties, that we all are reminded of the perishability and the dilapidation of this seemingly solid world order. "For this world in its present form is passing away" (1 Cor 7:31).

When we detect the fragility of that which daily can still fascinate us so strongly, the true desire for the imperishable aspects of God's kingdom can be awakened in us. This world simply cannot be everything, cannot have the last word. The haze has to be ripped to shreds and the majestic grandeur of God must break through all fog and darkness. This Jesus Christ, who has rescued us from the most frightening gloom and has reconciled us with God, this savior and Lord, who has borne death for us and has taken us along in his all-decisive triumph, he will at one time stand before us as the first and the last, the beginning and the end. When all these earthly matters will be wiped away in the whirlwind of the last judgments, then his throne will stand totally secure and then high above all realities the figure of the Son of Man will rise. With neck outstretched, standing on tiptoe, we long for that moment when he will destroy the shroud that enfolds all people (Isa 25:7) and all tears will be wiped from our eyes.

On and on the ages roll. We still stand at the entrance of God's ultimate act. Many generations before us have looked forward to what they knew would come. Wars, involving the entire world, were waged, empires rose and disappeared, cities were built and were ruined. New thoughts and new expectations were tried and found wanting. Science opened up new perspectives and new possibilities arose from everywhere. Current humanity proceeded at breakneck speed, became more powerful and richer and more self-conscious by the day, and at the same time also became more tired, more desperate, duller and more depressed. In the maelstrom of the world-happenings, we all are carried along and sometimes, in the middle of a nightmarish dream we awake and worriedly we wonder where we are and where we are going. Does all this doing and creating makes any sense?

Modern physics tells us that this earth is a temporary phenomenon, and that it, after many ages, will perish, perhaps by overheating or overcooling. Will that be the end of all human effort?

God's word tells us that straight through the matters that are perishable we will see that which is fixed for eternity: the greatness and glory of Him who sits on the throne, and of Jesus Christ, the faithful witness. If that is true—and it is true—then only one item is more important: "Wake up, O sleeper, rise from the dead, and Christ will shine on you" (Eph 5:14).

www.ingramcontent.com/pod-product-compliance
Lightning Source LLC
Chambersburg PA
CBHW030113170426
43198CB00009B/609